HE GIVES US AUTHORITY

Discerning and undoing the enemy's work in the name of Jesus

John Bardsley

'In that day, the LORD will punish with his sword, his fierce, great and powerful sword, Leviathan the gliding . . . coiling serpent; he will slay the monster! . . .' Isaiah 27:1 NIV

'Awake, awake, put on strength, O arm of the LORD; . . . Was it not Thou . . . who pierced the dragon?' Isaiah 51:9 NASB

WEC PUBLICATIONS

WEC PUBLICATIONS
READ MISSION

HE GIVES US AUTHORITY

John Bardsley

About the author

John Bardsley joined WEC International in 1972 and has served in Indonesia, Australia, on the team compiling the prayer guide *Operation World* in the UK, and as international prayer coordinator for WEC. During that time he found freedom from his own slavery to sin, and has delighted in helping others into freedom. He adopted a demon-fearing unreached people for prayer, asking God to teach him to pray, and what he learned is in here. He has preached on every continent.

With contributors

Antonio Alkimim, Janet, Colin Bearup, Traugott Böker, Mike Boling, Jill Chapman, Maurice Charman, Denise Christie, Jim Dawson, Stewart Dinnen, Joan Eley, Jean Goodenough, Jonathan Hacker, Norma Hunt, Dietrich Kuhl, Hellen Kulesky, Jane Larkman, Patrick McElligott, Thelma Mills, Walter Mohr, Arcanjo Rego Neto, John Oswald, Matt and Margaret Paton, Bruce and Annette Rattray, Richard and Roxanne Shawyer, Bhim Singh, Eddie Smith, Pondsius Takaliuang, Hazel Wallis, Brian Woodford.

CONTENTS

INTRODUCTION

This is not a theoretical book. It grew out of the experiences of Christian workers in WEC, an international, interdenominational mission agency. Nor do we imagine that we have nothing more to learn! We are hungry, eager to discover more about our majestic Lord and his ways, so that his kingdom can be accomplished, his bride can be complete, and his coming can be expected!

We are a pioneer mission working among the least reached peoples, where the enemy has had total control for too long. The contributors come from a wide range of locations and ministries, having learned things the church may not yet have faced in countries where it is more established. We share our experiences with each other, and with you, so that you too can exercise the authority of the Lord Jesus Christ over any enemy force you may find opposing your work for him.

How did I get into this? In 1986 I committed an hour a week to pray for an African people called Jola. I was angry that the Jola church was not growing, in spite of excellent workers and serious intercession. I asked God to teach me to pray, and began to search the scriptures for promises and guidelines. Our family experienced attacks, and we learned to protect ourselves. The African church began to grow, though not fast enough. (I still pray for them an hour a week). God also began sending me people who needed spiritual help in ways I had not met before. Each time, I grew some more.

God has commanded every obedient disciple to make disciples who obey, and has given us the authority needed to accomplish this task. This includes authority to overcome in prayer any opposition that we, as his church, might encounter in the process. We want to encourage all disciples to know their authority and to use it.

We see the tide of New Age rising, and a lot of old superstitions returning. God's people must prepare for this, and we believe this book can be part of that preparation. Pastors and lay Christian workers in their own and other cultures can learn to recognise demonic activity when it occurs, know how to deal with it, and have the courage to do so. Check the contents, the index and the definitions. If you are not already equipped, you can be.

I want to record my enormous gratitude to Dietrich Kuhl, who first suggested that I might compile such a book; to Patrick Johnstone who has used his experience of publishing to teach me to give attention to every detail, how to be ruthless where it needed trimming, and how to create an index and a table of contents.

I am likewise hugely grateful to the WEC Publications Committee in UK, comprising Andrew Bowker, Glenn Myers, Daphne Spraggett and Jean Goodenough, all of whom read the manuscript right through, encouraged me to keep going, and made excellent detailed suggestions.

Finally, my thanks go to all the contributors, who sent me their teaching notes and their stories years ago, and have waited – and waited – and waited some more, while I grappled with how to put it together.

Much of the teaching from various contributors has overlapped, so I have formed it into one seamless whole. There are no divisions between teaching sections from different contributors. At the head of each chapter is the list of those who contributed to that chapter, with the largest contributor first. Teaching sections are typeset in Mercury, a serif font. Stories, however, have been typeset in a sans font called Interstate, with the contributor listed.

John Bardsley
2011

MEET THE CONTRIBUTORS

Antonio Alkimim is a Brazilian pastor who, because of his deep experience of God and the power of his word, has been asked to teach at the Institute of Biblical and Inter-cultural Studies in Montes Claros, Minas Gerais.

John Bardsley has served WEC as teacher and editor in Australia, as a staff member in the International Research Office under Patrick Johnstone, and as International Director for Prayer. He is currently a mobiliser in West Australia.

Colin Bearup is British, and works as a translator in and out of Chad. His deep love for his Chadian friends is obvious in the 'Life in Chad' section of his letters.

Traugott Böker, a wise and gentle German, taught in a Bible School in Indonesia, was Director of WEC Germany, and is currently Deputy International Director of WEC.

Mike Boling is a medical doctor and linguist from USA who served in Cote d'Ivoire, West Africa before moving on to Chad.

Jill Chapman served in Brazil and has now returned to her native England.

Maurice Charman has taught Malachi to Chinese scientists in Taiwan, has led WEC Singapore, has been Dean of Studies at Worldview College in Tasmania, and was until recently Director of WEC New Zealand, where he was born.

Denise Christie and her husband Lindsay published a newspaper called 'Desafio' (Challenge) in Colombia, the profits from which were used to create schools and provide health care for inner-city children in Bogota.

Jim Dawson has been a church planter in Thailand and Cambodia, and is now a mobiliser in West Australia.

Stewart Dinnen was a major in the British army, principal of WEC Colleges in Glasgow and Tasmania, International Director of WEC, and a much-travelled preacher and writer. He is in heaven. His story is written in his book *When I say move*.

Joan Eley is a deeply loved church planter, preacher and counsellor in Venezuela. Her story is written in a book called *God's Brumby*.

Jean Goodenough served as a church planter in Cote d'Ivoire before returning to UK as an editor and writer for WEC.

Jonathan Hacker has been a church planter in Cote d'Ivoire and is now a pastor in UK.

Norma Hunt has been a pioneer church planter and translator for one of the Dayak peoples in Kalimantan.

Janet worked in an NGO in Nepal and Tibet.

Dietrich Kuhl is a medical doctor who taught at a Bible School in Indonesia and became a much-loved International Director of WEC for 12 years, and then one of our Regional Directors.

Hellen Kulesky published *Youth* magazine (now closed) for West Africa.

Jane Larkman worked in Senegal, and is now editor of the Fula magazines Booyata and Badare.

Patrick McElligott gained celebrity status in Japan with a PhD in Japanese literature and a televised course in parenting. His story is written in his book *On Giants' Shoulders*.

Thelma Mills has been a church planter and translator in Guinea Bissau, West Africa.

Canadian Walter Mohr serves the Indonesian church in every way possible.

Arcanjo Rego Neto is a pastor in Brazil who has served with WEC in Spain.

John Oswald is a consultant in Central Asia.

Matt and Margaret Paton are church planters in France, with four churches planted so far.

Bruce and Annette Rattray were church planters. Bruce was a Bible School principal in Kalimantan, travelling to many villages in an outboard-powered canoe. He has gone for his reward. Bruce and Annette's story is told in *Thousands: a church is born in the Indonesian rainforest*.

Richard and Roxanne Shawyer are friends of the Wolof people in Senegal, teaching them, writing and speaking for them, and preparing Biblical materials for them.

Bhim Singh comes from Mauritius and has served with WEC in Fiji and Tasmania. Rev Pondsius Takaliuang is an evangelist and speaker in his homeland of Indonesia, where he has preached in football stadiums in which converts have burned their charms.

Hazel Wallis was a church planter in Guinea Bissau.

Dr Brian Woodford has been a church planter in Burkina Faso, as well as International Director for Training in WEC, lecturer at East-West College in New Zealand, and is now translating the Old Testament for his beloved Birifor people.

1
HOW BIBLICAL IS SPIRITUAL WARFARE?

John Bardsley, Maurice Charman, Stewart Dinnen

Not only for super-saints

It was a perfectly normal weekend camp for students in the final two years of secondary education in civilised England. We were sleeping on the floor in a series of school classrooms and running seminars and Bible studies. There was a Bible teacher and a camp counsellor, and I was presenting a couple of missionary programmes. The camp counsellor asked me to join her in helping one of the young men. Suddenly I was on full alert when he said he had given his soul to the devil and now wanted us to help him get it back. No one had ever asked me that before! Here was an unexpected obstacle to building the kingdom of God in this young man's life. If he was to make any further progress, we had to deal with it.

Spiritual conflict is the normal state of every active Christian. The conflict began for humans in the garden of Eden. God had appointed mankind to rule the earth (Genesis 1:28). By his own act of disobedience Adam had given his kingdom to the devil, and had himself come under the influence of the devil. The devil had now become the prince of this world. But God had not accepted this transfer of power as the final state of things. He said there would be war between human kind and the devil and his kind. 'I will put enmity between you' (Genesis 3:15).

Our task as Christians is to build the Kingdom of God. Spiritual warfare is the process of pulling down whatever the dominion of darkness has built up to try and prevent the kingdom being established. It includes personal protection using the armour of God, intercession preparing the way for advance into new areas, counselling and deliverance, if necessary. It could include any of the chapter headings in this book.

Spiritual warfare describes the total conflict between Satanic forces and the Kingdom of God, a conflict which continues everywhere and at many levels. At the personal level, there are temptations from our own body's cravings, the world around us, and the demons themselves. In church, the forces of darkness try to cause disunity, religiosity, liberalism and doubts about the Bible and the supernatural, and above all, apathy about the lost! In the world at large there are strongholds of addictions like lust, pornography, gambling, violence, anarchy and many others; there are cults like freemasonry or the occult as tangents from the truth. There are false religions like communism, humanism, capitalism and materialism as well as Islam, Buddhism and Hinduism with their resistance to the good news and persecution of those bringing it.

Spiritual warfare is not only for super-saints, but for every believer, as promised by the Lord Jesus when he said, 'All authority in heaven and on earth has been given to me. Therefore go and make disciples . . .'; 'I have given you authority over all the power of the enemy' (Matt 28:18; Luke 10:19 NLT). It is not for special situations only, but for day-to-day survival: physical, moral, mental and spiritual; and day-to-day advance: unblinding darkened minds, opening hearts to the gospel, setting captives free.

Believers are all called to enlist in this war
1 Timothy 1:18 'Fight the good fight'
2 Timothy 2:3-4 'Endure hardship with us like a good soldier of Jesus Christ. No one serving as a soldier gets involved in civilian affairs. He wants to please his commanding officer.'

We are commissioned for this fight
1 Timothy 6:12 'Fight the good fight of the faith.'

We are equipped with all the necessary weaponry
2 Corinthians 6:7 'With weapons of righteousness in the right hand and the left...'
2 Corinthians 10:3-4 'The weapons we fight with are not the weapons of the world. . . they have divine power'
Ephesians 6:13-17 'Therefore put on the full armour of God . . .'

We are made aware of the nature of the struggle
Ephesians 6:12 (CEV) 'We are not fighting against humans. We are fighting against forces and authorities and against rulers of darkness and powers in the spiritual world.'

We are assured that we are totally adequate through our union with Christ
Ephesians 1:3 'every spiritual blessing in Christ'
Christ gives us victory in the conflict both now and in the final outcome:
Romans 8:35-37 'Who shall separate us from the love of Christ? Shall trouble or hardship or persecution or famine or nakedness or danger or sword? . . . No, in all these things we are more than conquerors through him who loved us.'
Revelation 17:14 'They will make war against the Lamb, but the Lamb will overcome them . . .'

Very few make a special ministry of deliverance full-time, but most people who go overseas planting churches will be faced with the need to see someone delivered at some time in their lives, and most of those who remain behind could very well face the same, as superstition returns to the West. I want to show that we do have the authority in Jesus Christ to set someone free. Please, don't just withdraw muttering 'I've never done anything like that.' Neither had I. Study the promises of God, and step out on them. All of us face the task of softening hardened people and seeing them respond. This may take more spiritual effort than freeing one individual!

I led a prayer walk to Senegal. We were ambling along the streets of Ziguinchor, praying for places we passed and people we met. A girl was approaching whom the local Christian worker said was well known as demonised. When we asked if she would like to be prayed for, she said 'Yes'. But at that time I did not even have the courage to ask her, 'Do you want to be free?' let alone to command, 'Come out of her, in the name of Jesus!' It could have been a major advance for the gospel in that city, with an effect similar to the deliverance of the slave girl in Philippi. Why did I fail? Firstly, I had never seen it done. Secondly, I had heard that it sometimes takes days, though for Jesus it was always just minutes. Basically, I was too chicken. I wanted my initiation into deliverance in a more private setting.

'My fear disappeared'
Jean Goodenough

We were staying in a village in Cote d'Ivoire for a conference with the Christians of the Gban people. In the middle of a meeting Marie came in. Her arms were stretched out, she was chanting. The Christians recognised her symptoms and said that she had an evil spirit. Immediately some began to tell the spirit to get out, while others prayed.

Dealing with evil spirits is not something I relish, and given half a chance I will avoid it, so I stayed with the praying group rather than the deliverance group. Then two people started to laugh, a mocking laugh, very inappropriate. One was an elder's wife who should have known better.

The other was Hortense, a teenage girl whose spiritual state was questionable. I felt uneasy about her staying in the meeting. I considered taking her outside, but decided against it. I have to admit, I was more concerned about not looking as if I was opting out, than about hearing the voice of God. My motives were not right. I was fearful, but did not want to show it.

Within moments of my decision not to take her out, her laughter abruptly ceased as a demon transferred its attention from Marie to Hortense. Instead of dealing with one case of demonic activity, we now had two. Hortense screamed as the demon took control. She marched round the church, stood at the front as if she was preaching, then sat down again.

I read her some scripture. She glared at me with a look of pure hatred. The Christians divided into two groups, one dealing with Marie, the other with Hortense. Eventually the spirit left Hortense, and I did what I should have done the first time, and took her home. Although she had no recollection of what had happened, she was very shaken and scared. The fear lingered for some weeks and she needed someone to sleep with her at night.

Marie was not totally delivered that day. The problem seemed to be her unwillingness to renounce the spirits and let God work in her life. We brought her in to town with us for ongoing ministry. One evening when the team met with Marie I was feeling resentful about something (I had a lot of resentment in those days!) and knew I would be vulnerable until I got right with the Lord, so I missed out on that occasion.

The next evening I joined the group praying for Marie. I had no excuse for not going, but a fair amount of apprehension. After a little while I began to relax a bit. Marie turned to me and said, 'You're scared of me!' Instantly the apprehension began to bubble into something more formidable, and I knew there was no way I could control it in my own strength. My only weapon was the sword of the Spirit. Suddenly it was in my hand and pointing in the right direction. 'No', I said. 'I am not scared of you. It is you who are scared of me, because the One who is in me is greater than the one who is in you.' The evil spirit had no answer for that, and my fear disappeared.

A need for authority

You too, wherever you live, may be faced with a need for spiritual authority over the powers of darkness in order for the church to grow in your area. All of these writers have been involved at some level in setting people free, and building the kingdom of God among them. Read on. Use the authority given to all believers. Exercise your birthright as a child of God.

STOPTHINK&DISCUSS
- Have you ever been faced with an issue which you felt had some demonic influence? Was there someone who could help?
- Were you able to help? If not, what would have to happen before you could help?

2
WORLDVIEWS: MATERIALIST, ANIMIST AND BIBLICAL

Traugott Böker, Dietrich Kuhl, John Bardsley, Hans Rothenberger

Our worldview is a set of presuppositions or assumptions which we hold about the basic make-up of our world, the thought system we develop to explain the world around us and our experiences in it. It is determined almost entirely by the society in which we grow up. It is something we absorb subconsciously more often than something we adopt after careful study.

Western, materialistic concept based on Greek philosophy

The industrial revolution, the age of enlightenment, the influence of communism and rationalism have all combined to dim our western experience of the spirit world. Many of us have never even seen a demon in a dream. So we read the Bible verses and believe them, but we have trouble relating them to our daily life. Spirits are not very real to us. Our Western worldview has a blind spot that makes it difficult for many Western believers to understand, let alone answer in a relevant way, problems related to spirits, ancestors and other spiritual powers.

A worker in China was living in the province of Xinjiang among the Uighur people, who in 1930 had slaughtered the Christians. Only now was the church being reborn. One night this worker had a dreadful nightmare, and dreamed she was being beaten about the head. When she awoke in the morning, she had been beaten around the head! She thought, 'Oh no! I've been burgled! What have they taken?' She searched and found nothing gone. She checked doors and windows, and found them all securely locked. There was only one other explanation. Could it be true? She had been severely beaten over the head by demons!

As I read her hand-written letter describing this attack, my blood ran cold. To this day it remains the most shocking letter I have ever read. But it would not surprise a Uighur or an African. They experience demonic interference in everyday life all the time. So do we, as evidenced by our compulsions (see p37), for example! But in the West, Satan is more subtle, and tries to conceal his tracks.

Daily life and practice

We need to be aware that there is a difference between the 'profession level of belief' and the 'practise level of daily life'. We often profess to a biblical worldview on the intellectual level but, if we analyse our daily life, in many cases Western Christians seem to live as any other humanistic and materialistic secular

Western person.

Those from a Western worldview have a strong tendency to analyse situations, dissect complexities into separate parts and to view all the different parts in their own little boxes. We need to remember that the biblical worldview is holistic.

You can see this clearly in Ephesians 2:1-3: 'You were dead in your transgressions and sins, in which you used to live when you followed the ways of this world and of the ruler of the kingdom of the air, the spirit who is now at work in those who are disobedient, . . . gratifying the cravings of our sinful nature, and following its desires and thoughts.' All the four enemy elements (sin, the world, the devil, and the flesh) are working together.

So we need to develop for ourselves, together with the churches, a biblical worldview which fully deals with the spirit world and which includes angels and demons as functioning elements in everyday life. Read 2 Kings 6:15-17. Elisha's servant saw the human enemy – troops massed on the hillside surrounding the city. Elisha told him, 'Don't be afraid. Our side has more than theirs.' When Elisha prayed, 'Lord, open the young man's eyes', the young man saw the hills full of horses and chariots of fire all around God's prophet. We need to pray for ourselves, 'Lord, open my eyes.'

In the West there is a huge revival of interest in the occult. Horoscopes appear in every magazine. New Age thinking is bringing back all sorts of superstitions and belief in the spirit world, astral travel, meditation, and lucky charms. Churches in the West must face up to these issues and know how to respond to people who have been involved.

But when is an ordinary Christian likely to meet such evil forces? Any time! Be prepared! A woman came for counselling after I preached. Her father was a Rosicrucian and an astral traveller. She was troubled by demons night and day. Her life was in ruins. A man asked me to disciple him. His father had been a Satanist and he needed deliverance. In another place a Satanist walked into church, straight off the street, and a church member rang me to help try to deliver her. New Agers, people who have had their fortunes told, those who have used horoscopes or have been to a séance may all need deliverance as they come to Christ. People traumatised by childhood abuse, people caught in entrenched social sin such as pornography, prostitution or gay rights may very likely need deliverance.

Animistic superstitious concept

For an animist there are no sharp dividing lines between 'natural' and 'super-natural'. Rocks, stones, trees and so on can have supernatural powers in them. All things material are at the mercy of spirit influences. They believe that the spirits can be influenced through ritual, magic and blood sacrifice.

The village where we lived in Java had gateposts but no gate. In fact, it had no fence either – just two massive brick gateposts. 'Why?' I asked one of the locals. He explained calmly, 'Oh, we don't need a fence if we have those gateposts. When we built them, we held a ceremony and invited a couple of spirits to come and live there and guard the village for us.'

There is a common belief in spirit beings who are involved in all aspects of life. As we walked the forest paths of southern Senegal, we often came across a clay pot at the base of a beautiful tree. It had held a sacrifice of palm wine for the spirit who lived in the tree. Notice I didn't say 'the spirit they believe lives in the tree,' because I believe it too, and you had better believe it. There are spirits who come to that tree to receive the worship of those people. If you were one of Satan's rebellious angels, wouldn't you?

Can the spirits be tricked?
John Bardsley

I was riding pillion behind a worker in Java and saw, just round a corner on the road, a circle of flower petals beautifully arranged. I wanted to know why someone would go to all that trouble. My driver explained, 'They want to get away from the influence of some spirit who they believe is bringing them bad luck. They put that arrangement just round the corner to the left, then dash off to the right, hoping that the spirit will be attracted by the beauty, and distracted from following them.' How tragic to imagine a spirit can be fooled so easily!

We face a confusion of truth, fable, and satanic lie. In the West we have to sort out what is true about leprechauns, trolls, witches and wizards, druids and water-divining. The same confusion also faces us in an animist culture.

One of the cornerstones of animist belief is that the actions of the spirits can be influenced through spells, incantations, rituals and sacrifices. (Western witches and Satanists seem to believe this as well.) Animists know the spirits are malevolent and are desperate to find some way to get them off their backs. They fear the occult practitioner, whatever he or she may be called. Their religions have rules about what they may and may not do so as to appease the ancestors etc.

Even in civilised, technological Japan, WEC church planters Shuichi and Elaine Kitamura wrote of the extreme difficulty any Japanese has to break away from the rest of the suburb and turn to Christ. 'It is a painful reminder' they wrote 'that Japan is in the grip of a spirit that is antagonistic to Jesus.'

Spirit of Kamphaengphet
Jim Dawson

I was walking through the town square in Kamphaengphet, and noticed well-dressed Thai business people going in and out of a beautifully-decorated pagoda in the centre of the square. 'Why are those busy people spending time in there on a Monday morning on their way to the office?' My Thai friend told me, 'Don't you know? The spirit of Kamphaengphet province lives in there. They are going in there to get its blessing on their work. That spirit is the reason the church cannot be built here, because it controls what happens in this province.'

Jesus said, 'I will build my church', . . . and the gates of Kamphaengphet will not prevail against it. Today there is a church in Kamphaengphet, and it is busy planting daughter churches in the villages around. But there was opposition to overcome before that could happen!

A new convert from an animistic background faces many tests. What happens when his child is ill? If he has no money for medicine, and we fail to teach him that Jesus can heal, what can he do but turn back to his folk beliefs and make a sacrifice to the spirits? In places where such issues haven't been sufficiently dealt with, syncretistic beliefs and practices have continued in the churches.

Biblical world concept

What is spiritual reality? The Bible speaks clearly of the existence of the unseen world. The unseen is not just in the future, the 'beyond', but it is part and parcel with our material world, part of creation. Creation is not divided into two separate worlds, one a visible, touchable material world and the other an invisible world of angels and demons. There is only one world, and we all live in it. However, we are not dependent on the demons nor at their mercy. What answers do we have? These are explored in the rest of the book.

CONSIDER
the following statements, and mark each with A for fact, B for fable, or C for lie. Check your answers below.

- [ ] 1 Angels and demons inhabit the same world we do.
- [ ] 2 A demon could make himself look like a leprechaun if he wished.
- [ ] 3 A spell or incantation can force a demon to obey a human.
- [ ] 4 Witches cook potions and ride broomsticks.
- [ ] 5 Witches and Satanists curse Christians.
- [ ] 6 Demons gather in places they receive worship.
- [ ] 7 Jesus can protect his people from Satanic attack.

Answers: 1A, 2A, 3C, 4B, 5A, 6A, 7A

STOPTHINK&DISCUSS
- What is false and what is true in the Western materialistic worldview as described here?
- What Biblical truth needs to be added to help us face reality?
- Pray for peoples whose worldview is animist, that they will hear of the One who defeated Satan and rules over the Spirit world.

3
CAN HUMANS HAVE AUTHORITY OVER SPIRITUAL FORCES?

John Bardsley, Stewart Dinnen

God is the Creator. He is greater than anything he made

'Who has measured the waters in the hollow of his hand, or with the breadth of his hand marked off the heavens? Who has held the dust of the earth in a basket, or weighed the mountains on the scales . . .' (Isaiah 40:12). Hold out your hand, palm up, cupped as if to hold water. Now tip out that palm full of water and say 'Pacific Ocean'. Some hand! Put your thumb down as the centre, and stretch out your fingers as far as you can to draw the circumference of a semicircle, an arc. Imagine the size of the hand necessary to draw the arc of the sky! OK, God is spirit, and he doesn't have a hand. It's a picture to help us realise how BIG God is! Imagine a set of bathroom or kitchen scales big enough to weigh the Himalayas! This is the Almighty reminding us, 'I'm BIG! I'm strong!'

'Let them praise the name of the LORD, for he commanded and they were created' (Psalm 148:5). Imagine a being with the ability to conceive the details of a human body, its brain, eye, ear, foot and hand, bone structure, muscular movement, a nervous system to communicate the commands from the brain to the muscles, hearing, sight, digestion, and procreation. Then imagine that being saying, 'Let's have one of those. I command it to be.' And Adam was. Pause and praise God for the wonder of your body.

A scientist said to God, 'We don't need you. We can create life in a test tube.' God replied, 'OK, let's do it. You make one and I'll make one. You first.' So the scientist began to gather proteins and amino acids. God said, 'Hey, I made all that. You create your own raw materials!'

'I am the first and the last; apart from me there is no God.' (Isaiah 44:6). 'Wait a minute,' I hear you say, 'There are millions of gods!' Certainly there are plenty who claim to be gods, plenty of spirits who demand the allegiance of mortals. But they are all created beings. What is your definition of God? We're talking about the first great Cause of all. We're talking about the only infinite, timeless, unchangeable Spirit, all-knowing, all-powerful, from whom all things begin and continue, and by whom all things will end. There is only one like that! We call him God. God is not threatened by demons. His power is immense! By comparison, the next nearest is infinitesimal!

There is the eastern concept of *yin* and *yang*, equal and opposite, both necessary to make a full circle. That is dualism! That is not the concept of good and evil as provided by the Bible. Satan is opposite God, but he is not equal. As a matter of fact, Revelation 20:1-2 contains an astounding insight. One angel bound Satan and locked him away a thousand years. Only one! It does not even tell us his name! And how many angels are there? Get out your calculator: 'Ten thousand times ten thousand, plus thousands of thousands.' For us, it's a titanic struggle and it often appears that Satan has the upper hand. That's exactly how he wants it to appear, for as long as possible! But when the time comes, God will flick him away like a pesky fly.

Job realised this. He said to the Lord, after all his suffering, and all the Lord had taught him: 'I know that you can do all things; no plan of yours can be thwarted' (Job 42:2). God's plan is always on a through-way, and no body (or spirit) can throw a roadblock across it and prevent its progress. Nobody is cleverer than God to trick him into making a mistake.

Psalm 19:1 says that the heavens declare the glory of God. I love the photos of the universe – the gases, the black holes, and the amazing shining suns, millions of suns that we call stars. David Cummings of Wycliffe said that if every star were reduced to the size of a grain of sand, the stars visible to the naked eye would fill a communion glass. The stars in the Milky Way, our galaxy, would fill a wheelbarrow. But the stars in all known space would fill one railway boxcar per second for three and a half years - or all the sand on all the beaches of the world. Why did God make so many stars? To show us that his power is infinite! His glory is infinite! His beauty is infinite! Revelation 4 is a whole chapter totally given to the worship of God as Creator. Let us join in that worship. Let us always keep that true perspective.

Back when there was war in heaven, as recorded in Revelation 12:7-11, it says Michael and his angels fought against the dragon and his angels, who fought back. But the dragon was not strong enough!

We know that Satan was hurled down to earth, our planet. He is called the prince of the power of the air, and this planet seems to be the only one with air. But the Almighty Creator has authority in every planet and sun, countless millions of them! That's how much bigger than Satan is our God.

Jesus the Conqueror is exalted above every other power

Jesus defeated the devil, who is now an illegal squatter. 'Having disarmed the powers and authorities, he made a public spectacle of them, triumphing over them by the cross' (Colossians 2:15). Paul must have written this after being in Rome. The 'public spectacle' refers to a Roman general returning from some war, being welcomed back in a triumphal march into Rome. His victorious troops are with him. Wagonloads of loot precede him, and the defeated kings, generals and troops of the enemies of Rome are dragged along behind him in chains. They will be slaves and gladiators. The cheering of the crowds giving praise to the conqueror is nothing but shame and embarrassment to them. Satan and his demons are defeated in just the same way.

'The reason the Son of God appeared was to destroy [undo] the devil's work' (1 John 3:8). The devil's work had been to tie us up, imprison us, and blind our minds. Jesus came to undo all that: restore our sight, untie us, and set us free. The devil's work had been to steal, kill and destroy (John 10:10). The idea is not extinction but ruin: loss of well-being, not of existence. He came to ruin us. Jesus came to reverse that ruin.

'Since the children have flesh and blood, he [Jesus] too shared their humanity so that by his death he might destroy [disarm] him who holds the power of death – that is, the devil – and free those who all their lives were held in slavery by their fear of death' (Hebrews 2:14-15). Jesus had to become mortal so it was possible for him to die. His death, planned before creation, was the battle to disarm the devil, to make Satan ineffective. Nineteenth-century explorers would sometimes bring a tiger home as a pet, but they would pull out its teeth and claws, making it ineffective as a killing machine. A boxer in a prize fight can sometimes land a knock-out punch. The opponent is not dead, but he's no danger any more. You may have seen a footballer at half time cut a small hole in the end of an orange and suck all the juice out, leaving the skin flat. Satan had all the stuffing knocked out of him at Calvary! Calvary was the battle ground where Satan was disarmed. Calvary was also a slave market where God paid the price in blood to buy us back from the plight our sins had left us in. How common is fear of death in the non-Christian world! How much hopelessness and despair is in their funeral services! What a contrast when they turn to Christ, and know they will meet their loved one on the other side!

'Jesus Christ . . . is at God's right hand – with angels, authorities and powers in submission to him' (1 Peter 3:22). 'Submission' is a military term meaning 'ranked beneath him', or even 'in subjection to him'.

'I pray also that the eyes of your heart may be enlightened in order that you may know . . . his incomparably great power for us who believe. That power is like the working of his mighty strength, which he exerted in Christ when he raised him from the dead and seated him at his right hand in the heavenly realms, far above all rule and authority, power and dominion, and every title that can be given, not only in the present age, but also in the one to come. And God placed all things under his feet . . .' (Ephesians 1:18-22). Paul prayed that we might wake up to the fact that the resurrection power of God raised Jesus from death and enthroned him, and that same power is available for us.

Just as the whole of Revelation 4 is given to worship God as Creator, so the whole of Revelation 5 is given to worship Jesus as the Lamb who was killed. These two facts about God the Father and God the Son become the two legs on which we base our right to engage in spiritual warfare, in submission to the King of kings.

Build worship into your daily life

All these wonderful Biblical facts are a huge rock for us to stand on. But sometimes in the midst of the darkness, with enemy activity flourishing all round, it doesn't look as though God is supreme at all. We see someone we love still hard and disobedient, or some ministry still struggling to find its feet. We wonder, 'Where is God in all of this?' That is the very time when we need to re-read some of these glorious verses, to appreciate again the victory Jesus won.

The value of praise
John Bardsley

As I prayed for the Jola people, I sometimes stirred up a hornet's nest of kickback from the dark forces that I must have been disturbing. Sometimes I would be discouraged when freedom did not come to someone, or if the church children did not manage to escape the initiation rituals. Like the generation of missionaries before me, I found it hard going at times. I thought, 'I could get depressed if I'm not careful.' That was how I learned another value of praise. Praise and worship remind me of how BIG our God is! Then I keep the enemy in his true perspective!

When the enemy has succeeded in making himself look bigger and stronger than the King of Kings, he has robbed the Christians of their confidence. Go back to the Bible, back to the song book, and re-experience the greatness of God.

Jesus demonstrated his authority over the forces of evil

'The people were amazed at his teaching, because he taught them as one who had authority, not as the teachers of the law' (Mark 1:22). 'A new teaching – and with authority! He even gives orders to evil spirits and they obey him' (Mark 1:27). It would be easy for us to assume that the authority Jesus demonstrated during his lifetime was because he was God. This is not the reason. In order to be 100% ordinary man, Jesus had relinquished the independent use of his divine powers. He relied 100% on his Father, just as he now expects us to do. The authority he demonstrated is available for us, not on the basis of our maturity, but on the basis of his cross.

Authority is a key concept

The dictionary definition of authority is 'power inherent or derived from position or appointment'. So our starting point is the objective truth of Christ's victory, and our linkage with him in it. We are talking about an experience of our union with Christ. When we realise the three dimensions of our union with him we are ready for the conflict. These dimensions are:

a. Union with Christ in his death (Romans 6:1-11)
b. Union with Christ in his resurrection life (Ephesians 2:4-6)
c. Union with Christ at the throne (Colossians 2:9-10; 3:1).

Greek words for power/authority are *dunamis*, (inherent power, ability), *ischus* (force, strength, physical power), *kratos* (dominion, manifested power), *energeia* (power in action, operative power), and *exousia* (authority, freedom or fight to act, from *exesti* meaning 'it is lawful').

Jesus delegated his authority to us, to build his kingdom

'When Jesus had called the Twelve together, he gave them power and authority to drive out all demons and to cure diseases, and he sent them out to preach the kingdom of God . . . ' (Luke 9:1). He did the same for the 72, and when they returned, he reminded them 'I have given you authority . . . to overcome all the power of the enemy' (Luke 10:19).

If it were just the twelve apostles to whom Jesus gave this authority, we might well assume it was meant only for those twelve men. But the 72 disciples are not named leaders. They were just disciples, people who spent time with Jesus, then went out to introduce others to what he said (Mark 3:14-15). By that definition, are you a disciple? Then surely this promise applies to you as well.

Such an important teaching should also occur in the epistles, and it does. 'And God raised us up with Christ and seated us with him in the heavenly realms' (Ephesians 2:6). I become very excited when I read this verse. We have already mentioned Ephesians 1:18-22 where Jesus is seated at the right hand of the Father, far above every other power. So I want you to imagine an awesome sight. God the Father – huge, covered in blinding light – is seated on the throne of the universe. At his right hand, seated also, because his work is finished, is Jesus Christ the Conqueror – risen, radiant, glorious. And at the right hand of Jesus, there on that exalted, authoritative throne, are millions of little itty-bitty Christians – you and me! We listen in awe to the battle plan of the Father and the Son; we double-check to make sure we have heard correctly; and then we command it to be done here on earth, as it is done in heaven. Utterly awesome!

Mark 13:34 contains one of the most puzzling parables. Jesus said the kingdom is like a man going away. He leaves his house and puts his servants in charge, each with his assigned task. Stop for a minute and try to work out what that really means. I was puzzling over it one day when I realised that only a few chapters further on Jesus went away. Before he did so, he said to his disciples, 'All authority in heaven and on earth has been given to me. Therefore go and make disciples of all nations, baptising them . . . and teaching them to obey. . . I am with you always, to the very end of the age' (Matthew 28:18). Does that sound like putting his servants in charge, and giving each their task? Our job is to establish groups of disciples in every ethnic group on earth, and our authority to do that is complete, total, 'all'.

Planned before creation

This plan was worked out by the Trinity before they ever gave that first command: 'Let there be light'; before the creation of the world. We know this because we were chosen in Christ before creation (Ephesians 1:4). Their intention was 'that now, through the church, the manifold wisdom of God should be made known to the rulers and authorities in the heavenly realms, according to his eternal purpose which he accomplished in Christ Jesus our Lord' (Ephesians 3:10-11). So the members of the Godhead are not dazed by the opposition nor daunted by the darkness. They have seen already what for us is still future, that this glorious kingdom will one day be complete; this radiant bride will one day be ready. All the powers of darkness will one day know that God's plan for twelve disciples to win the world has actually worked! They had the authority to make disciples, and had set up discipling movements in every tribe and language and people and nation. Hallelujah!

Imagine the smallest policewoman you can. She puts on her uniform, which today includes white gloves because today she will be on point duty, directing traffic at a busy intersection where the traffic lights are out of action. She holds up one lane, and waves another lane through. Soon, rumbling down the hill comes a 40-tonne Heavy Goods Vehicle, driven by a huge, hairy man in a blue vest. She holds up her little white hand, and with a hiss of his air brakes he comes to a halt. Why? He has a vehicle of enormous power! He could run her down! It doesn't suit him to put on his brakes and lose momentum! He would far rather roll straight on! Why does he stop? He stops because he recognises the uniform! She has the authority of the highest levels of government. If he defies her, the long arm of the law will punish him. We recognise police authority by the uniform, and the badge. Demons recognise our authority by Christ's indwelling, and the cleansing work his blood has done – the perfect sacrifice of Christ by which we stand. Praise HIM!

STOPTHINK&DISCUSS

- Discuss the awesome power of the Almighty Creator, and find some more scriptures to demonstrate it.
- Discuss the glorious victory of the cross. List who and what is conquered. List the benefits for us.
- Why does the Godhead delegate this awesome authority to us?
- Discuss this statement: Authority is based not on our maturity but on Christ's cross.
- Disciples spent time with Jesus learning his ways, then went out to create other disciples (Mark 3:14-15). The heart of discipleship is learning from the Master; the edge of discipleship is multiplication. By that definition, are you a disciple?
- Jesus said his kingdom is like a man going away, who leaves his servants in charge of his house, each with their assigned task. (Mark 13:34). Try to work out what that means.

4
WHY DO SO FEW OF US EXER
THIS AUTHORITY?

John Bardsley, Stewart Dinnen

If it is true that God has supreme power, that Jesus has all authority and has delegated it to us, where is the evidence? All this seems far removed from observable reality down here on earth. Let's keep our feet on the ground. How complete is this authority, really? How does it work in practice? Does it work in practice at all? It looks to many as if the devil is having a heyday, unhindered by the Spirit of God or the prayers of the saints. Evil is thriving here on earth, and no one can deny it. Crime pays. Sin earns big bucks.

Christian work in Japan is hard and discouraging. So it is in Europe. If you watch only secular news media, you see a depressing picture. But anyone who reads mission magazines and keeps in touch with the global harvest will know that the devil is not getting it all his own way! The kingdom of God is advancing. The church in China, while still enduring stiff persecution, has progressed to the stage of sending missionaries. A mission leader claims it is harvest time even in Tibet. India is demonstrating the first encouraging signs of vibrant life and growth, and now has the highest number of cross-cultural Christian workers of any country in the world. In most places where there are expatriate Iranians, there is an Iranian church. Hunger for the word of God has caused record sales of Bibles and JESUS videos across the Middle East. Latin American evangelical churches are sending missionaries.

So how can we put this picture in perspective? Read how Jesus explained it in Matthew 13: 24-30, 36-43. The Lord sowed wheat, the sons of the kingdom. The enemy sowed weeds, the sons of the evil one. The Lord says, 'Let both grow together until harvest – the end of the age.' Wickedness will thrive! And the church will thrive too! It is dramatically explained without parable in Matthew 24:9-14. Christians will be put to death, hated by every nation because of their faith. Many will grow cold and give up, or even betray their brothers and sisters. False teachers will deceive large crowds, but whoever stands firm to the end will be saved. Is that all? Just surviving by the skin of our teeth? No! Not a bit of it! In the midst of all that, the gospel will be preached to every people on earth! Hallelujah!

Is Jesus more powerful?
Lily Gaynor

Biombo is the centre of the Papel tribe of Guinea Bissau, West Africa. The people are deeply into spirit worship, which influences every area of their lives. Animal sacrifice, ceremonial dances, shamanism, divination and demonization familiar.

There is also belief in God the Creator who is represented by an idol in the form of a large box. This is bound in red cloth, has carrying poles running through it and is suspended from the roof of a rough 'temple'. It is taken out only by qualified priests to be consulted on important issues, and always with a blood sacrifice. No unauthorised person would dare go near it.

For twenty years we had worked in the area, very much aware that it is a Satanic stronghold. The battle has been fierce. Some early converts were forced to recant, others died mysteriously, but a successful medical work was slowly established, and as a result a little church formed.

One night we were awakened by a flashing light. It was coming from our ambulance parked outside the house. We went to investigate and found a young man, completely naked, sitting in the driver's seat. 'What are you doing?' we asked. 'I'm taking God away,' he answered. There in the ambulance was the god-idol in all its blood-stained wrappings!

With a struggle we got him out of the car and sent him home. Then what? 'We can't leave this here. We certainly don't want it on our premises.' We hauled it out of the ambulance. 'Let's sing,' said Brenda. As we struggled down the road with the god-idol, the night air rang out with 'Would you o'er evil a victory win, there's power in the blood of the Lamb!' We put it down beside the road and went back to bed.

What a commotion there was in the morning when the people saw it there! Nobody dared walk past it! They were even more amazed when they found out how it had got there. 'How did the senhoras dare to touch it?' 'How is it they did not die?' 'What sort of power have they got?' 'Is it true Jesus is more powerful than the spirits?'

Some are probably still waiting to see if we will die, but there are many others who have put their trust in Jesus.

Have you ever seen a disobedient child grudgingly giving in to his/her parents' authority? Parents say, 'Time for bed' and the child whines, 'Oh do I have to? Could I just finish watching this programme, or playing this game? Could I have a drink of water? Will you read me a story?' They try anything to postpone the dreaded moment. Likewise Satan does not give an inch until he has to.

The enemy is strong, but God is stronger
John Bardsley

Christian worker Johan Knol was starting a work among the Hanga people in Ghana. There was no church yet: the first Christians were just being born. Johan asked God to give him a disciple who could be to him as Timothy had been to Paul. Salifu, the first convert among his people, was proving to be just that, and Johan was discipling him to lead his people into the kingdom.

Salifu's young wife was not impressed. One weekend she went back to visit her parents some distance away. The parents took a dim view of this new religion as well, and the three of them took a chicken to the medicine man, and asked him to curse Salifu. The medicine man killed the chicken, poured the blood out to the spirits, then grunted with surprise and frustration. 'I can't touch him!' he muttered. 'There is some power round him stronger than mine. If I were you, I would stick with him.'

Mrs Salifu, however, was not quite so easily won over. She went back to the chief of her own village and reported that her curses had failed. He called a couple of warriors. 'Take your spears at tea time,' he said, 'when everyone is at home eating their evening meal. Salifu will be there. Go in and spear him to death. Perhaps a simple spear will do what black magic has failed to accomplish.' The men waited for the appropriate time, then headed for Salifu's one-roomed house. It held no place to hide. Then where was he? They checked the outside loo and the grain bin, but he was nowhere to be seen. They went back to the chief and reported that they couldn't find him.

Salifu had been in his house all along, eating his meal. He did not see them, either, which saved him an anxious moment. He learned about it later when his wife was converted and told him the story. Had God caused them not to see him? How? We don't need to know. What we need to know is that the power of God around Salifu is stronger than anything the enemy can throw at him. And the same applies to us.

What may be hindering my use of God's authority?

Authority is based on submission!

A centurion had asked Jesus to heal his servant, but he knew Jesus was busy, so he didn't think Jesus needed to actually go to his house. 'Say the word, and my servant will be healed. For I myself am a man under authority, with soldiers under me. I tell this one "Go" and he goes.' Jesus was impressed. 'I have not found such great faith even in Israel,' he said (Luke 7:9). This centurion illustrated more than faith that day. Notice he said, 'I am a man under authority, and my orders are obeyed.' Why didn't he say, 'I am a man in authority'? He didn't say that because the authority did not originate with him. He was in a chain of command. He had authority over a hundred men and answered to his captain who gave orders to ten centurions, thus commanding a thousand. Above him were higher ranks commanding cohorts, above them the general, and at the top, the emperor. The centurion was not wielding his own authority. His authority was much more glorious – it flowed down the chain of obedience from the emperor in Rome.

If he rebelled against the emperor, those of his soldiers who were loyal to the emperor would no longer obey him. His authority was dependent on submission to the source of the authority. And so is mine. I cannot wield the sword of the Spirit with authority if I am rebelling against the quiet prompting of the Spirit in some other area of my life. The two-edged sword cuts both ways! If I want my authority to be obeyed, I must be living in obedience to the powers above me.

I'm Australian. We Australians are not famous for submission to authority. That's how we got here in the first place! There has been a culture of rebellion against authority since the convict days. Civic, political and religious rulers were suspect. We tended to obey only those we respected and agreed with, and if it suited us. Usually in WEC that was not a problem. I managed a year in Indonesia with only one serious disagreement with my WEC leaders, and then fifteen more years in Australia living mostly in happy submission to my leaders. Then we were invited to serve in England.

It was our first time in UK. The culture is similar in many respects, but one facet of my culture shock was this business of submission. England seems to have a culture where 'play it by the book' is quite important. Follow the procedure, don't go making exceptions based on emotion, but stick to principle. And in the WEC centre called Bulstrode, where about sixty of us lived in a lot of flats dotted around a huge old mansion, it was quite pronounced. There were a lot of little rules set out in a document called 'The Bulstrode Handbook'. It didn't make scintillating reading. I couldn't initially see the sense in some of the rules at all. I thought 'I'm not gonna do that!'

For example, every family was allowed to have as many mattresses as they needed from the central furniture store. There wasn't a lock on the furniture store, and furniture of all descriptions flowed in and out at will. Later, for reasons you might be able to imagine, the management team felt it necessary to lock the door of the furniture store. Then it became a hassle for the staff member in charge of the store if, on Friday afternoon, a succession of families wanted an extra mattress for the weekend and on Monday morning they all wanted to return it. (We were in that group! We had three teenage daughters. They often wanted a sleepover for their friends.) However, a rule was formulated: 'You may have as many mattresses as you need. But you may not borrow a mattress just for the weekend.'

I wanted to go in shouting, 'That's not fair! You wait till you have teenage daughters of your own! Every normal family has sleepovers!' I even considered pulling one out of the window of the furniture store without permission, and putting it back again on Monday. It would have been quite simple. But actually I could see a reason for this rule, galling though it was. The staff member in charge of furniture was a busy missionary. Trips to the furniture store could become very repetitive. So was there a submissive solution? Of course! We asked for another mattress, permanently. She was delighted to give it. It was a bit of a nuisance in our compact flat, but we managed. And whenever we wanted a sleepover, we were equipped.

The same thing applies regarding submission to government. I began to have a conscience about speeding. Speeding is like lying – an abomination to the police, but a very present help in times of need. I preach a lot, and often need to drive to places I have never been before. I am incredibly forgetful and disorganised, so often I leave late. A last-minute phone call, or a daughter or wife who needs something might also delay me.

Then I would be in the car at last, with a choice. I have tried it both ways, and I recommend the latter. I could think to myself, 'If ever there was an excuse for speeding, it's today. Look at that clock. I have 35 minutes to cover a 45 minute journey. Let's go!' I'd plant my foot, and the most annoying Sunday driver would be ambling along taking his time or looking for his street, while I fumed behind him thinking, 'Are you trying to say something, Lord?' When I finally made it past him, there would be an amazing succession of red lights. Sometimes I would be going so fast I would miss the turn, and have to go back. I would arrive late, hot, flustered, and in no mood to preach!

After I had tried it like that a few times, I began to wonder if there may possibly be a better way. Eventually I would tell the Lord, 'Father, you know why I'm late again today. Some of it was unavoidable. Some of it is the way I am, and if I have done something wrong, I'm sorry. Remind me to study the map the day before. Teach me to plan to leave earlier. But now you can see my predicament today. I promise not to speed if you will help to get me there on time.' The lights would go green as I approached. Mr Slow Coach in front of me would find his corner quickly. I would wonder where the ground had gone, and find myself further on than I had dreamed. I would pray for help with map-reading, which is not my strong point, and find the street the first time instead of the third. I would arrive with peace in my soul. God is amazing, astounding, extravagant – you know that.

Humility is essential for spiritual authority
Who can participate when God moves?

'God opposes the proud but gives grace to the humble' (1 Peter 5:5). 'Who made you ruler and judge over us?' 'Who am I, that I should go to Pharaoh?' (Exodus 2:14, 3:11). The second question indicates that Moses is ready to be involved with on the work of God, without thinking he did it himself.

Once, I was surprised when another speaker was on the road more than I, surprised when I was not considered for a particular invitation. Suddenly it dawned on me – I am thinking of myself more highly than I ought! (Romans 12:3). That's why God dares not trust me with being part of a big move. I'd be thinking I did it.

'God chose the foolish things of the world to shame the wise; God chose the weak things of the world to shame the strong. God chose the lowly things of this world and the despised things—and the things that are not—to nullify the things that are, so that no one may boast before him. It is because of him that you are in Christ Jesus, who has become for us wisdom from God—that is, our righteousness, holiness and redemption.' (1 Corinthians 1:27-30).

'My greatest desire'
John Bardsley
Elizabeth Stewart, Thailand Field Leader, wrote in one of her newsletters: 'My greatest desire for the coming year is for a closer relationship to the Lord.' There's no pride in proximity to the King!

Authority is dependent on trustworthiness
More authority is given to those who use it well. 'Well done, my good servant! Because you have been trustworthy in a very small matter, take charge of ten cities' (Luke 19:17). When I was appointed prayer director for all of WEC, I was scared. What awesome responsibility! I had to teach spiritual warfare, but I had

never delivered anyone from unclean spirits. As I studied the verses about our authority, I gradually grew in my willingness to try. I had the opportunity to help a family smash an idol and burn charms, and we went through their house cleansing it and dedicating each room to God.

When a young man asked me to disciple him, I found he was troubled by a demon. Although I still had no experience, this time I did have the courage to help him discover how it entered, renounce the entry point, and then tell it to leave. I joined him in commanding it to leave, and it left. He never had any more problems, and his wife was elated.

Authority given is meant to be used!

Let Satan know he's defeated already! 'Encourage and rebuke with all authority. Do not let anyone despise you' (Titus 2:15). Titus was young and inexperienced, but youth and inexperience are not to stop us. This authority is not on the basis of age or experience, but on the basis of the finished work of Christ on the cross.

Is there a price for hours spent in prayer?

The disciples had driven out lots of unclean spirits, but one day they came up against one they could not drive out. They wanted to know why. Jesus told them in Matthew 17:19-21: 'This kind goes out only by prayer and fasting.'

But Jesus drove the demon out instantly! What does that tell you about Jesus? He had an established pattern of prayer and fasting! He was 'prayed up' all the time. It is now my ambition to be prayed up all the time, to be able to meet any challenge head on when it comes, in the power of Jesus.

WEC workers and their supporters had prayed for years that a church would be established among the Fula people of West Africa. Until the late eighties, there were just two struggling fellowships in eastern Senegal, nothing in the Senegal River Valley, or Gambia, or Guinea, or Guinea Bissau. Patrick Johnstone featured the Fula as one of the 'Gateway Peoples' on a video he produced. He suggested that if the Fula could be gripped by the power of the gospel, they could become a gateway for the gospel into all the rest of the cultures and languages of West Africa. This video had global circulation. The Fula were also featured in unreached peoples lists in the *March for Jesus* intercession, and in the prayer booklet of the movement to pray for Muslims during Ramadan. Millions of people must have been praying for Fulas. The person-hours had suddenly increased exponentially in just a few years. Was there any difference? Yes, praise God! Two Fula churches were planted in Gambia, one in Guinea Bissau, and one in Guinea, all lively churches with potential to multiply. Yet we cannot say that it was only the prayers of these extra millions that tipped the balance. The prayers of those pioneers were not wasted! They all went together to tip the balance!

Revelation 8:3: 'Another angel, who had a golden censer, came and stood at the altar. He was given much incense to offer, with the prayers of all the saints . . . The smoke of the incense, together with the prayers of the saints, went up before God. . . .'

A Fula couldn't say the Muslim prayers
Jane Larkman

During Ramadan, Wuuri found he couldn't say the Muslim prayers! The name of Jesus kept coming into his mind! His brother was a Christian, so Wuuri began to read the Bible instead. He came to us to say that he wanted to commit his life to the Lord. We stalled him, wanting him seriously to count the cost. But he was determined. After watching the Jesus film, he prayed a beautiful prayer of commitment and was immediately filled with joy. He publicly burnt his charms and openly testified in a large meeting of Fulas from four countries.

Is it FAITH we need?

Others have said, 'It's not the hours you put into prayer that make a difference. It's the faith in your prayer that makes God sit up and take notice.' Before Jesus said anything about prayer and fasting to those disciples who failed, he said it was 'because you have so little faith. I tell you the truth, if you have faith as small as a mustard seed, you can say to this mountain "Move from here to there" and it will move. Nothing will be impossible for you.' This famous verse in Matthew 17:20 is in the context of deliverance.

How do we develop faith? Romans 10:17 tells us that faith comes from hearing the message, and the message is heard through the word of Christ. 'Word' here is not the written word *logos*, meaning the scriptures, or the eternal living word meaning the Lord Jesus. *Logos* means the word for all time, for all cultures, true for ever, everywhere. 'My word shall never pass away' is *logos*. *Logos* is the eternal truth for all time. 'In the beginning was the logos and the logos was with God and the logos was God' (John 1:1).

'Word' here is *rhema*, a spoken word, a word for a specific person in a specific situation for a limited time. *Rhema* is local, applied truth. For example, God commanded Israel to march round Jericho silently, once a day, then seven times in one day with a final shout. He never seems to have used that strategy again. It was specific for that time and those people in that place. Sometimes a *logos* from the Bible can become a *rhema* to me specifically and unmistakably for a problem I am asking about. In any case, as we face the problems we are praying about, we need to be asking for a *rhema* to claim, to stand on, to speak back to God, to increase our faith.

God might cause a friend to write or say something. We might read something in a book or just get the conviction in our hearts as we are praying and agonizing about a situation. (So sometimes the faith might rise because of the time spent in prayer!) The most important thing is to get complete assurance that our prayer is answered.

Another way to develop our faith muscles is to use the ones we have, by praying something we can believe, and biting off more next time. George Muller did not begin with hundreds of orphans, but with one house. The first time he came to pray for a thousand pounds he really struggled, but eventually he discovered that it was easy to trust God for a thousand. His next faith struggle was to trust the Lord for ten thousand.

'Lord, save my neighbour'
John Bardsley

A French believer had been praying for months that God would save his next-door neighbour, but nothing seemed to be happening, and he complained to God, 'Why don't you save my neighbour? I'm sure it is your will. I've been asking for some time. What's the problem?'

The Lord replied, 'The problem is your faith. You don't believe I can save your neighbour'.

'Yes I do! You know I do! I believe you can do anything!'

'You think you do. But you don't believe. Can you imagine your neighbour a Christian?'

'Oh. When you put it like that, perhaps I don't.'

'No, you don't yet have faith for his conversion. Ask me for something you can believe.'

'All right then. Actually I've never even had a good conversation with him. Could you arrange that?'

The next weekend, they were both out digging their gardens, and they began to chat. So he said, 'Thank you, Lord! Can we go one step further? I've never ever been in his house.' Hey presto, next time they were both out in the garden at the same time, his neighbour said 'Why don't you come in for coffee?' The Christian thanked the Lord, and this time asked, 'Could you make him bring up the subject of Christianity?' and his neighbour asked 'Where do you go every Sunday morning at ten o'clock?' They talked a lot about various issues in Christianity, but eventually the day came when the Christian prayed again, 'Lord, save my neighbour!' And God did!

Is there a standard of qualitative holiness that makes our prayers more authoritative?

Demons knew of Paul, but not the sons of Sceva (Acts 19:15). After sin and confession, cleansing is immediate. It takes a little longer to restore my joy – the light in my eyes that makes me able to witness. But how long does it take to climb back up to the level of holiness I had? Purity is bought by the precious blood of Christ. Holiness is won in wrestling with the enemy – winning a series of moral choices. See the next chapter.

It is a continuing challenge to me that Jesus had instant and total authority over the dark forces of his day; and that he promised we would do greater things than he (John 14:12).

STOPTHINK&DISCUSS
● We have talked about submission, humility, faith, hours spent in prayer, and holiness, as factors in our ability to tap into the authority of the Eternal God. Ask yourself 'Do I have a problem with rebellion, pride, unbelief, prayerlessness, carnality?' Give it to God.
● Discuss these five issues, and help each other find ways to overcome.

5
PERSONAL PREPARATION FOR VICTORY

John Bardsley, Dietrich Kuhl, Hans Rothenberger, Stewart Dinnen

The whole Bible and all past history teach that battles are always won or lost before the armies take the field. The critical moment for any soldier is not the day he engages the foe in actual combat; it is the day before, or the month or year before, when he does his training. A boxer must win his fight weeks before he steps into the ring. The rule is, prepare or fail. The Duke of Wellington claimed that the battle of Waterloo was won on the playing fields of Eton College, where he went to school. Christ could endure the anguish of the cross because he had suffered the pains of Gethsemane the night before; there was a direct relationship between the two experiences. One served as preparation for the other.

The converse of this is also true. Battles are never lost the day they are fought. They are lost the day before, or the week or month or year before, and the results merely become obvious when the armies meet.

Preparation is vital. We can seek God today and get prepared to meet temptation tomorrow, but if we meet the enemy without first having met God, we can only lose.

Identify with Christ: you're crucified
Bruce Rattray

A young man at the back of the meeting had openly opposed the message, even standing to vent his feelings. At every mention of Christ's blood he would rage and blaspheme, his eyes glaring and his face contorted. After the meeting, I took him home to minister to him personally.

'Garth, I am going to pray for you,' I began. 'Pray? There is no God,' he raged. As he went on mumbling incoherently, I prayed, 'In the name of the Lord Jesus Christ I bind the spirit blinding Garth to the truth of the gospel, and I command you to release him.'

Instantly there was a transformation in his attitude. Sobbing, Garth turned to me saying, 'I want to know Christ more than anything else in the world, but every time I try to draw near to him I have these awful, blasphemous thoughts.' We worked on that. Within a few months he had come to Christ.

This incident raises several basic questions which demand an answer. Why did such a simple prayer have such a dramatic effect on Garth? What evidence gave Bruce the clue to Garth's problem? How did Bruce know what to pray?

Two pre-requisites for effective spiritual warfare

1. A revelation of our union with Christ in his death, resurrection and ascension.
2. A realisation that Christ has totally defeated Satan and the powers of darkness.

Bruce continues:

In my last year of Bible school the Lord called me to Borneo. When I graduated I received a letter from my Dad that said, 'I think the Lord is going to call you back to the farm for a while.' That was the last thing I wanted, but that very day God spoke from Habakkuk 2:3, 'The revelation awaits an appointed time . . . Though it linger, wait for it; for it will certainly come and will not delay.' While at Bible College I had been leading people to Christ in a Bible study group. Here I was back on the farm without even a Sunday School class. I had no ministry at all. But the Lord spoke through Psalm 139 where it says, 'You hem me in . . . you have laid your hand upon me.' It seemed the Lord was saying, 'I want you to stop. Stop while I deal with you. I want to teach you. I want to form you and prepare you.' It became two wonderful years of Divine preparation. Alone in the isolated farmhouse, night by night for hours on end, I would pore over my Bible from Genesis to Revelation.

The cry of my heart was for a true knowledge of his word and a life of holiness and victory, a life which until then had eluded me. I became so full of the Bible that God used to speak to me directly. I remember ploughing a paddock and throughout the whole day I don't remember turning a furrow. My mind was just running through the truths that God was showing me. I knew I was forgiven, I knew the power of the blood to forgive my sins but it seemed my life was a round of sin, confession, struggle, struggle, and falling again. I thought there had to be more in the Christian life than this. If I couldn't find anything more than this, what was the point of it all?

I hungrily read *Born Crucified* by Maxwell, *Bone of His Bone* by Huegel, *The Normal Christian Life* by Watchman Nee, all of which spoke about a life of joy and victory of which I knew nothing. Finally, at the end of my tether, I was led to do a wise thing. I prayed a scriptural prayer: 'Lord, give me a spirit of wisdom and revelation in the knowledge of Christ! Enlighten the eyes of my understanding!' I repeated this prayer many times, day and night, from the depths of my heart. My dilemma? I knew I had to die to sin, but the more I tried to put myself to death, the more I knew that I, the old I, was still very much alive. And that's when God showed me the truth of 'union with Christ'. I hadn't been able to see that before.

One morning I was reading John's account of the crucifixion, death and burial of our Lord. Suddenly the Lord asked me a question. 'Did Jesus really die?' I remembered the terrible scourging, the agony as he hung nailed to that awful cross, the loud shout as he died, the thrust of the Roman spear, the body wrapped in the perfumed cloths, the cold tomb. 'Yes, Lord, he really died.' Then, ever so quietly – it seemed almost as if time stood still – he spoke again, just a few words which totally transformed my Christian life, and from then on became the basis of my ministry.

'If he died, then you died, because you were in him when he died!' Suddenly I understood! Everything happened in Christ, and I was in Christ, so everything happened to me. All that Christ the head had experienced, the body had also experienced. I did not have to struggle to become a branch of the Vine. I was already a part of the Vine. The Bible came alive to me in a totally new way.

Then more dawned on me! If I have been crucified with Christ, I have also been buried with him. And if buried with him, I have been raised with him. And if raised with him, I have also been seated with him on his throne, which means that I now share in his victory over the world, the flesh and the devil. I am actually reigning with Christ!

Now I understood what Huegel kept repeating in *Bone of His Bone*: 'We are not imitators of Christ, we are partakers of Christ'. It was this revelation which enabled me to pray the prayer of deliverance for Garth.

After totally defeating Satan during the temptation in the desert, meeting every demonic suggestion with a 'word', Christ demonstrated his authority in such a way that people marvelled, saying, 'What is this? . . . He speaks with power even to the demons and they obey him' (Mark 1:27). On his way to the culminating moment of his mission, his substitution for us sinful humans, he called out, 'Now the prince of this world shall be evicted' (John 12:31, my own rendering). And so it was! Satan and his cohorts, drunk with blind rage and hatred, gloated at the sufferings they inspired evil men to cause him (John 13:2, 27). 'Many bulls have surrounded me; strong bulls of Bashan have encircled me. They open wide their mouth at me, as a ravening and a roaring lion' was David's experience described in Psalm 22:12-13 (NASB).

At Christ's death all hell threw an enormous victory party, never realising that his death as our representative forever sounded the death knell on Satan's claim to be the Prince of this world. All this Satan realised too late, on the morning of the resurrection! The only hope left to Satan then was to prevent the risen Christ from appearing in person before God as our representative, there in the heavenly Holy of Holies 'with his own blood'. Satan failed in this too. Christ stripped the power from these demonic powers, leading them as a train of defeated foes.

So Satan has been legally defeated! He is now a usurper, a mere squatter. When confronted by a disciple of Christ who knows this fact, Satan is forced to submit to his command in Jesus' name. 'In my name they will drive out demons,' Jesus said (Mark 16:17). When we left for Indonesia, we gave my sister the power of attorney over all our business. This meant that when she spoke on our behalf, she was using the legal right we had given her. Christ has given us power of attorney!

Confess your sin: be clean

What is righteousness? I am forgiven and cleansed, acquitted, clean. Christ the sinless one became sin for me, so that in him I might become the righteousness of God (2 Corinthians 5:21). God is light, pure light. There's not a trace of darkness in him. If we claim that we're free from sin, we're only fooling ourselves. On the other hand, if we admit our sins, make a clean breast of them, he is fair, and true to himself. He will forgive our sins and purge us from all wrongdoing. (1 John 1:7-9, adapted from The Message). On the basis of this, I am instantly white as snow the moment I confess.

Temptation

'Abstain from sinful desires, which wage war against your soul' (1 Peter 2:11). Is it from the world? Flee it! (I Timothy 6:11, 2 Timothy 2:22, 1 Corinthians 6:18 and 10:14.) Is it from the flesh? Crucify it! Ask Jesus for the will and the obedience! (Romans 8:13, Colossians 3:5). Is it from the devil? Resist him! Command him to take it away! (James 4:7-8).

Particularly be aware of any rebellion in your heart towards authority figures, because God includes it in the same category as witchcraft (1 Samuel 15:23; see also Romans 13:1-5, 1 Peter 2:13-21 and Hebrews 13:17). Confess and renounce it. Ask that any ground gained by the enemy in your life through rebellion will be cancelled and cleansed. Ask for a servant heart and a submissive spirit, and for grace to apologise to any leader who has suffered because of your rebelliousness. Watch out for subtle pride, superiority, and any area of self-confidence contrary to the teaching in John 15.

I never have trouble taking out the garbage or picking up papers on our drive or footpath, so I didn't suspect I was proud. I love preaching. One day, when I picked up a brochure for a WEC conference at Bulstrode where I was living, I noticed the line-up of speakers, and thought, 'They didn't ask me.' Suddenly the Holy Spirit hit me: 'That's pride.' I had to root out pride in that one area, and it was insidious! See also Philippians 2:1-5; Galatians 2:20; 5:24-26; Proverbs 29:23 and 1 John 2:16.

Forgive: be united

Any area of disunity will sabotage your prayer. Get rid of anger, resentment, jealousy and everything that contributes to disunity. Make things right with everyone. There are several whole chapters dedicated to unity: Psalm 133, John 17, Romans 14 and 15, and many powerful shorter passages like Philippians 2: 1-3. This shows just how important it is to God.

There is no substitute for the unity of the pastors of a city as a foundation for effective spiritual warfare. The reason for this is that the pastors are the spiritual gate keepers of the city, the spiritual authorities. Satan does his best to prevent pastors getting together, especially to pray. The unity required is not doctrinal, legal, philosophical, organisational, but spiritual. It is almost inevitable that certain pastors will be grumpy, indifferent, burnt out, hung up on some doctrinal issue, or even effectively screened out by the forces of darkness. Still, it is realistic to expect, after prayer and effort, a consensus of a majority of influential pastors who will agree for two hours a month. 'Summon the elders ... Cry out to the Lord' (Joel 1:14).

Reconciliation
John Bardsley

Edgardo Silvoso from Argentina visited Britain for Christian meetings. The first thing he said when he came on stage was, 'As a representative of Argentina I apologise for the war. Is there a Britisher who will come and forgive me?' There was. He came up, they talked a bit, then hugged. Then Edgardo said, 'Is there an Irishman who will apologise for the troubles, and is there an Englishman who will apologize for what the English have done there?' There was. They met at the front, talked, hugged. Edgardo went on, 'Is there a Scot who will be reconciled to the English, and an Englishman who will be reconciled to the Scots?' There was. They were reconciled. Then Edgardo demonstrated how well he had done his homework before he came to UK. Not everyone in the world knows that the northern Englishmen speak differently from those in the south, earn less money, and some tend to resent the wealthier southern English with their posh accents, while some of the southern English may tend to despise their 'country cousins'. Edgardo said 'Is there a Northerner who will make peace with a Southerner?' The place erupted in surprised laughter. He touched a nerve. Two people went forward, met at the front, talked, hugged, as representatives of all of us.

Then Edgardo stated, 'As a man, I want to apologise to all the ladies present for the way we men don't listen to you, and the way we withdraw emotional support when there is a disagreement. If any of you other men here agree with me, will you kneel down and apologise to a woman near you?' I turned, and saw a woman I had never met before. I kneeled down and apologised to her, but then I didn't know what to do, because she burst into tears, with huge, gut-wrenching sobs that shook her whole frame! I stood up and hugged her, and eventually her heaving sobs subsided. The same thing was happening all over the auditorium. Slowly silence descended on the auditorium as people began to sit down again. Edgardo began to give his message about reconciliation. He didn't really have to say any more. The Holy Spirit had fallen on us as we had become reconciled to one another.

What misunderstandings lie between you and your spouse, ignored because they are too difficult to solve? Is that limiting your authority in prayer? Will you try again? Buddhism teaches about getting rid of your passionate desires so you can be more peaceful and united. The world is hungry for this unity. Among us we have the Prince of Peace! We have the answer! We must demonstrate that we do.

Take it to heart: be committed

Whatever we pray for had better be what we want, and want badly. Sometimes our wishes are our real prayers, and God may well grant a burning wish in preference to a lukewarm prayer. Prayer is wanting something badly enough to ask the most powerful person in the universe. But if the most powerful person in the universe is my Father, I'd ask him anyway!

Bringing it all to God
John Bardsley

When our daughters were teenagers, they had the usual teenage issues. I would often wonder what to do. Sometimes I would write to my mother. Mum does not have email, and I knew a letter from us to her would take six days to arrive. I don't know how many times it happened that the problem evaporated on day six! I would be thanking God. Then the penny would drop, Mum must have received the letter! She's taken it to the throne. Grandmothers are committed!

Our prayer must be persistent, not to persuade God, but because of the opposition of the enemy. Daniel discovered this. In Daniel 10:13 and 20 the angel who came to Daniel admitted he had been delayed because of obstructions from the Prince of Persia.

James 5:16 in the Amplified Bible reads, 'The heartfelt, continued prayer of someone right with God makes tremendous power available.'

Heartfelt: There are eight different biblical words for prayer. They range in meaning to include plead, beg, demand, beseech, call, ask, wish. They are all emotional words, filled with longing and desire. Our English word 'prayer' is weak, emasculated. To be real prayer, it must be heartfelt (How much do I care? What difference does it make for me?) and continued (Is this a one-off, or am I committed to pray until it happens? Can I hang in there?). To be effective, I must be righteous. See website for an example of each of the passionate words for prayer (details on page 229).

Continued: The Greek for endurance is *hupomeno*, meaning literally 'staying under'. I was reminded of a competition held by the physical education lecturers for the 300 male students at our teachers' college. We were given several weeks to train, and told that we should all aim to swim the length of the swimming pool under water. There would be a competition to see who could swim the farthest under water. I was flat out against swimming across the pool under water! But I began to train. It is amazing what training will do! On the day I didn't quite make the full length. My lungs were screaming for oxygen, my brain was saying, 'Get up! Air! Air! Get to the surface!' but my will was saying 'One more stroke! Pull! Pull!' It was an endurance test, a test of staying under. Many others did make it to the end. One man touched the end, turned under water, and continued. His huge arms and hands and legs made great sweeps under water. He surged onwards and completed almost two laps under water! We need to ask God for the same steady endurance in the face of opposition as we pray for our faith goals.

Righteous means simply 'right with God'; a clean heart, everything confessed, forsaken and forgiven; nothing between us (1 John 1:9). Bishop John Owen described to a reporter for *The Western Mail* his experience of the Welsh revival in 1904. He said, 'The power of the Holy Spirit is given to the Church in proportion to the reality and purity of its prayers.'

A man about to be elected as a church elder was deeply disturbed about the church, and his attitude was negative and critical. Stewart Dinnen showed him that he could turn his concerns into prayer. When he realised that prayer was doing something practical about the problems, he began to pray for the church instead of criticising, and his whole attitude changed.

Claim the protection of the blood of Christ

What has it done for us? The blood has gained everlasting life for us. Christ 'entered the Most Holy Place once for all by his own blood, thus obtaining eternal redemption.' The blood of goats made an Israelite ceremonially clean. 'How much more, then, will the blood of Christ, who through the eternal Spirit offered himself unblemished to God, cleanse our consciences from acts that lead to death, so that we may serve the living God!' (Hebrews 9:12,14).

The blood has made us God's friends. God was pleased through Jesus to reconcile to himself all things, 'by making peace through his blood, shed on the cross' (Colossians 1:20).

The blood has paid the slave price for God to set us free. 'You know that it was not with perishable [biodegradable] things such as silver and gold that you were redeemed from the empty way of life handed down from your fore-fathers, but with the precious blood of Christ, a lamb without blemish or defect.' (1 Peter 1:18-19).

The devil visited me in hospital
Jean Forbes

One night the devil visited me in hospital. He stood beside my bed, quiet and dressed in black. I knew who he was. I told him that I loved Jesus and that he was to go and leave me alone. He went over to the window and I went back to sleep. Then he appeared again with a black blanket in his hands. I knew he wanted to smother me. He had a nurse with him (not one from the ward) and said that I must be cold and that he would cover me with the blanket. I told him I was not cold and I said once more that I loved Jesus and belonged to him. He was to go in the name of Jesus. He did, and I have had no trouble since. We don't have to be afraid of him, though we must have healthy respect for what power he does have. He is a loser and he hates the name of Jesus. 'Do not be afraid. I am the First and the Last. I am the Living One. . . I hold the keys of death' (Revelation 1:17-18).

Expect reprisals. Be alert: refuse them
According to temperament

When I began to pray for the Jola people in Senegal, every member of my family was attacked in some way, each according to temperament. One came in one day saying, 'I like to be angry! It makes me feel strong!' I was so alarmed I rushed straight into the bedroom and fell on my knees to pray. Another struggled with depression, yet another with fear. I seemed to have extra powerful temptations to lust, with filthy thoughts injected from nowhere, then the accusation, 'You're rotten'. It was a great comfort to me when a fellow worker testified that as he had been praying for the conversion of one of the girls at a summer camp, he had been attacked with images of her in her bathing costume. He had commanded the enemy to take his lust with him and leave. Another worker, in a lonely front-line evangelistic position, had also been plagued with lustful thoughts and images. As she resisted the enemy, he fled, and she had made the delightful discovery that she herself, filled with Jesus, was actually clean in her imaginations.

Ignoring Satan's lies
Patrick Johnstone
When my wife Jill Johnstone was dying of cancer, she came into the office one day and said, 'Satan came and told me: "You're depressed, Jill." I told him, "I'm not depressed, Satan. If anyone is depressed around here, it must be you, so you take your depression and leave".' How glorious to recognise the enemy's tactic so quickly.

Out of sorts
Carolyn Pinke
I am not normally a moody or depressed person, but I discovered that occasionally I could be emotionally 'down'. If I can't seem to snap out of it, I assume it may be spiritual. I can't bear that feeling of a heavy, depressing weight on my spirit, so I respond something like this:

'If this is from my flesh, I refuse it in Jesus' name! I don't like it and I will not continue this way. If it is from the Evil One, I resist him in Jesus name! The Lord rebuke you! Get away from my life! I have been bought by the shed blood of Jesus Christ and I am free! Jesus is the Lord of my life. Lord, I worship and praise you, the King of all the earth!'

Sometimes I have to speak under my breath, but I try to go where I can speak out loud, at least quietly, but very energetically. Whether it is my flesh or the Evil One, I can put the whole force of my spirit behind my declarations. I continue declaring my position in Christ and his greatness, as necessary.

After this, I sense the heaviness lifting off me. I continue to praise and worship the Lord. I have prayed in the same way for my husband when I could tell that something was making him feel out-of-sorts. I have seen some distinct changes, as if he suddenly relaxed and was at ease.

Falling in love
John Bardsley
When I was still single at Bible College, I was helping one of the lady students push a trolley of food from the dining room back into the scullery for washing up. Our eyes met, and I experienced falling in love. I was in my first year, and the rule then was that relationships could not be initiated without checking first with the staff. I went to the Principal and told him. He said, 'John, do you plan to be a missionary?' 'Indeed I do,' I replied. 'She is not going to be a missionary,' he said. 'If she were not graduating next month she would be asked to leave. Are you sure this is from God?' I had promised God that I would marry nobody who was not called to the

field I was called to! But that promise had gone completely out of my head in the pools of those beautiful eyes!

Extremes

Avoid an over-emphasis on the demonic. Territorial spirits are not to be a primary focus of our ministry and prayer, but don't underestimate the enemy and your frailty. Some years ago 18 evangelists demonstrated and preached daily against pornography in front of the conference location of a Copenhagen pornographic festival. Every one of these 18 subsequently succumbed to pornography. A Ghanaian pastor ordered a sacred tree to be cut down, and he dropped dead when the tree fell. Be aware of spiritual arrogance (Zechariah 3:2; Jude 8-9) and looking down on others who might have a different view of spiritual warfare. Don't concentrate on techniques, but follow the plain teaching of the Bible. Don't move alone, but involve a group of intercessors or, preferably, the church or churches in the area.

Was there not enough prayer?
John Bardsley
Pastor John Kipo in Ghana had been a pillar of the church for twenty years. In 2001, an elderly relative became a Christian and burnt the family fetishes. This caused a great deal of persecution to the old man and to the local pastor, Inusah. Within three months Pastor Inusah killed a child in a car accident, Pastor John had a stroke which affected his memory, and another close relative, Rasaku, cut off four of his fingers in a circular saw. Was there not enough prayer? Or were all these things really just accidental?

Reclaim footholds: be God's!
John Bardsley
Do you have any area of regular defeat? Do you feel a compulsion to do something you afterwards hate having done? Then perhaps you have given Satan or one of his demons a foothold in your life.

The most significant spiritual experience that had happened to me for a decade happened in October 1991. Sometimes I had experienced incredible compulsion to sin. I really used to wonder what happened to the promised way out. 1 Corinthians 10:13 says: 'No temptation has seized you except what is common to man. And God is faithful; he will not let you be tempted beyond what you can bear. But when you are tempted, he will also provide a way out, so you can stand up under it.'

One afternoon I noticed that another missionary was absolutely shining, and I said to her, 'What's different about you?' She said, 'I have just got free from compulsions that have dogged me for years!' I said, 'Tell me about it!' A pastor had visited her field and explained how these footholds are established, and helped her to freedom.

What is a foothold?
Is there reference in Scripture to footholds? Ephesians 4:26-27 reads, 'In your

anger do not sin. Do not let the sun go down while you are still angry.' 'Don't give the Devil that kind of foothold . . .' (The Message). A foothold is literally a place, a small beachhead or landing pad. 'Do not take revenge, my friends, but leave room [again literally a place, same word] for God's wrath' (Romans 12:19).

These references describe wilful persistence in anger or unforgiveness. The devil loves it. He emphasizes it, strengthens it, so you do it again. 'Each victory will help you another to win' is true, and so is the reverse: 'Each defeat strengthens the bondage.' Jesus said to the Pharisees: 'My word has no place in you' (John 8:37 NASB).

Eventually, it seems, a demon specialising in that sin was assigned to hang around me to try to make that sin part of my character, part of my way of life.

As well as anger (Ephesians 4:26), other footholds explicitly mentioned are unforgiveness, one of the schemes by which the devil tries to outwit us (2 Corinthians 2:4-11), pride, which incurs the same judgment as the devil (1 Timothy 3:6), a quarrelsome spirit, a 'trap of the devil' (2 Timothy 2:23-26).

When Jesus was on the way to the cross, he said, 'The prince of this world is coming. He has no hold on me' (John 14:30). We want to be able to say the same! There is no foothold for any demon in my life!

Specialist demons?

Is there such a thing as a demon that specialises in one particular problem? Yes, sins and sicknesses and mental states. Not that I believe all sickness is related to a demon! But it can happen. Jesus said so:

'My son has a dumb spirit.' 'When Jesus saw that a crowd was running to the scene, he rebuked the evil spirit. "You deaf and mute spirit", he said, "I command you, come out of him and never enter him again"' (Mark 9:25).

'A woman was there who had been crippled by a spirit for eighteen years. She was bent over and could not straighten up at all. When Jesus saw her, he called her forward and said to her, "Woman, you are set free from your infirmity." Then he put his hands on her, and immediately she straightened up and praised God' (Luke 13:11-13).

'We were met by a slave girl who had a spirit by which she predicted the future. . . Finally Paul became so troubled that he turned round and said to the spirit, "In the name of Jesus Christ I command you to come out of her"' (Acts 16:16,18).

'For you did not receive a spirit that makes you a slave again to fear, but you received the Spirit of sonship' (Romans 8:15).

'God gave them a spirit of stupor, eyes so that they could not see and ears so that they could not hear' (Romans 11:8). 'In later times some will abandon the faith and follow deceiving spirits and things taught by demons. Such teachings come through hypocritical liars' (1 Timothy 4:1).

'God did not give us a spirit of timidity' (2 Timothy 1:7). Also mentioned are a spirit of Antichrist (1 John 4:3), a spirit of falsehood (1 John 4:6), a garment of praise instead of a spirit of despair (Isaiah 61:3), a lying spirit (1 Kings 22:22), a haughty spirit (Proverbs 16:18), a spirit of foolishness (Isaiah 19:14 NLT), a familiar spirit (1 Samuel 28) and a spirit of prostitution (Hosea 4:12).

Some of those listed seem like actual evil spirits, while others seem to be using the word 'spirit' in the sense of 'atmosphere' or 'emotional context". But that emotion could also be caused by that spirit.

What gives a demon a foothold?

Be aware of bad moods, touchiness, rage, prolonged fits of anger, hatred, worry, persistent negativism, emotional upsets, bitterness, jealousy, hardness, criticism, or any excessive emotional upsets, swearing, blaming God, because through all these things the enemy will try to gain entrance.

A foothold is usually the result of:
a. childhood trauma which you may have experienced, or
b. something that may have been passed down the generations, or
c. wilfully choosing one particular sin, alone or in a group. Group agreement makes bondage even stronger.

Any of these gives the devil a foothold, a beachhead, landing rights on the island of your mind from then on, year in, year out.

Do we have a theological basis for such a claim?
a. Childhood trauma: 'Jesus asked the boy's father, "How long has he been like this?" "From childhood," he answered' (Mark 9:21).
b. Generation curse: God does not condemn us for the sins of our ancestors. 'Each of us will give an account of himself to God' (Romans 14:12). 'The soul who sins is the one who will die. He will not die for his father's sin; he will surely live. But his father will die for his own sin' (Ezekiel 18: 4,17,18).
We do suffer the results of our fathers' sins, up to four generations. If my father is an alcoholic, I am poor, possibly beaten, possibly with a tendency to alcoholism or fear or violence myself. The daughter of a Satanist is likely to be brought up to be a Satanist, and her daughter too. Children who live with criticism learn to condemn. Children who live with bitterness echo that bitterness.
'I, the Lord your God, am a jealous God, punishing the children for the sin of the fathers to the third and fourth generation of those who hate me, but showing love to a thousand generations of those who love me and keep my commandments' (Deuteronomy 5:9-10). 'Because of their fathers' sins they will waste away' (Leviticus 26:39). 'Your children will be shepherds here for forty years, suffering for your unfaithfulness' (Numbers 14:33). 'Our fathers sinned and are no more, and we bear their punishment' (Lamentations 5:7). 'You show love to thousands but bring the punishment for the fathers' sins into the laps of their children after them' (Jeremiah 32:18).
c. Wilful sin: Deliberate sin gives the devil a foothold (Ephesians 4:25-28).

Footholds ignored grow into strongholds
If I don't do anything about my habit, it becomes ingrained
Imagine an island in the Pacific. Troops are guarding it against invasion, particularly from one particular direction. The enemy lands a small force in an

unexpected position, and that gives the enemy a foothold. If discovered in time, the small enemy force is easily overcome. The longer it remains undiscovered, the more it can dig a trench, erect a palisade, build a blockhouse, construct a fort, develop a well-defended stronghold.

But even well-defended strongholds can be taken and destroyed. The description of a stronghold in 2 Corinthians 10:4-5 includes disobedient thoughts, (false) arguments and pretensions that set themselves up against the knowledge of God. What is a pretension? It's a cunningly presented lie. It's false statements dressed up to look like truth.

A child makes a mess of a project, and someone tells him, 'You'll never be any good.' If he is regularly criticised, that can grow from a foothold into a stronghold in his life. In Christ, everyone has potential, and no failure is final.

How do we remove footholds and destroy strongholds?
Treatment is incredibly simple and fast! A three-step process:
1. Identify lies you believe the stronghold may have been based on, and counter them with truth: e.g. 'Sex satisfies', 'I can sin and avoid the consequences', 'I need more money than God gives me' or thinking I am something I am not.
a. Dissociate yourself from that sin that disturbed your childhood. In the name of Jesus cut off its influence on you, and refuse it. Or
b. Honour your parents and your ancestors but refuse and renounce any evil influence that has come to you from them. Or
c. Confess that original wilful sin by name. This removes the beachhead!
2. Tell Satan (or the spirit of _____ he sent) that he now has no foothold; everything is cleansed by the blood of Christ. Command him, in Jesus' name, to leave.
3. Give that area of your life to the Holy Spirit to flood and control.

How it happened for me
John Bardsley
I knew it applied to me, as soon as she spoke. I had compulsions. I used to sin, feel rotten, and confess it, over and over again. When I was clean, God used me. But in between were times of defeat and despair. I said to the missionary, 'That applies to me too. Can we talk?' I told her my compulsion, and immediately she said, 'That's a spirit of_____.' Then she gave me a sheet with lists of sins (below). She said, 'Sometimes other related sins come with it. Check to see if there are more.' I found two more.

'We've identified the spirits,' she said. 'Can you remember a childhood trauma, or a time when you wilfully chose to do one of these things?' I paused and prayed right there. Into my mind came an occasion when I had gone out of my way to sin, way back when I was a lad about ten years old. I confessed it right there and then. It was embarrassing, but freedom is worth it! That got rid of the foothold, the entry point for the filthy spirits.

Then I calmly told the spirits of those three sins that their landing pad was gone. 'I am cleansed by the blood of Christ,' I said. 'You have no place in me any

Compulsions that have sometimes been caused by a spirit

Compulsive eating/ slimming/ working/ talking	Mental torment Anguish	Hypocrisy Confusion Guilt	Perfectionism Impatience Criticism
Addiction: nicotine/ drugs/ alcohol/ medicine/ coffee/ betting/ music/ TV	Disillusionment Rejection Abandonment Loneliness	Condemnation Poverty Jealousy Greed	Mockery Division Impure thoughts Nudity
	Desire to die Suicide	Hurt	Fantasy Sex Masturbation
Fear of death Fear of rejection Fear of making mistakes Fear of self- revelation	Family reputation Shame Worry	Hostility Hatred Bitterness Revenge	Sexual perversion Homosexuality Lesbianism Fornication Adultery
Fear	Self-pity Inferiority Insecurity	Rebellion Arrogance Pride	Prostitution Incest
Indiscipline Procrastination	Doubt Indecision	Attention getting Manipulation Self-justification Self-righteousness	Witchcraft
Helplessness Apathy	Compromise Rationalisation Spiritual blindness	Cursing	
Sadness Depression Despair	Deceit Lying	Blasphemy Coarse jesting	

more. I command you to leave me alone in Jesus' name.' It took only about seven minutes.

I wondered if I could be really free after all this time. Seven minutes, to be free from all those years of intermittent misery. Over the next two weeks it did not seem to be working the way she said it should. Then I remembered two other major occasions when I had wilfully chosen the same sin. The first was in my first year as a missionary, the second four years later. I confessed them both, told the spirit to stop bugging me, and I knew I was free. I am free. I really am free. I can say 'No' to that temptation. The temptation still comes, of course. And I could say 'Yes'. The joy is in being able to say 'No'.

Breaking free
Another level of joy and freedom was gained after six or eight weeks. These sins had become habitual, with lots of little supporting habits and ways of thinking. Habits take time to break. In fact, it takes time to recognise what is a habit or a thought process that needs breaking! But the Lord is interested in setting us free. As I identified them, I asked God to help me create new ways of thinking or acting.

A few times since then I have been tricked again. Immediately I have felt the old ways begin to reassert themselves. Immediately I have fled to Jesus in repentance. If necessary, I have gone through the three stages again. The freedom is wonderful. I wish someone had told me years ago! Why don't we teach this stuff in church?

Renounce: is this a Biblical term?
Psalm 89:39: 'You have renounced the covenant with your servant and have defiled his crown in the dust.'
Proverbs 28:13 'He who conceals his sins does not prosper, but whoever confesses and renounces them finds mercy.'
Ezekiel 14:6: 'Therefore say to the house of Israel, "This is what the Sovereign LORD says: Repent! Turn from your idols and renounce all your detestable practices!"'
Daniel 4:27: 'Therefore, O king, be pleased to accept my advice: Renounce your sins by doing what is right, and your wickedness by being kind to the oppressed. It may be that then your prosperity will continue.'
2 Corinthians 4:2: 'We have renounced secret and shameful ways; we do not use deception, nor do we distort the word of God. On the contrary, by setting forth the truth plainly we commend ourselves to every man's conscience in the sight of God.'
Revelation 2:13: 'I know where you live—where Satan has his throne. Yet you remain true to my name. You did not renounce your faith in me, even in the days of Antipas, my faithful witness, who was put to death in your city—where Satan lives.'

We see that renounce is a strong word indicating a total change of direction and attitude. It is useful for wilful sin. I can renounce an old covenant I made with the devil, and initiate a new covenant with God. I can renounce sins of various kinds. I can renounce my old faith and adopt a new one.

Build positive habits to replace harmful ones
Break detrimental habit patterns and establish good habits instead. As I say 'No' to a bad habit every day, it is like dying to my craving; but the good thing is that every time I say 'No', the bad habit becomes weaker, until there will be a neutral period when I can choose to establish a good habit to replace it.

Even if you have been delivered from a demon that had been compelling, driving or enslaving you, the flesh continues and you must continually be putting it, together with its desires, to death on the cross, as in Colossians 3:5-9 and Galatians 2:20. What you are delivered from is being driven to sin against your will.

Getting into good habits
John Bardsley
Sidlow Baxter was a pastor with a much-appreciated teaching ministry. He told us a story about himself. 'I had promised the Lord the first hour of every day. We had good times together. One day a little voice whispered to me, "Sidlow, you haven't

visited the widow X for a long time. Make sure you do your visiting." So I took that on board, and tried to squeeze things to get out among the people more. Another day the quiet voice said, "Sidlow, your people love the word when you preach. That's what they come for. Don't rob them. Make sure there is thorough preparation." So I sighed, and squeezed things a bit more, to give more time for research.

'It was strange. After a while, it seemed there was less blessing in my sermons, not more. More wood, but less life. They were dry. I began to wonder if that quiet voice was not from the Lord at all, and then I did hear the still small voice, the voice of the Master, asking, "Sidlow, didn't you promise me the first hour of every day?" It had slipped, you see, under all these other pressures.

'The next morning I got up and said to my will, "Will, will you come with me to meet the Lord this morning?" Will said, "I'll go if you'll go, Sidlow." We headed for my quiet corner. Emotions screamed, "No! Don't do it! Don't go, Sidlow!" But Will and I plodded off to spend time with our Father, dragging Emotions along behind us. And the next day it was the same. For about two weeks it was like that.

'At the beginning of the third week, I said to my will, "Will you come with me to meet the Lord this morning?" "I'll go if you'll go, Sidlow," said Will. Emotions grumbled: "That's boring! Not that old stuff again! You've done all that before!" But Sid and Will set off, dragging Emotions as usual. The smell of freshly brewed coffee wafted under the door, but Will and Sid met the Lord. That went on for about two weeks as well.

'At the beginning of about week five, I said to my will, "Will you come with me and meet the Lord this morning?" "I'll go if you'll go, Sidlow," said Will. And Emotions said, "Hallelujah anyway!" I think it was Wesley who said, "Choose those things that are best. Habit will make them the most pleasant."'

Holy God, holy people

What does it actually mean to be holy?

Staying clean
Righteous means right with God. It's being made clean. Then what is holiness? Holiness is staying clean. It's walking around close enough to God to be able to say 'No' to the tempter. It's winning a series of moral choices. It's the set of your will that your body is only for God to use. The devil will always push you as hard as he can. He will make you think it's impossible to change, it's inevitable to sin. All God asks is that you genuinely want him instead of the tempting dirty bait that Satan is offering.

Holiness is beautiful
'... O Lord, who is like you – majestic in holiness, awesome in glory, working wonders?' (Exodus 15:11). 'Worship the Lord in the splendour of his holiness' (1 Chronicles 16:29). What is majestic about holiness? What is demeaning about unholiness? You see the expression on the face of someone who is filled with

hate, or lust, or rage. Look into the eyes of a gossip with a juicy bit, or someone who despises you, or a child who is telling you a lie, and you can see that sin demeans us.

The opposite works too. Two sisters grew up into young women, one beautiful, one plain. The plain one thought, 'I'll never get married if my face is my only fortune. I'm going to be the kindest person in the room.' And she was. Nothing was too much trouble. She grew into a person who loved helping people. People just loved being with her (obviously!). I don't remember if she got married or not, but in her old age everyone remarked how beautiful she was.

Holiness is difficult
'Speak to the rock,' commanded the Lord. Moses raised his arm and struck the rock. Water gushed out. But the Lord said to Moses and Aaron, 'You did not honour me as holy in the sight of the Israelites' (Numbers 20:2-13). 'You did not uphold my holiness among the Israelites' (Deuteronomy 32:51). How had they not honoured God as holy? They had expressed pride, anger, arrogance and irritation as representatives of God. Do you not represent God to your children? To your neighbours? To your colleagues at work? Of course you do! Then represent God as holy.

'They will keep my name holy; they will acknowledge the holiness of the Holy One of Jacob, and will stand in awe of the God of Israel (Isaiah 29:23). When will I stand in such awe of God's holiness that I, who call myself one of his, will live holy like him? We can be as holy as we really want to be. So often we hanker for something else, something from the old life.

God promises holiness
'I will show the holiness of my great name, which has been profaned among the nations... Then the nations will know that I am the LORD ... when I show myself holy through you before their eyes' (Ezekiel 36:23).

'Praise be to the Lord ... because he has come and has redeemed his people ... to enable us to serve him without fear in holiness ...' (Luke 1:68,74).

'"Touch no unclean thing, and I will receive you. I will be a Father to you, and you will be my sons and daughters," says the Lord Almighty. Since we have these promises, dear friends, let us purify ourselves from everything that contaminates body and spirit, perfecting holiness out of reverence for God' (2 Corinthians 6:17-7:1). Perfecting? Working towards it, building it bit by bit.

From darkness to light
Carolyn Pinke
It has been fantastic to see that when I bring a darkness in my life to the Light, confessing it to the Lord and renouncing it, rejecting it and refusing to let it have any further hold on me, I receive freedom and deliverance from that. I have had to ask the Lord to give me a cold heart towards someone for whom I recognized that I was developing an unhealthy emotional attachment. I was completely dead-serious, horror-struck at the hideousness of my sin in God's eyes, and the Lord

gave me a cold heart overnight and completely delivered me. One must be serious.

Holiness is gradual

Holiness is gradual, and hellishness is gradual too. It's a spiral, a continuum, and we're climbing up or slipping down. 'Just as you used to offer the parts of your body in slavery to impurity and to ever-increasing wickedness, so now offer them in slavery to righteousness leading to holiness What benefit did you reap at that time from the things that you are ashamed of? But now that you have been set free from sin and have become slaves to God, the benefit you reap leads to holiness, and the result is eternal life' (Romans 6:19-22).

I can never be holy by myself, but I must cooperate with God.

'God chose the foolish things of the world to shame the wise; God chose the weak things of the world to shame the strong . . . It is because of him that you are in Christ Jesus, who has become for us . . . our righteousness, holiness, and redemption.' (1 Corinthians 1:27-30).

Why does God want us to be holy?

'You are to be holy to me, because I, the LORD, am holy, and I have set you apart from the nations to be my own' (Leviticus 20:26). Why does God want us to be holy? So we can be with him, to be his own. Holiness is so God can be near us, in us, with us, close.

What does it mean to you, this word holy?

The Hebrew word for holy basically means to cut or to cut loose from something. Being holy really means to cut loose from sin, from Satan, from the world, from what my body wants, from legalism, from myself, from my right to be the boss of my life, and to be totally given to God and available for the Lord. I am not my own. I have one purpose, one longing, to glorify him.

Imagine a great big chocolate cake for a party. I cut a wedge for someone I love who can't be there, and put it aside just for them. You are God's wedge of chocolate cake, set apart only for him.

Cut loose from sin

'Put to death, therefore, whatever belongs to your earthly nature: sexual immorality . . greed. . .' (Colossians 3:5). The passage goes on to tell us to rid ourselves of all such things as anger, malice, slander, filthy language, lying, racism.

Removing the problem
John Bardsley

I taped a film. In some ways it was a beautiful film. God did not seem to think it was good for me. I know why. The thought came very strongly to me as I was going to sleep, 'Wipe that film.' I got up in the morning and taped anything over it so it would be gone. I knew it would be useless to try to have my time with God while that film was still in my house. I'd rather have God's righteous joy like a bride and groom; I'd rather have praise springing up.

It might be my favourite sin I need to cut loose. Do you have an Achilles' heel – a sin the devil can get you on most times? There is no sin in heaven, not even my favourite.

Sin doesn't belong here
John Bardsley
In his book *The Great Divorce* C S Lewis describes a day trip on a coach from Greytown (read Hell) to the lower regions of Heaven. Everyone who stepped off the coach had the option of going further into Heaven if they took nothing from hell in with them. Each person seemed to have brought one thing they could not part with. One man had his pet lizard on his shoulder which suggested 'fun' activities for them to do. An angel chatting with the man asked, 'Let me kill it!' There is nothing from hell in Heaven! Choose!

Hosea 4:17 says it in a frightening statement: 'Ephraim is joined to idols; leave him alone!'

Cut loose from Satan
'Let the mighty strength of the Lord make you strong. Put on all the armour that God gives, so you can defend yourself against the devil's tricks. We are not fighting against humans. We are fighting against forces and authorities and against rulers of darkness and powers in the spiritual world' (Ephesians 6:10-12 CEV). 'He has rescued us from the dominion of darkness and brought us into the kingdom of the Son he loves' (Colossians 1:13). It says he has already rescued us. Yet it also says, 'Be strong. Keep the armour on. Take your stand. Struggle!' Which is true? Both are true. God can do it, but we have to participate fully by being truly willing, for that bit of enemy contact to go.

Cut loose from legalism
Let the peace of Christ be the umpire in your hearts when you are deciding if this or that is OK or if it has to go. It's not a list of don'ts! It's letting the peace of Christ choose. It's doing everything you do in the name of the Lord Jesus. It's having him with you whatever you do. (See Colossians 3:15-17).

Cut loose from yourself and your rights to be boss in your own life
'Clothe yourselves with compassion, kindness, humility, gentleness and patience.' Make allowances. Forgive. Love. Unite. (See Colossians 3:12-14).

The problem solver
John Bardsley
While Dieter Kuhl was our International Director, he visited about 30 of our teams. He said, 'Almost all the problems I have seen could be solved, at least to some degree, if that core issue of holiness were resolved.'

Caricatures of holiness

'Here we go. No fun any more. All my sense of humour purged away.' Actually holiness doesn't say anything about giving up your sense of humour! In fact, the opposite is true. There's an enormous link between joy and holiness. When are you the most full of joy? When your conscience is clear, and your fellowship with God is fullest! And there's an enormous link between sin and depression, confusion and misery.

'If I have to be holy all the time, whatever will I do to relax?' If it feels stressful working towards holiness, we should ask ourselves if we are trying too much in our own strength. The way to holiness is simply saying 'Yes' to God every time he wants to cleanse us of something, inviting him into every corner of our life.

'Holiness means being no earthly use any more, mooning around in spiritual clouds and not having time for ordinary stuff and ordinary people.' Was Jesus holy? Is that what Jesus was like? Holy people help around the house more, not less. Holy people are more natural, relaxed, friendly and approachable, not less.

Holiness is joyful!

Be thankful. Sing with gratitude in your hearts to the Lord. (See Colossians 3:15-17). Holiness always ends up with singing! When I'm holy I wake up singing! 'I delight greatly in the LORD; my soul rejoices in my God. For he has clothed me with garments of salvation and arrayed me in a robe of righteousness' (Isaiah 61:10).

'A highway will be there; it will be called the Way of Holiness. . . Only the redeemed will walk there, and the ransomed of the LORD will return. . . with singing; everlasting joy will crown their heads. Gladness and joy will overtake them, and sorrow and sighing will flee away' (Isaiah 35:8-10).

One purpose

'One thing I do: Forgetting what is behind and straining toward what is ahead, I press on toward the goal to win the prize for which God has called me heavenward in Christ Jesus' (Philippians 3:13-14). 'One thing I ask of the LORD, this is what I seek: that I may dwell in the house of the LORD all the days of my life, to gaze upon the beauty of the LORD and to seek him in his temple. For in the day of trouble he will keep me safe . . . At his tabernacle I will sacrifice with shouts of joy' (Psalm 27:4-6).

The one thing I'm after today is God, but at 11 o'clock tomorrow night when I arrive home tired, what will be the one thing on my mind? Next time I have a free evening at home, what will be the one thing on my mind? Sometimes I seem in a civil war. Sometimes the one thing I want is the opposite of what God wants. But I've found another prayer in the Bible to help with that problem: 'Give me an undivided heart, that I may fear your name' (Psalm 86:11). Lord, make me holy when I'm tired, holy instead of feeling sorry for myself, holy when I'm tempted, holy when I'm hungry, holy when I'm hassled and overworked, holy when I'm treated unfairly, holy when I'm relaxing.

But does holiness actually give more authority? Read this testimony of how

God turned failure into authority when sin was dealt with.

Revival in Congo
Dietrich Kuhl

I was invited to have a full day of teaching the word to all the pastors from the Ibambi area, the subject being 'Evangelism in the power of the Holy Spirit'. We looked at the church in Jerusalem when God poured out his Spirit, what happened in her early days, and what is happening today. We taught the promise of Jesus to pour out his Spirit on all flesh (Acts 1:5,8; 2:17; Matthew 3:11).

Pastor Timoté gave his testimony on how the Lord spoke to him through Acts 16:6-10. He asked the Lord, 'Why does the Holy Spirit speak to Paul and guide him, and he doesn't speak so to Timoté?' For three weeks he sought the Lord and wept before the Lord. He realised he was empty on the inside. As another Pastor was giving a seminar, the Holy Spirit fell on Pastor Timoté and showed him the sins of tribalism and many other things. He wept and wept and prayed for the whole church.

As Pastor Timoté gave this testimony, the Holy Spirit fell on all the pastors. They fell on their knees with loud crying, asking Jesus to forgive them. All were renewed. The word spread. We came to Ibambi for three days with the Bible School and secondary school students. God came to meet with them. Since then the Holy Spirit has fallen on the Ibambi church communion service while Pastor Ikabu was preaching. The church has been changed. Prayer meetings occur night and morning, there is a love for the word, the church is out witnessing. The same thing happened when we went to Nebobongo during a week of teaching the word. The Holy Spirit came. The church is changed. Praise the Lord.

Revival for us too?
Hazel Wallis

News of the Congo revival began to reach Guinea Bissau in 1953. If revival had come elsewhere, why not here as well? The first week in January was set aside for prayer. In 1956 there was a week of special meetings in the central church. The Lord blessed his people.

'Because I didn't really want to go, each night I would arrive later and later so that one night I arrived just as Pastor Tarrant had finished preaching. People were on their knees praying. Suddenly I fell to the ground. I could no longer resist the power of God. I saw my sins clearly: the pride in my heart, envy, jealousy and anger. I fell down, afraid but unrepentant. The Spirit spoke to me: "I have been crucified with Christ and I no longer live, but Christ lives in me" (Galatians 2:20). I surrendered my life to Christ. The weight of my sin disappeared. Great joy filled my heart.' Domingos Dias lay on the floor, but he rose up a new man. His wife discovered the difference immediately. Twenty years later he would be the leader of our whole denomination.

Intercession, unity, and the resultant anointing

It's not easy, but it's simple. Here is how it worked for one of our Bible school principals.

Renewal in a Brazil Bible School
Jill Chapman

While I was acting Field Leader, a phone call came in from Rosifran, the Bible School principal, to say he had expelled two thirds of the students for rebellious attitudes. I felt I should visit the college, but the staff felt I should not go alone. Our Regional Director Bob Harvey was rumoured to be making a flying visit, so John, our techie, kept ringing on the hour till he caught Bob at home in Australia. Bob said he would be delighted to come. God had said to him, 'You have to go to Brazil. You have to visit the college.' He came immediately.

When we arrived at the College, Rosifran told us quite calmly what he had done. We asked if we could speak with the students, and he was perfectly relaxed about that too. Those who had not been expelled were thinking of leaving too. They came to Bob and said, 'Can't you veto his decision?' Bob said, 'In theory I can, but that is not how it is going to happen.'

Seto, a staff member, confided that he had not been in agreement with the decision, but had gone along with it for the sake of unity. Rosifran wanted to call a full meeting because he said Seto had been disloyal, and he wanted to get it out in the open. I said, 'The Bible way is to speak with him alone, first.' Rosifran felt it was too late for that, but I repeated, 'It's the Bible way. It's never too late.' Eventually Rosifran agreed to speak to Seto in front of Bob and myself. He accused Seto of three things: disunity, speaking out of turn, and something else. Each accusation Seto was able to completely and frankly explain. In the end Rosifran broke down and wept and told Seto how sorry he was. A lovely bond was restored. Later, at a staff meeting, other staff members came out with things that had bothered them; explanations were made and apologies accepted. Suddenly, the staff realised with joy: 'We're united!' On the basis of that unity, Rosifran was willing to rescind his banishment order.

Everyone was called to a meeting, and Rosifran told the students the good news. He said, 'You can all stay. But you will need a new principal, because I am resigning.' More shock and tears. We went back to the staff room. 'Why did you not tell us before?' 'Because I knew you would try to talk me out of it.'

Then student after student began coming to Rosifran to confess their rebellion or disloyalty. Eventually another meeting was called, led by Rosifran. Suddenly he went all stiff, began groaning, and eventually Seto and others laid him down on the floor. His wife Alicia thought he would die. He went totally quiet for several minutes, then got up and began to give specific words to individual students, such as: 'You need to forgive your father.' Eventually every student in the college had met with God in a new way. Alicia, with her charismatic background, had often prayed that God would fall down on Rosifran, a Presbyterian, but she had not asked for such a visitation as this.

Suddenly one of the students said, 'Oh, I have to go and preach in my church, and I haven't prepared a sermon.' I suggested, 'Tell them what has just happened to you'. 'Oh no. I must have a message'. But there was no time. He went, and shared what God had done for him, and for the college. Then the Spirit came on him too, and he began to have specific words for members of the congregation, and they too were changed.

The next day Rosifran confessed, 'I had been praying and agonising for the students. There was a spirit of rebellion, and we could not go on like that any longer. God said three things to me: 'Expel the whole student body, then take no other action. I will take charge, but you will resign.' So that explained his wonderful calm throughout the ordeal.

Joan was staff nurse at the college. She recalled that the night before Rosifran expelled the students she had heard fearful groanings coming from his house long into the night. She went to see what was the problem. Alicia told her, 'It's OK. He's just praying for the students'.

What can we expect when God moves?

We can expect the supernatural, in the midst of trouble, hardship and opposition. We can expect death and danger as well as deliverance and delight. We can expect wisdom to know what to do in baffling circumstances. And all of it will add together to further the purposes of God in bringing in the lost. (See Hebrews 11:33-37).

STOP THINK&DISCUSS

- List all aspects of our preparation for warfare. Tick the ones in which you are already prepared. Put down an action point for each of the ones in which you are not yet ready.
- Discuss the meaning of 'foothold'. Share examples of footholds in the Bible and in modern life.
- Discuss the value and the price of unity.
- Is revival a sovereign move of God unaffected by human hearts, or how does it work? If it is possible for humans to influence when and where there will be revival, discuss what we must do.

6
KNOW THE ENEMY: WORLD, FLESH, DEVIL

Traugott Böker, Trevor Kallmier, Dietrich Kuhl,
Alastair Kennedy, Pondsius Takaliuang

The spirits who rebelled

By contrast with the Creator God and the Conqueror Jesus Christ, the created beings who rebelled are powerful but not all-powerful, cunning but not all-knowing, unseen spirits but not omnipresent, everlasting but not infinite.

Satan
His origin: a beautiful, highly positioned angelic being (Ezekiel 28:12). His fall: Because of his sin of pride, and his desire to be Lord, he was banished from heaven along with those angelic beings who followed him in his revolt. (Isaiah 14:12-15; 2 Peter 2:4; Jude 6; Revelation 12:3-4). His current position: He is still god of this world (2 Corinthians 4:4). Those without Christ are unable to be freed from his control.

Satan is limited; he is not in any way equal to God. His destiny is already fixed. At the end of the age when Christ returns with power and glory, 'the devil, who deceived them, was thrown into the lake of burning sulphur, where the beast and the false prophet had been thrown. They will be tormented day and night for ever and ever' (Revelation 20:10). Satan is fully aware of this, but is remorselessly seeking to take as many with him as possible. Demons are aware of it too. Demons asked Jesus, 'Have you come here to torture us before the appointed time?' (Matthew 8:29).

The key term for describing the relationship between humans, and especially believers, and Satan is enmity and hatred. 'I will put enmity between you and the woman' (Genesis 3:15). 'Be self-controlled and alert. Your enemy the devil prowls around . . .' (1 Peter 5:8). 'The dragon was enraged at the woman and went off to make war against the rest of her offspring – those who obey God . . .' (Revelation 12:17). So there we have it clearly. Not only is Satan our enemy, but he has declared war on us.

'I am Durga. I want to kill him.'
Deepak
Do you know that God is not only a God of love, but is also a God of hate? Because of his love for human beings, he hates those things which destroy human beings. Because he is morally perfect, his nature is to hate evil. Read

more about this in Hebrews 1:9, Proverbs 6:16-19, and Deuteronomy 12:31.

I will never forget the evil force that gripped Kishore, a young Chamaar from North India, making him roll around and foam at the mouth. 'I am Durga,' one of those spirits said to me that day. 'Durga' is the name of a Hindu goddess. When I asked her what she wanted with Kishore, she said she wanted to kill him. Since then, every time I see a statue or a picture of Durga, it gives me chills. I hate Durga.

Young Sunil is also learning to hate what God hates and love what God loves. He is eighteen years old, from a Hindu family. For quite some time he has been a truth seeker, visiting various churches in his city. Unfortunately most of their services are in English. Finally he found our church, where everything is in his own language of Hindi.

He looked a bit strange that day. After the service I went over to say hello. 'How are you?' I asked. 'Not so well,' he replied. 'What's the matter?' 'The last couple of days have been horrible,' he went on, 'It seems I am not able to think. I feel as if my mind is shutting down.' The pattern sounded quite familiar. Similar things have happened to the young university student who visits us. He too is from a Hindu background.

When a Hindu starts thinking about Truth, he becomes dissatisfied with the idolatry, superstition, oppression of women and low-caste people that he finds around him. He feels as if he has been betrayed. Going deeper into Hindu philosophy, he is told that the mind is a hindrance to spirituality, so he must stop thinking and do whatever his guru says. If he studies the Bible, he gets headaches and nightmares, and feels as if someone is literally jamming his thought processes. When I first heard people relating such experiences, I thought nothing of it, but now I am beginning to wonder.

I said to Sunil, 'Satan is not happy that you are using your mind to search for Truth. But no one can force you to do anything you don't want to do.' Putting my hand on his shoulder, I prayed, asking God to protect him. By the authority of Jesus I rebuked any evil powers that were attacking him. When I was done, he said 'While you were praying, I heard a voice in my mind telling me, "Tell that man not to pray like that".'

I said, 'Sunil, have you worshipped any idols in the past few days?' He said 'No, I have decided to stop idol worship.' 'What about your family. Do they still worship idols?' 'Oh yes!' he said. 'What do you expect? We are a Hindu family. There is much idol worship in our home.' Then I explained that idols are nothing, merely representations of characters from mythical stories. But on the other hand there is a real Satan, a being who is the ultimate source of all evil and who leads a demonic host. These demons associate with idols in order to receive the worship which people think they are directing towards God. If an idol worshipper reasons his way out of idolatry, Satan will lose the worship he has been receiving. That is why he interferes with the very process of reasoning.

'Do you want to follow the Truth, Sunil?' I asked. 'Yes,' he said. Wanting to make sure he was not rushing into anything, I said, 'But what if following the God of the Bible means that you may face opposition, hardship and cruel treatment?

It won't be easy.' He replied, 'I'm ready. No matter what, I want to follow God.' 'Then you can commit yourself to him right now,' I said. 'No special words are necessary. Just say whatever you want to say.' He began to bow his head ready to pray. Then he stopped . . .

Next thing I knew, he was reaching inside his shirt and pulling out a black cord which was hung around his neck. On it was a picture of the monkey god, Hanuman. Grabbing the cord in both hands, he gave a strong jerk and ripped it from his neck. I could hardly believe what I was seeing. Feeling a bit numb, I took his hand in mine and gave it a congratulatory shake. (Later Sunil told me he was surprised at how resistant that cord had been. Though only a weak cotton cord, it was surprisingly strong that day, and he had to use all his strength to break it.)

Sunil bowed his head and committed his life to his new Lord. Later, church members took the cord and burnt it. From that very day, Sunil has been coming for Bible study, bringing a young Hindu friend with him. He has begun to write songs about his new faith, and reads the Bible avidly and intelligently. He has a sharp mind and is a natural leader. Several months later his young Hindu friend came over to see us with another friend. They too have committed their lives to God.

Unmasking Satan

The Bible calls Satan:

- the tempter (Matthew 4:3)
- a liar and the father of lies (John 8:44)
- a murderer from the beginning (John 8:44)
- a destroyer (Revelation 9:11)
- man's enemy (Matthew 13:39 – the Greek term denotes his strong hatred of us)
- the accuser and slanderer (used 34 times in the New Testament, diaballo means 'to throw into disarray')
- a counterfeiter (2 Corinthians 11:14 says that 'Satan himself masquerades as an angel of light')
- a hinderer (1 Thessalonians 2:18)
- a blasphemer (Revelation 13:6)
- a misleader or false guide (1 Timothy 4:1 – the Greek term *planao* means 'to lead off the track, to create a tangent')
- a wily trickster (Ephesians 6:11 speaks of 'the devil's schemes')
- a stimulator of lust, i.e. stimulating perfectly normal desires into inflamed, compulsive and uncontrollable passions (Ephesians 2:2-3)
- a stimulator of pride (1 Timothy 3:16)
- an ensnarer (1 Timothy 3:7 speaks about 'the devil's trap')
- a deceiver or a master at creating false impressions, spreading misunder-standings and leading the whole world astray (Revelation 12:9)
- a worker of false miracles (Revelation 16:14, 2 Thessalonians 2:9)
- a promoter of pride, discourager and troubler and trouble-maker (2 Corinthians 12:7)

- a blinder of man's mind (2 Corinthians 4:4)
- a corrupter of minds (2 Corinthians 11:3-4; Ephesians 2:2-3)
- a strong man armed (Luke 11:21), the ruler of darkness (Acts 26:18)
- the director of demonic activity (Ephesians 6:12; Matthew 12:24)
- the suppressor of the Word of God (Matthew 13:37-39; Luke 8:11-12)
- the prince of this world (John 12:31)
- the ruler of darkness (2 Corinthians 6:14; 1 John 2:9-11)
- a creator of divisions (2 Corinthians 2:10-11; Galatians 5:19-21)
- the evil one (Matthew 12:43-45).

This gives us a fairly good picture of the kinds of traps and schemes Satan may design in order to get the servants of the Lord into trouble or to render them ineffective.

Satan:
- prevents people from receiving God's word: 'The devil comes and takes away the word from their hearts' (Luke 8:12).
- tries his best to negate the work of God in the redeemed: 'I was afraid that in some way the tempter might have tempted you and our efforts might have been useless' (1 Thessalonians 3:5).
- causes subtle doubts about God and his word: 'Has God said . . .?' (Genesis 3:1,4).
- provokes us to go against God's will: 'Satan rose up against Israel and incited David to take a census of Israel' (1 Chronicles 21:1).
- was rebellious in heaven and he is still rebellious: 'that day will not come until the rebellion occurs and the man of lawlessness is revealed, the man doomed to destruction. He opposes and exalts himself over everything that is called God or is worshipped' (2 Thessalonians 2:3-4).
- is completely presumptuous, boldly going into the very presence of God (Job 1:6).

The aim of Satan's work is the destruction of life in some form. Jesus makes this clear in John 8:44 'he is a murderer from the beginning.' In every form and shade of his workings, Satan always keeps this one aim in view – to destroy every kind of life – earthly life (contentment, peace, happiness, body, soul) as well as eternal life.

In comparison to God, Satan is a midget. But in comparison to me, Satan is a giant.

He tempts us to sin, often focusing on a specific weakness in our personality or lifestyle to strengthen the weakness and make it part of our character. Sow a thought, reap an action, and harvest a destiny. We need to be careful, but not introspective. He tries to push us into an over-strong desire for position, possessions, or power. This distorts our perception and can lead us off on to tangents. The rich young ruler of Matthew 19:21-22 went away sad because he loved his possessions too much. Paul warns Timothy about the love of money

(1 Timothy 6:9-10). Diotrephes used to love to be first (3 John 9-10). Satan also tries to keep us from doing what is right, often by getting us too busy doing something else that may even be good. Sins of omission can be as damaging as sins of commission.

He attacks us physically with sickness of body (2 Corinthians 12:7; Luke 9:38-42; Matthew 12:22-23). He attacks our mind (2 Corinthians 10:5). He tries to instil fear (Hebrews 2:14-15). He is a master of false accusation (Revelation 12:10).

The church in France, Japan, and among the Uighurs, has been wiped out once. Other persecution has stimulated the growth of the church. The scriptures warn us that persecution will happen (John 15:20-31; 2 Timothy 3:12).

Satan attempts to cause division through slights and misunderstandings, pride and rebelliousness. Increased pressure produces increased probability of relational tensions (2 Corinthians 2:10-11). Beware of ignoring your need of rest and renewal. Beware too of ignoring your need of self-discipline, though we should avoid being driven people.

He creates deception by counterfeiting genuine ministry of the Spirit. In this way he tries to discredit what is true and gain control of lives through lies. Mormons and Jehovah's Witnesses are good examples. Note 2 Corinthians 11:13-15 and Revelation 13:14.

The Bible insists that this redoubtable enemy is conquered (Colossians 2:15). In the desert Jesus showed himself already stronger than the tempter. In spite of incessant attacks on him throughout his ministry, Christ remained the conqueror, even sending an army of demons fleeing with a single word – 'Go!' (Matthew 8:32 – 'legion' was a Roman army term designating 8,500 soldiers).

Free from fear
Deon, with Hellen Kuleskey

I heard a woman's laugh in my bedroom. Mum was the only woman in the house, and she was already asleep in a far room. I heard it again, louder and clearer. My whole body trembled with fear. I shouted for my mother to come quickly. I could not get my mind off the incident.

Not long ago I had broken away from Hinduism, a religion which pronounces a curse on those who leave. Mother told me the voice was that of the Hindu mother-goddess Durga. She was laughing in my room and was terrorizing me because I had stopped worshipping her. She pleaded with me to deny my Christian faith and return to Durga. Rather than turning me back to such darkness, this frightening experience opened my eyes to the deceit of the evil one.

My great-grandparents had migrated to Guyana, taking their Hindu gods with them. My grandparents continued this Hindu worship, but when they died none of my four uncles would make the sacrifices. All four suffered many tragedies. One committed suicide. The villagers warned my mother that these tragedies were the result of failing to continue the ancestral religious practices. My mother was not prepared to risk the curse. She pledged to revive Hindu loyalty. I never saw a woman so deeply committed to her religion. She dedicated me to Shiva as a baby. Before dawn she taught me to face the rising sun and recite a mantra to the sun god Suruj. She would take me to the river for ablution for remission of sins. On Sundays she took me to Hindu gurus. One day I saw my guru slapping and cursing a boy. There was no mercy or forgiveness in his heart. I decided never to bow to him again.

In my early teens I visited a Christian Sunday School. My mother believed all religions led to God, and that Jesus was a reincarnation of Krishna, so she was happy about it. My guru was not. He warned me not to read their New Testament. My stepfather, also a staunch Hindu, set up taboos which prevented me from going to Sunday School any more. This was one of the loneliest periods I have ever experienced. I took comfort in my tiny New Testament. Jesus' words challenged and made sense to me. Even though my mother practised Hinduism to the fullest, she was still tormented by the superstitious belief in the curse.

The yearly family puja, which involved the sacrifice of a goat to the demon goddess Kali, shook my life. I knew there was something diabolical about it. At the age of fifteen I visited a small church, went forward and surrendered my life to Jesus. I went home with joy and the promise of eternal life. I felt a completely different person. My stepfather told me it was impossible to change a sheep into a goat – 'Born a Hindu, die a Hindu,' he had said. Now he accused me of selling my old religion and threatened to put me out of the house. The neighbours laughed at me; my friends hated me. I was called the black sheep.

Even after my conversion, I experienced a deep fear of the idols, and the generational curse. The thought of dying a contemptible death terrified me. I knew something must be done to overcome this paralysing fear that was destroying my trust in the Lord. I felt an urge to visit the pastor. To my amazement, he was about to leave to visit me! I began to praise God. I left with a complete Bible and scripture verses to build my faith in Jesus and help me overcome fear of the devil.

Satan wanted to dominate me as he had my ancestors, but he did not succeed. I thank Jesus for delivering me whenever I called on him. I thank God for teaching me that Jesus' power is far greater than any evil power in the universe.

Voodoo
Name withheld

I helped an African refugee family with many problems. I later felt the Lord was warning me that a curse had been placed against me. I prayed against it and didn't feel too concerned.

Shortly afterwards I became ill. It was wrongly diagnosed and wrongly treated. First my kidneys were in a mess, then my liver, and on top of that, a dose of flu. I had never experienced such extreme physical weakness. I felt evil was attacking me, especially late at night (I live alone) when it was too late to get prayer help. I could only repeat the basic Bible truths of my identity in Christ until the pressure lifted.

I then got a picture of a hand moving a voodoo doll. I realised that I must be under a death curse. I prayed against it. I emailed a ministry dedicated to problems of this kind. After quite a delay they confirmed my assumption, and said that the curse had been broken and measures had been taken to prevent any recurrence. I was asked to break the curses over me daily.

It was coming up to Easter. I came under a burden to pray, spending days in prayer in which every aspect of my life, feelings, thoughts and behaviour came under scrutiny. I repented of everything the Lord brought to mind, expelling all wrong influences and replacing them with Jesus Christ's Holy Spirit. It felt good.

A pastor then met me and told me he had a prophetic word for me. This was an affirmation, from a completely objective external source, of God's love for me and the promise that he would use me to save many. Next I had another strong spiritual attack, this time on my identity in Jesus. It was as if the enemy was trying to prove I was wicked and would not stand in righteousness. Again, I restated the biblical truths about my identity in Christ.

I found Jessie Penn-Lewis's The Cross of Calvary and Eileen Crossman's Mountain Rain most helpful, with classic descriptions of this kind of attack. I remembered someone's remark that this is a hand-to-hand fight against all the forces of evil. The good result is that my capacity to help those around me is increased.

Dark world of the Birifor
Alex and Kezia Schoonveld
The Tuna area of north-west Ghana near the Burkina Faso border is infamous as a spiritually heavy area. Most people are involved in ancestor worship, worship of the Black Volta river god, land gods, hill gods and so on. So many are involved in black magic that witches and wizards are common. We came across a phenomenon called a witch market. It is supposed to take place weekly, but is invisible. In the market, purchasers can pay with human souls. If they do not have money, they can offer a human being. That person suddenly becomes very ill, without any explanation. They say, 'His soul is being eaten. When it is all eaten, he dies.' It doesn't happen to Christians who are under the protection of the Lord Jesus Christ.

Between their seventh and fourteenth birthdays, Birifor children in Ghana have to travel across the Black Volta river into Burkina Faso for the initiation rites, which take place every seven years. While there, they take off their clothes, are washed in the Black Volta river, and are given new clothes and a new name. Their old name becomes taboo for them even to say. They are told many secrets and taboos. Their front teeth are filed to a point. They are filled with fear and become deeply involved with demons.

Praise God that the Birifor church is growing, the Birifor scriptures are being translated, and all this darkness cannot extinguish the light.

What attracts human beings to Satan?

Fear of death
Genesis 3:4: 'You will not surely die.' Humans fear death. Not just old people, but young ones too in every situation in life. This fear of death and the longing for life

governs Animism very strongly. For every stage and time of life there are prescribed rites to give or preserve life. There are pregnancy taboos for the mother, and ritual washings. At birth a Javanese mother might strew rice on the placenta to distract the demons from the baby. The afterbirth is then buried in front of the house and an electric torch is shone on it. The child is given a repulsive name which can be changed later, when he or she is big and strong. An amulet is worn because they hope it will give protection. Young people undergo initiation rites which dedicate them to a demon. In their search for a partner they use sacrifices. At marriage people throw rice over the pair, a fertility rite. The newly wed couple tread on an egg for the same reason. The husband carries the woman over the threshold so that house-demons do not attack her.

Too afraid to pray
Traugott Böker
Ina, who lived on the island of Nias, was always overcome with fear when she prayed. She felt as if she was going to fall into an abyss. She told her husband and he prayed with her until all was well. However, she still had the problem when alone. It stemmed from her childhood. She was often sick as a child, living in an area without medical aid. Her parents took her to a so-called Christian healer who made the sign of the cross all over her body. She was healed. When she confessed this before Jesus as white magic and renounced all influence and help except that of Christ, then she was healed of her fear.

In some places it is taboo to work for a period after the death of a relative. All kinds of labour which provide our daily bread are also thought to be 'made safe' by spirits. Before sowing, a sacrifice is made in the fields. Sacrifices are made before harvest, before going fishing or hunting, before setting off on a journey or before visiting the grave of a near relative.

Wish for power
One factor in the appeal of occultism is the wish for power: '. . . you will be like God' (Genesis 3:5). People of power may keep others under their thumb by using occultism. Nobles or the upper class, who have often obtained their position through use of evil powers, often find it particularly difficult to come to believe in Jesus. This wish for power is specially true of all people who are not very strong, but want to protect themselves from others.

Hidden practices
Traugott Böker
Sitoli was converted in the Nias revival, became a teacher, but feared cheeky children. Someone taught him a mantra which would make him invulnerable and with which he could even kill someone. Though he had never dared to use the mantra, he could never get to sleep before 2 a.m.. Only when he had confessed this to Jesus and renounced it completely was he able to sleep normally – but by then he was an old man! What a mean cheat Satan is!

Mr Sihombing's child suffered from dreadful headaches, though no illness was to be found, even when the child was examined in Jakarta and Singapore. An evangelist came to his house and said with great certainty to Mr Sihombing that he was depending on evil powers. In the end he had to admit it: he kept ceremonial swords (keris), washed himself several times a year with flower-water, and had buried certain objects in front of his house. When he renounced all this in Jesus' name, his son was healed immediately.

Longing for knowledge

A third factor in the appeal of occultism is the longing for knowledge '... your eyes will be opened, and you will ... know good and evil' (Genesis 3:5). A man wants to know his future. Who will be my marriage partner? What will happen to my family? Mr Camat had someone read the lines on his hand. The predictions were good and bad: all his children would be clever, but at some time he would get into difficulty and have two wives. This worried him very much. What a disgrace for him, a respected person both in the public eye and in church. So he made the wish that his wife should die before this came to pass.

Who is the thief?
Traugott Böker

A Bible school student in Indonesia wakes up screaming in the night. He feels he is being choked. Others come and pray with him and all is well, but it happens again and again. He asks a teacher for a private talk, and this story emerges: Some time ago, a lot of money had disappeared in the Bible school. No one knew who was responsible. Someone told this student that a person in the village could help to get at the truth. He went there. The person was a medium. A name was given him. He didn't believe it, but from then on he was troubled at night. 'Do not turn to mediums or seek out spiritists, for you will be defiled by them. I am the LORD your God.' (Leviticus 19:31).

The worship of parents and ancestors is an integral part of animist culture. This appears most strongly as the fear of parents in their position as representatives of the spirits of the ancestors, and so possessing supernatural powers.

Occult practice from birth to death
Pondsius Takaliuang

Occult practice can be used when a baby is in the mother's womb. The mother might drink special water, eat special food, wash in special water for the good luck of the baby. Sometimes the baby is surrendered to a certain spirit and given a certain name. That spirit will guard that person all his life unless Jesus sets them free. In counselling, we must be aware of this reality. We need to know the meaning of every name, because sometimes the devil hides behind a strange name given by the witch doctor when the baby is still unborn. There is cleansing for occult names.

Occult practice is used at the time of birth. The baby may be washed with special water, given an amulet for his/her future, or 'protected' by a special ceremony.

As children grow, occult practice is to hang charms on their necks or wrists or waist for their 'safety'. The life of the child is under the power of darkness. When boys and girls go to school, amulets are used so they will be successful in their study.

When a young man falls in love, there are charms or spells used for flattering the one they admire. There are special charms for young widows and rich young men. Occult practice is used at the wedding and when moving into the new home. There are charms to keep spouses faithful in marriage. Strange but true, marriages are bound by the power of Satan.

Occultism is used when people face difficulties, troubles and challenges in business, military service, sport, in court, on the plantation, fishing, fighting, when smuggling, and in every area of life.

Occult practices are used when people die to 'deliver this human soul into heaven'.

For these reasons, in deliverance ministry, the occult involvement of a person must be traced precisely via the patient's information, through his grandparents and parents, and through God's Spirit using the gift of discernment. The Holy Spirit gives the ability to distinguish the spirits of darkness and the Spirit of God.

Fetishes

Primitive fetishes may be made from stone, iron, gold, silver, antique or ancient coins, cloth, relics, or any kind of bottle with liquid or oil. They may be handed down by ancestors to their descendants. Other fetishes can be made from the bones of pigs, the teeth of tigers, the claw of a lion, the tusk of a boar, the quill of a porcupine, the skull of a buffalo or a cow, or even a fish bone. A skull is commonly buried under a house. There are fetishes written on paper, cloth, animal skin, written in Arabic, Chinese or a tribal language.

Nature fetishes can be made from a leaf, a root or a flower. A tree is planted in the garden to resist sinister events. Ask someone what kind of tree that is, and you will find what they believe about it.

Modern objects can be made into fetishes too, including lipstick, perfume, hair cream or a mascot. The devil is always up to date. Love fetishes can be spectacles, handkerchiefs, photos, rings, cigarettes or cloths used to charm an intended spouse or to prevent a partner from being unfaithful.

Among religious people without Christ in their life, they use the Bible, the cross, the bread and wine as fetishes. Bible verses or the name of the Trinity may be written on paper 'for luck'. Catholics may use the bones of saints and holy water. Muslims may use Koranic verses, or a holy book wrapped in special paper. Hindus use statues and flowers. Satan deceives religious people according to their religion.

A fetish may be placed in the door, window, the apex of the roof, in the wall, or under the floor. It can be worn round the person's neck, wrist or waist, on their finger, in their ear or hair. It can be buried under the skin. It may be in their boat or car. Some drivers cannot drive without the mascot.

Tied to the occult
Pondsius Takaliuang

After an interview with a man who had been strongly tied to occultism, I discovered he had a white and a black belt used for defence, and quoted the name of an ancestor who was supposed to have magical power. He had a keris, the Javanese dagger. If he was fighting, he had a talisman for it, and a magic singlet supposed to stop a bullet; he would drink the blood of a dog to make him brave. By biting a feather duster he hoped to become invisible when entering into a forbidden area in the harbour. He had a 'magical' staff for casting out demons and preserving a house, a rattan cane for helping people with disease, and a ring for both defence and healing. He put the ring into a glass of water and the patient drank the water while mentioning God's name or his ancestor's name. He had a magical stone taken from the well for defence and healing, and soil from a tomb for protecting the family.

When he first received these fetishes, he swore using the Bible, the name of Jesus, and the name of his ancestor, then faced the wall and stabbed using a Japanese samurai sword. He promised to keep a long list of taboos. He was not to eat bamboo shoots or young sprouts, pumpkins or gourds. He was not to eat shrimps, because they move backwards. He was not to wear clothes inside out or back to front. He was not to pass over a washing line. He was not to cut down a banana tree. He was not to put any fetishes under his feet or take them into the toilet. And he was not to marry for ten years!

If he went anywhere with his fetishes, he felt confident and strong. Without them, he felt fearful. Although he went to church, he could not understand the word of God. His marriage was on the rocks. They had no joy, and it was difficult for them to agree. Their children were suffering from strange diseases. He struggled to make a living.

His wife was a diligent member of a keen Bible study group, and she warned him about the dangers, and challenged him to throw all his fetishes away. He strongly refused. Then a Bible study group came to his own home, and after hearing the word of God about occultism, he was fearful. His wife challenged him again to repent. He took a clear decision and earnestly repented, renounced the devil and received Christ in his heart. He burnt every fetish.

His family life now had joy and happiness. He began to understand the word of God, studied it, and with his wife became involved in evangelism, prayer and deliverance ministry. Their home is a place of prayer and Bible study, and a place of counselling for many people.

Auspicious days

An animist has a complicated method to decide on the day for a marriage, feast, or for building a new house. In Java there are many practices of significant days and dates for marriage, but there is still a high divorce rate. In marriage counselling, it is wise to ask these people about the date of their marriage. Many nominal Christian families are broken up because of such practices, because the devil operates in the family instead of the Lord.

There is a widespread fear of the 13th date. In Kalimantan there are certain days when people are forbidden to come down from their house, because these are supposed to be days of purification, cleansing the village from sinister fears or faults. If they break the rule, they will be punished by their leader.

Afterlife beliefs
Pondsius Takaliuang

There are important days following a funeral in Indonesia. These include the third day after the death, when the soul of the dead is believed to be still at home; he leaves on the seventh day. By the 40th day, he is believed to be far from home. By the 100th day, he is believed to be in heaven. By the 1000th day, it is believed he has come to his place.

There are special ceremonies on each of those days. Nominal Christians will call a pastor to lead the fellowship, calling it a day of 'thanksgiving'. But be careful! In one room you might find food prepared for the dead, some of his favourite food. What should the pastor do?

Ask them why they have that fellowship on the third, seventh, 40th, 100th or 1000th day. If they answer that it is just for thanksgiving, ask them if they would have it on the second, fourth, sixth, 39th or 41st, 99th or 101st, 999th or 1001st day. If they refuse, they still believe in the significant day.

How can we help them? Preach the gospel to them, emphasising the hope of a true Christian. Pray for them. Take time to speak with them personally about the relationship between the dead and those still alive on earth. Never rebuke them from the pulpit or in public. Be patient, because they do such practices because of lack of knowledge of the Bible.

Wonderful verses to help those who practise significant days are in Genesis 1, where we discover that all days are good. Ecclesiastes 3:1-8 is not concerned with occult practices, so it cannot be used to defend significant days. Paul opposed such days strongly: 'You are observing special days and months and seasons and years. I fear for you, that somehow I have wasted my efforts on you' (Galatians 4:10-11).

Spells, charms and incantations

The practice of spells and charms is well-known throughout the world. Snake charming is an ancient practice – it is referred to in Jeremiah 8:17 and Psalm 58:4-5. All spells are forbidden in Deuteronomy 18:10-11.

Traditionally, spells or incantations use mixed or obscure language with ancient words which are difficult to understand and with dark meaning. They must be memorised before they are used, and are often whispered or mumbled.

Spells are used for demonic healing and problem-solving; for defence in war or success in fighting, sport, hunting, business or examinations; for finding mercy before the authorities or influencing or controlling other people. Black spells or curses, perhaps in conjunction with stabbing a voodoo doll, may be used to destroy human lives.

One man had many spells written in his books. If his children were ill, he spelled a charm. The result was terrible. In that house there was no prayer or Bible reading, no worship, no happiness, peace or joy. They found it difficult to memorise the word of God, because the word of Satan filled their hearts. After repentance, confession and cleansing through Jesus' blood, it was transformed. They could understand and memorize the word. They needed 'brainwashing' to remove occult words from their minds.

Invulnerable magic
This practice is used by people who have to go away to fight a war. They are washed with special water, stabbed with a sword, then sometimes drink animal blood and receive fetishes, spells or taboos. It is a terrible occult bondage, because in this way they give their lives totally to the power of Satan. Such men are uncommonly brave, but easily angered, and experience problems when facing death. They have difficulty understanding the word of God.

Confessions
Pondsius Takaliuang
A nominal Christian serving as a soldier came to be counselled. He honestly confessed that he had fetishes, charms and invulnerable magic. I recognized that he had no peace in his life, no happiness in his family and that it was difficult for him to know God's will for his life. He repented, gave up his fetishes, and renounced the devil behind the invulnerable magic, and received Christ into his life. He went home with joy, a real Christian.

A businessman had invulnerable magic strong enough that when stabbed he was not wounded. But his family was in confusion. In counselling he confessed his practices, renounced the devil and received Christ. Now he is a born-again believer and lives happily with his wife and children.

Spiritism
Spiritism is the belief that the dead survive as spirits which can communicate with the living, especially through the help of a medium. The spiritist can call the spirits by means of a ouija board, a glass that moves without being held, through special dances, music, séances, meditation, or a medium who loses his own personality and voice. Other spiritists might visit a cemetery to speak with the dead and ask a blessing, to remove and rebury bones with an occult ceremony, to offer sacrifices, flowers and food to the dead, or to sleep near a certain tomb to gain magical power from 'the dead'. The island of Bali has visits from people who want to contact spirits, because so much spiritism is practised there.

Spiritists have performed levitation and table lifting, automatic writing, alleged materialisation of dead people, astral travel, and necromancy.

A rich man studied spiritism through mysticism. As he meditated on a certain day, a spirit came to him. He asked, 'What is your name?' 'The spirit replied falsely,

'I am Jesus Christ.' From that time the man became very wicked, and tried to kill his wife. He railed at people around him, and eventually he went mad. He repented when a pastor challenged him to forsake all his practices, and the Lord healed him. He received Christ and has since led many other people to Christ.

Astrology and horoscope

Astrology is based on an earth-centred universe. God created the sun, moon and stars for three purposes: to separate day and night, to mark seasons, and to give light to the earth (Genesis 1:14). There is no mention that they may be used to foretell our future. Human lives are totally dependent on the Creator, not on creation. At the end of the world the sun, moon and stars will be changed. They will fall from their place (2 Peter 3:7,10; Revelation 6:12-14). It is foolish to rely on such things. In heaven there will be no sun, moon or stars (Revelation 21:23). If those things will pass away, why depend on them? We trust in our eternal God, who holds our future and our destiny.

Some astrologers have tried to use scriptures that mention stars as biblical support for astrology. God has spoken to man by the stars as a symbol: 'Count the stars—if indeed you can count them. So shall your offspring be' (Genesis 15:5). 'The sun and moon and eleven stars were bowing down to me' (Genesis 37:9). 'A star will come out of Jacob . . . a sceptre . . . a ruler' (Numbers 24:17,19). 'Where is he that is born King of the Jews? We have seen his star . . .' (Matthew 2:2 KJV). None of these occurrences indicate any influence by these planets in human lives, so these verses cannot be used as biblical support for astrology.

Astrologers failed to tell or interpret Nebuchadnezzar's dream. Daniel, who lived among these astrologers, never used astrology to explain the will of God or to interpret the dream (Daniel 2:10,18-19). A girl called on three pastors for help. She had experienced nightmares, and had found it difficult to pray and read the Bible. In counselling she confessed that she read her horoscope and practised some occult things. She repented and received Christ.

Why do people practise occultism?

We have three basic needs in human life:
1. Physical needs: food, clothes, home, rest, sleep, sport, sex, medicine.
2. Psychological needs: education, art, aesthetic sense, knowledge, skill, music, love, satisfaction.
3. Spiritual needs: forgiveness, peace, joy, power, authority, hope, faith, prayer, assurance of salvation.

Many people who practise occultism seem to have their physical needs met, but their spiritual needs are not satisfied. If they do not meet the Lord, they will seek to satisfy these needs through some other power. Humanity can live without electricity, television or cars, but we cannot live without love and assurance of salvation.

Biblical excuses

Many occultists will misquote Bible verses, taking them out of context. Satan misused scripture too, to try and trick our Lord (Matthew 4:6). These people are wrong in the way they use the Bible. They can be helped through more accurate explanation of the Bible, and the testimony of the entire Bible.

Cultural excuses

There are cultures, customs, traditions and philosophies that are controlled by the devil. Some people claim they must practise occultism to identify with their friends in the hope of drawing them to Christ, and quote 1 Corinthians 9:21-23: 'To those not having the law I became like one not having the law . . . so as to win [them]. To the weak I became weak, to win the weak. I have become all things to all men so that by all possible means I might save some. I do all this for the sake of the gospel.' They compromise with people around them, attend occult ceremonies at the birth of a friend's baby, practise occultism before being blessed by the pastor in marriage, offer sacrifices to the gods when sowing their fields, and contribute towards the building of temples for the gods, because they are afraid of losing face.

Religious excuses

Many witchdoctors use the name of God, and don't oppose religion, even honouring every religion by saying each is good for its own people. Sometimes a witchdoctor will keep a Bible, a Qu'ran, the Vedas and other holy books. Nominal Christian witchdoctors will use the Bible, the cross, the wine, the bread. People will be taken in because 'he heals by prayer'. How can we discern who is divinely healed and who is healed by the devil? Someone who cannot understand the Bible, is bored with the Bible, or even hates the Bible, may have been treated by white magic. Occult practices make the heart stubborn and rough.

Practical excuses

People argue that occultism must be from the Lord, because it brings success, wealth, help, authority and power. This argument originates from lack of Bible knowledge and understanding. We must be patient towards such people. We must show them that Satan can do miracles (Exodus 7:11-12; Matthew 24:24; 2 Thessalonians 2:9-10).

The devil can give almost everything except salvation. He gives glory and power (Matthew 4:8-9), he can make fire fall (Job 1:16), or create a storm (Job 1:18-19). He can make people rich (Acts 16:16). To this argument we can quote Matthew 7:20-23: 'Not everyone who says to me "Lord, Lord," will enter the kingdom.'

To some, practising occultism is simply a job to earn their daily bread. Occultism is a practical road and sinners tend to enjoy it. We must challenge them to repent. We can promise them that the Lord can help them in their need, because he is faithful. We have a great responsibility to warn them, because that road ends in destruction (see Matthew 7:13-14).

Living in anger
Pondsius Takaliuang

A woman attended a gospel meeting, but could not concentrate on the preaching. She was disturbed. Yet she wanted to be set free from fear and anger. During counselling she revealed that her grandfather had practised occultism and killed a girl by it. As a result, her father didn't like the church, the Bible or anything spiritual. That night she honestly repented and received Christ after renouncing all her own occult practices. She was released from the curse of her grandfather and father. Now she is a happy woman with her husband and three children.

Another woman lived in anger and hatred. She had no peace in her heart. She was counselled by a Christian, and the Lord revealed that she had buried fetishes. When asked about fetishes, she strongly declared, 'I have no such fetishes.' The counsellor told her, 'The Lord has revealed your practices. It is better to repent than to talk lies and perish.' At last she confessed. They dug in the floor of her house and found a fetish made from a Bible wrapped in a certain paper. That woman earnestly repented and received Christ, and her life has been changed by the Lord. She opened her house to become a place of fellowship, and from that fellowship four young men have gone out to serve the Lord.

The way of deliverance

Make sure those being counselled are serious and have a strong desire to be delivered. Never counsel those who are unwilling to be set free. It is a waste of time and energy. It is impossible to help those who are not serious. Wait. Jesus knocks at the door but he doesn't push it open himself. Make sure they are willing to give open honest answers to counselling questions. It is impossible for them to be delivered if they hide sin. It must be honestly confessed and brought to light. When God walked in the garden and asked Adam, 'Where are you?' did God not know? Of course he knew. God asked because he wanted Adam and Eve to be honest. Sometimes the Lord reveals someone's sin. Sometimes he waits for them to be honest.

Totally rely on, trust in, and obey the Holy Spirit. The Holy Spirit will enable us in counselling to discern the other spirit and the real problem. There may be physical problems, mental or psychological problems as well as spiritual problems. Among the spiritual problems learn to differentiate between Satanic attack, occult involvement, and full demonization (see chapter 15). There is madness, and there is demonization. There is sexual immorality which is not always a spirit of prostitution. There are headaches from malaria as well as from occult problems. Discernment is possible because the Holy Spirit is in us (1 Corinthians 12:10). Observe and analyse occult symptoms (1 John 4:1-2). Expose and bring to light occult practices (Psalm 90:8). Lead them to confess sin by name in prayer (1 John 1:9). Ask them to renounce the evil spirits behind occult practices. Deliver them from occult bondage in the name of Jesus. Ask them to receive Christ into their heart (John 1:12). Have them destroy all occult articles by fire (Deuteronomy 7:25-26). Ask them to yield their life totally to the Lord (Romans 12:1-2). Let them thank the Lord for salvation and deliverance (Psalm 103).

STOPTHINK&DISCUSS

● In what ways have you experienced enemy opposition in your life and work for God?
● In which of Satan's roles have you seen him in action?
● Which story from this chapter impacted you the most? Why? What is God saying?

7
DISCERNMENT - AN ESSENTIAL GIFT

John Bardsley

In the list of spiritual gifts in 1 Corinthians 12:8-10 we find 'discernment of spirits', 'word of wisdom' and 'word of knowledge'. I have felt a huge need for at least one of these if I am to be used for any deliverance ministry at all. One experienced worker told me, 'You don't have the gift all the time, only when you need it'.

The rest of this chapter is devoted to story after story where discernment of one kind or another was the key to knowing what to do.

Sensitive to the leading of the Spirit
Bruce Rattray

Mr Y, who had come clearly through to salvation a month before, came to visit, desperate for help. He was a government official in the education department, and also the son of a powerful witch doctor. His condition seemed serious, and had not responded to treatment, even from the best hospital on the island. Now he was almost breathless. He grabbed my arm and gasped, 'Quick! Pray for me! I think I'm dying!'

We sat him on a chair, with my wife Anne standing on one side and a fellow lady worker on the other. I stood in front of him and tried to pray, but I did not know what to pray for. So I stopped and asked the Holy Spirit to guide me.

Suddenly I said in a loud voice, 'In the name of the Lord Jesus Christ, I command the evil spirit to come out of Mr Y!' He made a loud noise, and began sliding to the floor in a daze, sweating profusely and struggling to open the top buttons of his shirt. Then he stood to his feet, raised his hands to the heavens, and with beaming face repeated over and over, 'Praise the Lord, praise the Lord!' He had been instantly delivered.

Without help I would not have prayed such a prayer. Only the Holy Spirit knew what the problem was. Evil spirits lie and deceive and will use all their guile to sidetrack us. We must be totally dependent on the guidance of the Holy Spirit.

Another time we were asked to help a young woman with obvious symptoms of demonic oppression. After explaining to her from the word the basis of Satan's defeat, and our authority over evil spirits in Christ's name, we asked Jesus' cooperation in evicting any demonic squatters which might be holding ground in her life. Several named themselves, with one giving the name 'Saigon'. I was immediately suspicious of this, so we stopped to talk about it. Anne expressed the same suspicion, so we prayed and forbade the spirit from lying to us. Numerous others gave their names and were evicted, but 'Saigon' did not come up again!

A thank you gift with a hidden menace
'Janet'

The area where my people group live has tight security as the government is very strict regarding political and religious activity. Living there in a potentially hostile environment and knowing that you are being watched produces a great deal of caution in what you say and do as a tentmaker. Added to this was the spiritual battle that was going on in ways more subtle than I was prepared for. One particular experience warned me how careful we need to be when living in areas that practice idolatry.

During my first year as a language student in that restricted area, I also taught English. At the end of the year my student gave me a farewell gift. It was a large picture painted on cloth. Normally these pictures have all kinds of demonic figures and occult symbols which are very much part of what the people worship. Knowing that I was a Christian, he had asked his friend to paint a historic building instead of a 'religious' painting. It wasn't until later that I noticed six inconspicuous Buddhist deities. Normally, if I received any gift that was obviously an idol or some kind of religious object, I would wait for a discreet opportunity to throw it away or destroy it. Could I ignore those small additions and use 'the freedom we have in Christ' or should I take it down and risk offending my student? I was leaving shortly, so I decided to leave it hanging up until I returned for my second year.

During my time away I completely forgot about the picture. On my return, a number of locals asked me about it. Even though to Westerners it is only a famous building, to this people group it has religious and political significance. They wanted to know if I had beliefs the same as theirs. As a Christian I didn't want to give the impression that I believed that our religious beliefs could be mixed (syncretism). I was certain that some people's attitude had changed towards me since they noticed the picture hanging up. It was confirmed when one of my teachers warned me that the authorities were suspicious of all foreigners, believing that some were involved in political activity.

One day an incident occurred which was obviously spiritual in origin. During a lesson, I could clearly smell a particular bush burning which is specifically used in the practice of local religious rituals. I stood up and looked outside expecting to see someone burning it, although I had never seen it burned on our campus before. There was no sign of any fire nor smoke of any kind, and I knew that it couldn't be coming from outside.

I realised that I was leaving myself open to enemy attack because of that picture. I took the picture down. I asked the Lord to forgive me for spiritually compromising myself and renounced any (unknowing) spiritual bondage that I had placed myself in. I asked him to wash me in His blood. The Lord's peace just washed over me again and again. I felt His presence and had a freedom to pray, which I realised I hadn't had in the past few months.

During a time of prayer, I sensed that I needed to ask the Lord that my student would offer to take his gift back again! On his next visit, I explained that as I didn't worship idols I couldn't keep his picture on the wall, otherwise I would be disloyal to Jesus. He said that he understood. I also explained that having the picture brought me under suspicion regarding my political views, so I thought it better to remove it. He agreed with me and said that his family had also been questioned about my relationship with them.

Next followed an hour of talking about our different beliefs. Then he said, 'And so I should take it back?' I replied, 'Yes.' Inwardly I sighed with relief and gave thanks to the Lord for turning this situation around and making it an opportunity to share about Him. My student later opened up and shared with me that he had evil thoughts. I told with him that 'in my religion' the Blood of Jesus washes our minds from sinful thoughts. He understood that and said that he also believed in Jesus! I knew that he probably meant that he would put Him alongside all his other gods and deities. But at least there was an admission that his religion didn't help him in his practical struggle to overcome sin!

It made me realise that by trying too hard to be friends with these local people and not offend them, I had compromised myself spiritually by being disloyal to the Lord. If accepting certain types of gifts or being involved in some 'harmless' religious practices is compromising our faith in Jesus, then we should find some culturally acceptable way of declining. We need to realize that the enemy will try to make spiritual compromise more plausible for those of us who would usually be on our guard.

Some may say that we have freedom in Christ and don't need to worry about objects that we don't use for worship, and quote 1 Corinthians 8:4-13. It appears from the context that whenever the 'weak believers' ate 'such food', meaning a particular type of food, 'they think of it as having been sacrificed to an idol' (verse 7) - it doesn't say that they were eating food that had been sacrificed to idols - only that they thought of it like that! There are other verses such as Acts 15:29; 21:25 which clearly forbid eating food sacrificed to idols. There are also numerous references in both the Old and New Testaments concerning the hatred God has for idols and idolatry. Usually, because there was spiritual significance attached to them, all objects associated with idolatry had to be destroyed by God's people when they conquered the land. Such objects could be the means of turning God's people away from him, as happened to King Solomon (1 Kings 11).

Soon after arriving back in the West for home leave, the Lord confirmed to me the seriousness of having these kinds of objects in our possession through a book that was lent to me. Elizabeth-Ann Horsford relates a similar experience in her introduction to the book *Created To Conquer*, which teaches principles of spiritual warfare from the life of King David.

Pray in the Spirit
Bill and Meg Lapworth

While working in the Senegal River Valley, we experienced days when the drums beat to call the spirits. We could feel the atmosphere thicken as the demons gathered, and the power of darkness become so intense we could not pray with our minds. But we could still pray in the Spirit. At times like that how much we need worship to remind us how great our God is.

Ready, steady, go!
A church-planter in Central Asia

'Spiritual warfare? No problem.' Bible College diploma in hand, I was all set for the mission field. Although my experience was limited, I'd read all the right books, watched other people carry out deliverance ministry, and listened as friends related how they had been involved in breaking bondages. I realised I had a lot to learn, but I was confident of my position and authority as a child of God. Unfortunately, I put two and two together and made five. I mistakenly assumed that the Lord would automatically protect me from the attacks of the enemy. I also had the idea that any demons present would come running out to meet me. (That's what happened with Jesus, wasn't it?) I expected them to be forced to flee or to reveal their presence when confronted with the Holy Spirit in me or in a group of believers. So no need to bother about them till they showed up and announced their presence. Well, I had more to learn than I realised!

Close encounters

Confidently I headed off to Central Asia. It was spring 1995 and I was joining a church-planting team in one of the republics that had recently gained independence from the Soviet Union. Our focus was one of the nominally Muslim, Turkic peoples of the region that had been kept from the gospel, both by their geographic isolation and then by 70 years under the communist regime. Until independence in 1991 there were few known believers and no known churches. Since then there has been an amazing response to the gospel with churches springing up almost overnight. But nearly all of these are in the capital cities of each republic, and most of the population remains unreached. Although foreigners can now live and work in these countries as teachers, businessmen and students, it is still not possible to go openly as a missionary.

Our first task was to learn the local language. Quickly realising that the lack of materials (the 'Teach Yourself' series doesn't quite stretch to Uzbek or Turkmen) and the amount of Russian spoken in the capital made this easier said than done, I decided to live with a local family. Having learned how to say 'thank you' and 'good', I moved into a chaotic household consisting of mum, dad, five kids and various cousins. With those two words and the creative use of hands and feet we began to make ourselves understood. Each day (and often well into the night) visitors came and went. I was so culturally naive that when a sheep was slaughtered (in the kitchen) the day I arrived, I didn't realise it was in my honour!

During that first week one visitor, an aunt, stood out among the rest and immediately caught my attention. I sensed evil in her, and knew that she sensed the Holy Spirit in me. Somehow I knew, and I knew that she knew. In the heavenlies the battle lines were drawn. I surprised myself. Never having been particularly sensitive or discerning, I wondered if I was just imagining things. But I didn't wonder for long. That same evening I heard a strange noise as she began to summon demons and then fell into a trance. Afterwards she took a shovel full of burning grass and wafted it into each room, opening the windows to drive out the evil spirits. When she entered my room I protested as best I could, but after only three days' language study, I couldn't manage much more than 'No, this doesn't please me.'

Later in the year she returned. This time I locked myself in my room, and sang praise songs loudly - partly as an act of spiritual warfare, but mainly just to block out the noise. (As she summoned the demons she sounded as if she was continually and violently throwing up.) When everything quieted down, I went out to find all the children unconscious in the living room and the aunt nowhere to be seen. She had returned to the village. Eventually the children came round, and a few months later I moved out of the family. That was the end of that - or so I thought. It wasn't until a year later that I realised she had placed a curse on me.

During that year, several of us moved out as a team from the capital and began to plant a church in a regional city. After the stresses and strains of life with the family I was now enjoying the space and privacy of my own flat. I'd learned the language and we were beginning to disciple the first believers. But my own spiritual life was a mess. It was only while on holiday in a neighbouring country that the root of this problem came to light. My room-mate commented that I screamed each night. (Perhaps I'd been doing this for a while, but I hadn't had a room-mate to tell me!) Then a couple of times when I tried to pray, I experienced physical difficulties - once I couldn't get down on my knees, and another time I came out in a cold sweat. At this point someone who knew nothing of this, nor about 'auntie shaman' as I used to call her, suggested that I had been cursed. We put two and two together and this time made four! Some friends came to pray for me and break the curse. Immediately after they finished I was released in praise.

My new-found freedom was wonderful, but I was left with unanswered questions. Why had this woman been able to put a curse on me in the first place? Am I not a child of God? Isn't He who is in me greater than He who is in the world? Why doesn't Jesus just automatically protect us? As I dug around for an answer, the first one I came up with was sin. Paul implies that ungodly anger gives the devil a foothold (Ephesians 4:26,27). At the same time as rebuking the curse I confessed and dealt with sinful attitudes in my heart that had no doubt given space to the evil one.

But that's only part of the picture. I am also learning that exercising authority, like praying, is part of the role that God has given us on earth. In fact, we could ask the same question about intercession - why can't God just do X anyway? Why do we have to ask Him to do it? Because He has chosen to delegate His authority to us as His representatives here on earth. What a privilege - and responsibility. Suddenly I realised I was being inconsistent. I had assumed that only defence, not offence, was automatic. I didn't expect to see God plant a church in a dark city without intercession to prepare the way, so why should I expect automatic protection while there? In the same way that we are told that we don't have because we don't ask (James 4:2), we are told not to ignore the devil but to actively resist him (James 4:7).

Another incident reinforced the message that the authority we have in Christ must be exercised.

A steel door had slammed shut on my foot, and even after a couple of weeks it was still swollen and painful. As I hobbled home one day, a neighbour invited me into her flat, saying, 'I have just the thing for that.' Naively I expected a bandage! As soon as she started waving her hands about over my ankle I realised she had something different in mind. Immediately, I declared quite loudly, 'I don't need that', and left hurriedly.

It was to my surprise then, that when I woke the next day my ankle was covered in pink spots. (Previously it had just been swollen). In Jesus' name I renounced the woman's incantations, and within an hour the spots had disappeared. (It took another few weeks for the original swelling to go down though!) I had thought that my rejection of her 'help' at the time was enough, but the appearance of the spots showed me that something more was required. So in a way I was thankful for the spots - at least they indicated that there was a problem and I needed to do something! Perhaps the more dangerous situation is when there are no obvious symptoms and the work of the evil one remains hidden. Although there are occasions when the devil likes to be the centre of attention, at other times he realises it is wiser not to make his presence too obvious. In other words, he likes to play hide and seek.

Hide and seek

When we moved out from the capital to a regional city, our first regular cell group meeting began in a home where the daughter and daughter-in-law were believers. Granny, as head of the household, had invited us to use the living room for our meetings. Each week we came together with about 15 believers and not-yet-believers to worship God and study the book of Genesis. Granny was usually present too. By the time we got to Noah some more people had put their trust in Jesus.

After a few months the son came in drunk during a meeting and threw us out. So the cell moved to the flat of a young couple who were both believers. Immediately I noticed a difference. Teaching the group suddenly became easier. Instead of a 'wall' (which I had put down to cultural or language difficulties), the believers were responsive and the Word of God seemed to hit home. What had happened?

I continued to visit our first meeting place in order to disciple the daughter, and often ended up drinking tea with granny as well. I began to sense darkness each time I entered the home, and gradually I uncovered the cause. As I listened to the ramblings of the old woman - half the time I didn't know if she was recounting a dream or something that had actually happened, and the rest of the time her lack of teeth made her hard to understand - I realised she was a shaman. Neighbours, and occasionally those from further afield, would come to her for healing or protection. Her grandson's wife confirmed this and added that when the son had died suddenly granny had cursed three people she suspected of causing his death. Within a year all three were dead.

But how could this be? How could a shaman sit week after a week in a room full of worshipping believers without the demons in her either manifesting themselves or causing her to leave? Why had the two believers in the family not told me before that she was a shaman? Why hadn't I sensed it before when talking to granny? Why did I only begin to sense darkness in that house after we stopped meeting there? How was it possible that while I had sensed a 'wall', several people were actually converted there?

Questions remain, but one thing has become clear - the enemy's tactic is often to remain hidden. After all, if his presence is undetected it is also unopposed. Many complain of headaches when they first come to a cell group meeting. We're glad if they do so, as we can then pray and bind the spirits that are troubling them. Many more just leave never to come back. With time we are growing in discernment and learning to ask the right questions.

One example of this is a young girl whom I'll call Mary. When she turned to Jesus, I began to disciple her. Like most of her people she had thought that prayer was only for those who had been to 'prayer school' or for 'holy men' or the like. I showed her from the Gospels that we can approach God as our Father, and with a little encouragement from me she prayed out loud - brief and a little falteringly, but it was a start. The next time we met, there was no stopping her! I was surprised then, when a few weeks later we sat down to pray together and she said, 'I can't.' Going back to the passages I'd shown her before, I explained again about coming to God as Father. 'I can't pray,' she kept saying. It was only when a more discerning team-mate asked the right question ('Why not?') that a demon was revealed. 'Because there's a snake around my neck about to strangle me if I do,' she replied. Once uncovered, the problem was easily dealt with. Well, I say easily - binding a demon was the last thing I felt like doing after a sleepless night caused by the neighbours' new Yamaha keyboard! The devil does choose his moments. But the victory was won nonetheless, and a child of God found freedom to pray to her Father.

Truth under attack

Other times the attack has been on the level of truth. The evil one has been a liar from the beginning (John 8:44), and loves to whisper in the ears of believers, attacking the truthfulness and integrity of God's word.

I open the Bible and read, 'God is faithful,' but immediately the thought comes, 'No he isn't.' Or I wake up in the night with such ideas running through my mind. On these occasions an audible declaration of truth: 'God is faithful,' has usually done the job. It took a while for me to realise that, unlike God, the enemy and his minions cannot read my thoughts. At other times, I have struggled to open my mouth, and have had to call on Jesus silently first.

The new believers are also attacked as they read God's Word. Many complain of headaches, and others cannot understand even the story line, never mind the spiritual truths. Confusion is a trademark of the enemy.

I once sat for hours, trying to prepare a lesson for the cell group the following day. Somehow it wouldn't come together. Frustrated, I got up and started to praise the Lord out loud instead. At first it was hard going – an act of the will – and I had to almost force myself to keep going. Then suddenly the breakthrough came. Praise began to pour from my lips, and I eventually had to pull myself away to go back to my desk. Within 30 minutes, the lesson was completed. My previously confused thoughts had become a clear idea of what I was trying to teach, and how I could best communicate it.

On other occasions since then, stopping to praise when I reached a seeming brick wall has been the key to moving forward. My prayer life is including more and more declarations not only of who God is, but of his word which is truth.

So how do we deal with seeming contradictions between what the word of God says and what we so confidently call 'reality'? What do you say to a woman who has no work, no money and not even bread to eat? Her neighbours mock her, saying, 'What has believing in God done for you?' And all the time the temptation is there, either to make money illegally or to pay a bribe to obtain work. In the past I would have been tempted to 'excuse' God and his word. But which is ultimate – our circumstances or our infinite Creator God? Recently the mundane issue of daily bread for the believers has been the focus of many prayers, declaring that God will provide. It is the circumstances that must conform to God's promises, not the other way round. But perhaps the most dangerous type of attack is slow attrition.

The first time I visited Central Asia (on a three-week trip), I was not at all aware of an 'oppressive atmosphere'. It was only when I returned to Heathrow, and felt praise welling up within me and a lightness in my spirit, that I realised what a spiritually dark place I had just left. Since then I have noticed the difference when arriving in Central Asia, but after a few weeks I've got used to it. Even so the effect on me has continued. Apathy, fear, lack of joy, all these things creep in unnoticed. It takes a conscious effort on my part to counter these with declarations of God's goodness, faithfulness, and other truths from his word. Praise music is one means I've used to fill my mind with truth. A guitar and a song book, together with my Bible, are part of my survival kit.

Yet I want to do more than survive. Is it not better to do away with the oppression than learn to live with it? Victories such as with Mary, though precious, are not enough. Rather than plucking ones and twos from the prison of the evil one, we long to see the doors opened so that all may come out. Jesus has won the victory on the cross, but we need to take the land.

Perhaps you are reading this in a country where there is already an established church, and where to some extent the darkness has been pushed back by the light. Yet the evil one is on the doorstep seeking to reclaim it. Will you stand against him? And if you have the privilege of living without having to continually stand up against the oppressiveness of Central Asia, will you join with those of us who do? While we are forced to expend our energies on surviving and 'fire-fighting', we need an army of intercessors to concentrate on the big breakthrough that is needed. Who will be part of the troops enforcing Jesus' victory and exercising His authority on earth and in this dark city?

I asked the Lord for the gift of discernment
Jean Forbes
I joined a Spiritual Warfare group when I was a five-month-old Christian and I thought it was perfectly normal to fight the devil. I wanted to pay him back for all the years he had kept me in bondage. I prayed for discernment of spirits for myself – that is one of the gifts listed in 1 Corinthians 12:10, yet I have hardly ever heard this mentioned by Christians. Many mention 'discernment' and seem to relate it just to wisdom. Soon after asking for this gift, I asked the Lord to show me its effectiveness.

Late the next night, from my second-floor window I heard a big argument going on. There were two cars, two young men and two girls in the road below me. I did not know what the argument was about. There was much bad language and the men were pushing at each other, ready to fight. I bound the spirit of aggression and dissension, and loosed the spirit of peace. The effect was instantaneous. Both men lowered their hands, got into their respective cars, each with a girl, and drove off. I was amazed.

Next day I asked the Lord to confirm that he could use me in this way. That afternoon, while I was shopping, I saw a drunk man weaving from side to side of the pavement. He had a bottle in one hand and was shouting and singing. I bound the spirit of alcohol in him and loosed a spirit of peace. He immediately dropped the bottle into a waste bin, straightened himself up and walked normally up the road.

Binding and loosing go together. It is good to remember that on these two initial encounters the spirits were only bound until let loose again by the persons. When the drunk passes a pub with the door open and smells drink in the environment he is used to, he may go in, and then the spirits are free again.

Discernment is like radar
Antonio Alkimim
Discernment is like radar. You can feel a presence. There is an uneasy sensation. You can say immediately, 'Go out. You have no right in my house.'

One night I was asking God why my kids were becoming rebellious. I dreamt that our doorbell rang, and at the gate were two kids, a boy and a blonde girl (my kids). Before I touched the doorknob the two of them went through the gate, ran into the house and went to my children's rooms. When they reached them, I woke from my dream with that sensation of evil. God said, 'Go and pray for them now.' I stood in the corridor and in a low voice I commanded the spirits of rebellion to leave. I saw the kids writhing in bed as they left. Then I thanked God for his kindness to us, for showing and leading me.

Everyone has a gift. Ask God for that gift. Then act as if you have it. It will start in a small way, to help you believe. I was asking God for the gift of discernment. As I was praying for a lady, I suddenly had a vision of her with darkened eyes. I made the comment to her husband, and he said, 'She doesn't believe.' So as you practice it, the gift will grow.

Congo light
Philip Wood

There was no doubt that Mukulungando wanted to go to the nursing school at Nyankunde. Since 350 students had sat the entrance exam from all over the country and only 25 had passed, it was an honour to be among the four from his region. A major inconvenience was the uncomfortable three-day journey through the jungle on the top of a broken down truck – the only available transport for the long journey from where his family lived.

Fortunately this journey needed to be repeated only once each year – during the summer holidays – the one significant holiday the school allowed. These holidays were filled with hunting, fishing and visits to relatives. 'Oh, he is getting to be a man,' said his grandfather. 'Time to find him a wife,' said his grandmother. 'We will need to find someone from our tribe,' and she went on to say, 'We could not accept a woman from out east.' 'I will ask the witch doctor who we should suggest as a wife,' said his grandfather.

Mukulungando had made a profession of faith in Christ before he went for nursing studies and was therefore uncomfortable that his relatives were asking for this kind of spiritual guidance. He was even more uncomfortable when he learnt that negotiations had started with the family of a girl he had never met. The young lady in question was thrilled to be promised to an educated fellow with every prospect of a well-paying job. Naturally she was concerned that she might lose him to an attractive student at the school he was attending. She threatened to curse him if he did not marry her immediately.

Back at the school Mukulungando was uneasy about the turn of events at home, but he tried not to let his apprehensiveness affect his studies. Being an honours student he never found studies difficult, but over the next couple of weeks he found more and more difficulty in completing his practical assignments. He dropped a glass syringe in the paediatric ward. He broke a thermometer in intensive care. Then I got a report that Mukulungando was acting very strangely in the dormitory. He was shaking uncontrollably and seemed very agitated.

As a doctor this looked to me like a nervous breakdown; I prescribed a heavy sedative and took him off his work on the wards. There was some improvement but for several days in a row we needed to increase the dose of medication to control his shaking. After a few days he was taking a huge dose of chlorpromazine, a knockout dose for most of us, but he did not seem to be the least bit drowsy.

We were forced to make plans to return him somehow to his family, but then, out of the blue, we had news that he was completely better and asking to go back to work. What had happened? Mukulungando had some inkling as to what the problem was and he had gone to the leader of a bible study group that he had been involved in. 'I think my problems come from my family's involvement with the occult in relation to my marriage,' he said. 'Will you pray that I be released from whatever it is that is controlling me?'

The bible study leader called in another leader, and together they prayed for him, anointed him with oil and he was healed.

Involvement with spiritism and the occult is very common in Africa. People have discovered these powerful forces and have been using them for centuries. Drugs and medicines are not the way to combat them. Spiritual forces need spiritual weapons, and we and many Africans praise God for the Holy Spirit, who can overcome the darkest power the enemy can throw at us. I did not have the discernment to see what was going on, but praise God for the power of prayer.

Discernment and curses
How to recognise a curse
Joan Eley (additional material from Derek Prince)
A curse is something like a dark shadow, oppressing you, pushing you down, obscuring the sun of God's grace and blessing, propelling you in directions you do not really want to take. It is like an evil hand from the past, and every time you break through it gets hold of you and pulls you back, or it catches you and trips you. It is like a negative atmosphere that surrounds you, which seems to be stronger at some times than others, but from which you cannot seem to be totally free.

One key word is 'frustration'. You are aiming for a certain level of achievement in your life, you seem to have all the needed qualifications and gifts, yet something goes wrong. You start again, reach the same level, then something goes wrong again. The invisible hand drags you back. There is no obvious reason for it. This pattern may occur in any area: business, personal relationships, career, finance, health, marriage and family. 'He shall not see good when it comes' (Jeremiah 17:5-6).

If you were telling your life story, would you be likely to recognise the same pattern in previous generations? 'The same thing used to happen to my father' or 'I remember my grandfather telling me about that'. You become aware that this thing did not begin in your lifetime. That curse may go back several generations.

Where might a curse have come from?
Deuteronomy 28:1-2 states that the gateway to God's blessing is obedience. If we want to be blessed, we obey God. Conversely, Deuteronomy 28:15 makes it clear that disobedience is putting ourselves under a curse. Specifically, Deuteronomy 27:15-26 lists four major areas of disobedience: idolatry (verse 15), dishonouring parents (verse 16, Ephesians 6:2), illicit or unnatural sex (verses 20-23) and injustice to the weak or helpless (verse 25).

The cause of the curse mentioned in Jeremiah 17:5 is trusting in yourself, making flesh your strength, relying on your own natural ability, cleverness, talent or education. The result is that your heart slips away from the Lord. Both individuals and churches can lose the blessing in this way.

Malachi 1:14 lists another possible cause. Have you promised something to God and failed to give it, or have you given poor quality to the Lord? Malachi 3:8-10 spells it out as stinginess, withholding tithes and offerings. The remedy is to bring them, with the right motive – gratitude, not so that he will give to us.

Those in authority, like parents or teachers, can unwittingly curse those under their authority with negative statements like 'You will never succeed. There is no hope for you. You're stupid.' It can become a self-fulfilling prophecy. One grandfather used to say of his granddaughter, 'Where is the little devil now?' and she thought to herself, 'All right, I'll act like a little devil, if that's what you think of me.'

We can curse ourselves. Two biblical examples are Rebekah (Genesis 27:13) and the mob shouting, 'Let his blood be on us and on our children! Crucify him!' (Matthew 27:25). Soon after Rebekah cursed herself she said, 'I am weary of my life because of the daughters of Heth ... what good shall my life do me?' (Genesis 27:46 KJV). You become sick with sadness that never can be diagnosed. Instead, make a positive confession: 'I shall not die, but live, and will proclaim what the Lord has done' (Psalm 118:17).

Curses can come from people who serve Satan: witches, sorcerers, fortune tellers, mediums, whatever they call themselves.

Deliverance from curses
Appropriate for yourself the work of the cross when Jesus was made a curse for us. Try to discover the source or cause of the curse. Repent, if it was your own sin, or renounce it, if it came from others. Revoke all curses in Jesus' name. Commit yourself to obedience to God.

'My parents cursed me'
Thelma Mills
'Please pray for me. I have to go to Mansoa,' begged sixteen-year-old Maria, the youngest present in the women's meeting. 'My parents have summoned me home to marry me to the man I've been promised to since babyhood.' A keen Christian, recently baptised, she had a Christian boyfriend of her own, called John.

Her father would already have received her dowry from the bridegroom's family, and probably had spent it too. We knew this would be spiritual warfare, and we were not wrong. The women encouraged her to stand firm against this, and explain to her parents that now she had to obey God, and could not marry a non-believer. She set off. How we prayed!

Weeks later she returned, looking thin and ill. She seemed to have lost her joy in the Lord. 'What happened?' everyone clamoured to know. 'On the day we went in procession to the groom's house, I pretended that I needed to relieve myself in the woods, gave my family the slip, and came back here,' she explained with a woebegone expression

Maria became thinner and weaker as the days went by, yet I could find nothing medically wrong with her. Eventually she admitted that her parents had cursed her to die for bringing shame on them and landing them in debt. She knew of nobody who had been cursed like this who had not met a miserable death. She was convinced she was going to die. Fear and the power of evil seemed to grip her. Gone was her vibrant faith, the bounce in her step, her fearless witness for Jesus.

We brought her into our home, and spent every available moment reading or quoting scripture, especially verses exalting the name of Jesus and proving his power to be greater than that of the enemy. My co-worker at that time was an illiterate Balanta widow. She knew all too well the power of the spirits, but she knew the power of God was greater.

For three days or so Maria was soaked in the scriptures until she said she was ready for us to pray with her for release from the demonic power strangling the life out of her. We three knelt by the bed. Young Maria prayed, confessing her lack of faith, asking cleansing by the blood of Jesus, and asking for his Spirit to empower her. Then we laid hands on her, and she was gloriously filled with his Spirit, and delivered completely from the curse. She rose from her knees a different woman. Soon she began to regain her normal weight. Her joy in the Lord returned, and she became a powerful witness for Jesus.

She married John. Today she has a family of five and is a leader among the local women believers. The power of the curse was broken through prayer and being immersed in the scriptures until faith in the power of God replaced fear of the spirits.

Bewitched to love a Muslim
Bruce and Annette Rattray

Samsia belongs to the Serawai, a Malay people group in Sumatra. She and most of her family, along with many others in her village, were converted from Islam. After high school, Samsai went to Bible School and had just completed her studies when she met Colleen, a language student, and agreed to work with her in Kalimantan. Samsia was a lovely young lady and became like a daughter to us.

Pak Robin, the head of the primary school in our little township, approached her about marriage. This culture requires parental consent which has to be obtained through a third party. We acted as the third party for her, so he had to come and be "looked over" by Bruce. We were hesitant at first about giving our consent because we weren't very sure how keen he was as a Christian, but eventually we agreed to their engagement.

However Samsai's home church in Sumatra was not in agreement; they felt it was a very big step down to be marrying a Dayak. We did not know until later that they had tentatively arranged her marriage to an up-and-coming church leader, and that she had already refused because she considered him a ladies' man. The missionaries and the national leaders felt that she should return to Sumatra to visit her family. We gave her a letter saying that we were in agreement with her marriage to Pak Robin, and asked them to give their permission and blessing.

Samsai stayed with her parents. They were believers, but they were illiterate and knew very little about the Christian way. Her brother, a Muslim, decided that he would thwart Samsai's plans. He had a particular fellow in mind for her and when she went to visit her brother this man was sure to be there. When her brother's friend came round to Samsia's home she refused to see him. Her brother, however, resorted to the occult, and arranged to have a spell put on her which would give her an insatiable desire for this man. Sadly, the church was in a bad state spiritually and the members were not praying for her. In fact, they were ridiculing her for wanting to marry a Dayak, even though he was a well-educated person. As a result, the enemy gained a foothold.

This spell had a powerful effect. Whereas before she could not stand the sight of this Muslim man, now Samsai had an uncontrollable desire to be with him. She wanted to pray, but just could not. When he visited she asked her parents to lock her in her room and not let her out however much she pleaded with them. Several times, this satanic urge was so powerful that she even tried to knock the door down. But her parents were faithful and kept her locked in her room.

Samsai became very ill. No one knew what was wrong with her, and she ended up in hospital. Ruth Loan, a WEC worker in Sumatra, heard about Samsai. She visited her in hospital, ministered to her, and broke the spell. Very soon afterwards she was well enough to go home and immediately arranged to return to Kalimantan to complete her training.

Discernment and ancestral spirits
Manohar
Ram was spiritually weak and relied on his illiterate wife's solid faith. An ancestral spirit calling itself 'fairy of Delhi' troubled him at night. The same spirit had haunted his grandfather and his father. Now, as the oldest male in his family, he fatalistically reasoned that he could do nothing about it.

I encouraged him to be strong and fight it himself. As the oldest male in his family, Ram had to choose to take a firm stand and not pass the responsibility on to others. One night he was wakened several times by the spirit. As he normally did, Ram woke his wife and asked her to pray for him and tell it to go away. She refused! She reminded him that he needed to take a stand himself. She did pray silently, of course, but did not tell him. Within half an hour he was asleep. This happened several times. Early one morning he woke his son (I guess he gave up on his wife!) and his son also reminded him that he needed to take authority himself. When they shared the night's happenings with me at breakfast, I firmly told Ram again that he had to make the choice between being whole and happy or being weak and driven crazy. The message began to get through.

Later that day he went to the dentist and told him some of what had been going on and asked his opinion. The dentist, who was not a Christian, told him he was causing his own problems and would have to get over it. Ram came back a changed and determined person. He told me, 'Now I am going to fight.' He has begun to pray fervently and changes are beginning to take place. He now understands that he has the power to resist the ancestral spirit even though his ancestors did not. He has taken a stand to reclaim his authority as head of his family, and has asked forgiveness for the sins of his ancestors who brought this trouble on them.

On the day he took this stand my wife asked him, 'What is today?' He told us the date, 31 May. She told him to fix this date in his mind, so that if the spirit came back to trouble him, he could remind himself that he renounced it on that day. My wife and I feel a major breakthrough has been made, and we are sure that if Ram walks in this way of truth he will be greatly used by God. His wife Mata needed prayer as she adjusted to the changes in her husband who had been dependent on her for the past 30-40 years.

Health of the worker
Name withheld

Suddenly I was taken ill and I was hardly able to move. My body just refused to function normally. At first a viral infection was suspected, but the doctor was puzzled and couldn't find a real reason. As I slowly recovered I felt up to listening to tapes and reading. One song really touched me: 'Rejoice greatly, O daughter of Zion! Shout, O daughter of Jerusalem! Look, your king is coming to you. He is a righteous Saviour and he will speak peace to the nations!' My heart was filled with wonder and joy – yes there IS hope for the people of this sensitive nation. The Lord is righteous and hasn't left them out of his plan of salvation.

Three months later I had the opportunity to share at a prayer group. While preparing, it dawned on me what (or who!) had been bothering me out there. How often had I felt confused and unable to think clearly, tired or had a headache when talking to local people. What fear and loneliness I had experienced, such as I had never encountered before. During the night (usually between one and four o'clock in the morning) there were physical attacks. What mental battles had gone on in my head and heart!

I attended a so-called 'Time-Out' week in another country for workers like myself. There the beautiful morning sky made me cry, and suddenly my thoughts were back in 'my' country. I realised that there the sky – heaven – seemed to be an enemy, not a friend. Normally the sky is hardly seen in its beauty because there is so much dust in the air. But there was also a spiritual dimension to it. Somebody is trying to keep the people bound in the belief that heaven is closed up for them. That same morning the Bible reading was from Mark 7 where Jesus healed a mute man. While praying, Jesus looked up to heaven and said: 'Ephatha,' which means 'Be opened!' For me these words spoke into my situation out in 'my' country. I am so thankful that Jesus opened heaven to us by shedding his blood on the cross. And this is the truth for the peoples of 'my' country as well.

Over-contextualised
Dietrich Kuhl

Some years ago a worker was very much attracted by the contextualisation emphasis. He learnt some Arabic. He started to observe the fast, at least partially. He had long interactions with Muslim village leaders. One day he came to me and shared that he increasingly slipped into a depression. He realised that Islam is not just a religious system of beliefs but that there are realities and spiritual forces behind Islam.

STOPTHINK&DISCUSS
- Do you have a natural gift of discernment? Share an event in your life when it was useful.
- Discuss the giving and the use of the gifts of spiritual discernment, knowledge and wisdom.
- Share more stories where you needed spiritual discernment, knowledge or wisdom, and what happened.

8
WHY PUT ON DEFENSIVE ARMOUR?

Traugott Böker, Maurice Charman , Stewart Dinnen, Trevor Kallmier

'Put on the whole armour of God.' Note that it is always God's armour, never ours. Only as we are dependent on the Lord and in close relationship with him can the various parts of the armour be effective in our lives. But Christians are not merely passive receivers of God's protective resources. We actively 'put on' the armour. It is our responsibility to clothe ourselves with this armour so that we are not wounded in the fight.

We put on truth, righteousness, the gospel of peace, the shield of faith, the helmet of salvation. What is the belt of truth, and why is it first? Is God demanding an honesty factor? What is the breastplate of righteousness? What is foot-readiness that comes from the gospel? Is there a need to prepare for witnessing and then make the effort and begin? What is the shield of faith to extinguish flaming arrows? What is the sword of the Spirit, the word of God, and why is it last?

Stand firm, with the belt of truth buckled

Why is truth first? Because God desires truth in the inner parts (Psalm 51:6). God expects us to be open and honest with him.

Girded with truth! Sometimes a wrestler or someone about to lift a heavy weight will tie something tightly around himself. It helps to protect him from ruptures. It is a strengthening thing. Truth is like that. When you know you are in the right, it gives confidence. Before a race or before going to work in the fields, a Hebrew would 'gird himself' – that is, he would tie up his long flowing robes so they did not entangle his legs while running. Truth is like that too. Lies trip you up sooner or later. Truth sets you free from that danger (John 8:32). 'Your word is truth' (John 17:17). We need to know the truth so well that we recognise and contradict the lies and deceptions of the enemy. Paul spoke of 'the knowledge of the truth that leads to godliness' (Titus 1:1).

How we need truth in our speech! How easy to fall prey to the great danger of exaggeration. An evangelist estimates the number of converts too generously. A pastor is tempted to exaggerate the number of worshippers present in church 'for God's honour', or to alter facts about the early history of the local church in order to give himself a good position.

The Indonesian Missionary Fellowship had Indonesian and foreign staff on an equal footing. Gifts were received from Germany, Indonesia and Canada. All the money was pooled, and all members received the same allowance. Building projects were ambitious, beginning with a campus for hundreds of students complete with accommodation, administration and education facilities. How exciting it would have been to say that all the money came from Indonesia! But we had to keep to the truth.

Clothed with the breastplate of righteousness

There are two aspects to this. The first is the righteousness of God, given to us through the work of Christ on the cross. 'Christ Jesus who has become . . . our righteousness' (1 Corinthians 1:30). 'God made him who had no sin to be sin for us, so that in him we might become the righteousness of God' (2 Corinthians 5:21). God's standard is perfection.

The second aspect is practical righteousness in everyday living. Eventually the righteousness of Christ that is credited to us goes to work in us, and begins to produce itself in us. It is an armour, a protective wall. Satan finds no way to accuse us of hypocrisy or to lead us astray. Admit anywhere you have failed. Humble yourself. Put the breastplate back on. Both these aspects are a great protection from the enemy's attacks in the area of evil and sinful desires.

Take the shield of faith with which you can extinguish all the flaming arrows of the evil one

Faith shields us from attack in a bewildering number of unexpected ways! Facing a new and daunting task, we may be tempted to fear, like the men sent to spy out Canaan: 'We seemed like grasshoppers' (Numbers 13:33). But Caleb was not tainted with that fear (13:30). Why not? Caleb's faith strengthened him. When people jeer at us, our faith keeps us going. 'The God of heaven will give us success' (Nehemiah 2:20). Faith counters unbelief and nullifies the accusations of the enemy.

Take the helmet of salvation

We need protection in the thought world because temptation begins as a thought; feelings of rejection, despair, fear or resentment begin as thoughts. All Satan's attacks begin in the mind, with lies carefully disguised as truth, or mixed with some truth twisted. Martin Luther once said that our mind is like a prostitute, willing to serve whoever. That's why we sometimes need to drag our thoughts back into captivity (2 Corinthians 10:5). For example, liberal higher criticism attempts to destroy or discredit the authorship of every book of the Bible, and to explain away every miracle, because of an underlying assumption that the supernatural does not exist. During his theological studies, Traugott came to confess as sin some of the critical thoughts about God inspired by such lectures.

Your feet fitted with the readiness that comes from the gospel of peace

The word used for boot describes a special army shoe that enabled the soldier to travel long distances comfortably and prevented his foot from sliding. Sharing the Good News is protection for us. One reason for the decline of the church in North Africa was that they only had theological disputes, and no longer any missionary work. There was a 'Pro Christ' Billy Graham Mission in 1993, but many evangelicals took no part, being preoccupied with internal issues. We can be so aware of the world that we are in danger of spending all our effort on separating ourselves from it and do not evangelise together.

Ready to tell the gospel
John Bardsley

I was going to Korea for some meetings. As I packed, the Lord clearly put the thought in my mind, 'If you want to share my life with someone, put literature in your pocket'. I took a copy of *Why Jesus?* by Nicky Gumbel, and put it in the pocket of the jacket I would be wearing on the plane. But nobody initiated a conversation on the plane. As I was waiting at the bus stop outside the terminal in Seoul, and checking carefully to ensure I had the right bus, a friendly voice beside me said in English, 'May I help you?' I was grateful to have her confirmation that this was the right bus stop for the coach going to the suburb where the WEC office is located. She said, 'I'm going on that coach too.' We had an hour and a half to talk. She was an art student in America, but was returning home to Seoul because her mother had been diagnosed with terminal cancer. She was fearful, and very open. We shared about how to get to heaven, and I gave her the booklet.

I was driving home from Birmingham after a day teaching in a Bible school. Two motorways diverge from one point: the M40 going towards Oxford and on to my home, and the M5 going to Wales and Bristol. Fine misty rain was falling. I saw a man hitch hiking. I don't pick up lots of hitch hikers any more, but I had that familiar nudge from the Lord to say, 'Stop for him.' He was so grateful.

When I asked him where he was going, he said, 'I had a row with my wife last night, and slept outside in the trees. Now I am going to Bristol to pick up my unemployment benefits cheque'. I said, 'No you're not. You're on the M40 heading for Oxford.' 'Oh, I see. Never mind, at least it's warm and dry. I'll get out at the next petrol stop and go back.' Then I knew I had about twenty minutes.

We started talking about that old saying: 'Strife between man and wife and faults on both sides.' I asked him if he would be willing to say sorry for his faults, even if she did not say sorry for hers. He said he would. I reminded him how difficult it would be, and suggested he needed help from Jesus. He said, 'I'm glad I got into this car today.' I always keep leaflets in the car, and this car had a pocket for them on the door. I couldn't choose one, because I had to watch the road, but I reached in and took one, and gave it to him. We both burst out laughing. It was covered with road signs, and said, 'Turn back! You are going the wrong way!' I left him at the petrol stop, sitting with a coffee, reading it.

Another time, after a weekend in Birmingham, it was I who had to turn back. There had been a rebellious teenage girl in the Sunday night meeting, the daughter of a church member. I slept the night, but to miss the traffic I woke at 4 a.m. and left quietly. As I passed the local petrol station, a nudge: 'Get petrol.' 'Lord, I don't need petrol.' So I drove past. But the feeling grew stronger that I had to get petrol. I turned the car round, and stopped at the petrol station. The voice said, 'Put two tracts in your pocket'. When I got to the night window to pay, that disruptive teenager was inside chatting with the attendant, a Pakistani lad. I gave him the money and the leaflets, saying, 'One for you and one for your friend.'

The power of the blood of Jesus

The blood is the basis of our approach to God. 'You who once were far away have been brought near by the blood of Christ. For he himself is our peace' (Ephesians 2:13-14).

The blood is the means of the atonement. 'God presented him [Christ] as a sacrifice of atonement through faith in his blood' (Romans 3:25).

The blood is the ground of our justification. 'Since we have now been justified by his blood, how much more shall we be saved from God's wrath through him!' (Romans 5:9).

The blood is the basis of the new deal God makes with us. 'After supper he took the cup, saying, "This cup is the new covenant in my blood"' (1 Corinthians 11:25).

The blood is the means of redemption. 'In him we have redemption through his blood, the forgiveness of sins' (Ephesians 1:7).

The blood cleanses the conscience. 'The blood of goats and bulls . . . sprinkled on those who are ceremonially unclean sanctify them so they are outwardly clean. How much more, then, will the blood of Christ, who through the eternal Spirit offered himself unblemished to God, cleanse our consciences from acts that lead to death, so that we may serve the living God!' (Hebrews 9:13-14).

The blood is the key to forgiveness. 'Without the shedding of blood there is no forgiveness' (Hebrews 9:22).

The blood is the basis of Christ's identification with humanity. 'Since the children have flesh and blood, he too shared in their humanity . . .' (Hebrews 2:14).

The blood is essential for our fellowship. 'If we walk in the light, as he is in the light, we have fellowship with one another, and the blood of Jesus, his Son, purifies us from all sin' (1 John 1:7).

The blood is the ground of victory over Satan. 'They overcame him by the blood of the Lamb and by the word of their testimony; they did not love their lives so much as to shrink from death' (Revelation 12:11).

Cultural entertainment
Mike Galpin, East Asia

The university used to take its foreign students out on a weekend away once a semester. This particular time part of the trip was to a village, to see dancing and other activities. There were at least three bus loads of us, many of whom were Christians. One of the items was to be done by a shaman, or witch doctor, who said he wanted to bless us. Spontaneously all the Christians realised they did not want his type of blessing. So all over the place Christians were praying, many in tongues, against this blessing. Sure enough, God answered our prayers and the shaman could not continue. The announcer said he was sorry, and that this had never happened before. We not only need to know our authority in God, we need to use it.

Oppression near the temple

Another time two workers were going up a hill towards a temple when an old lady came down the hill towards us, begging money for the temple. She could not speak English and at that time we could not speak Chinese. Marian said in English, 'The only thing I can give you is my Jesus.' At this the old lady turned and fled up the hill.

Living in Thailand, we are within the sound of the temple monks chanting every day. This can bring oppression. To keep us covered, we put on the armour of God and, even more important, we worship. In Thailand it is very easy to become complacent because the monks and saffron-robed children are everywhere and we found that after a while we weren't seeing them. So it is vital that we stay in prayer and worship to the Lord. Now we are attending a very live fellowship, so with many voices and with one accord we often pray and worship the one and only living God together.

As sons and daughters of Christ we are targets of the enemy. The spiritual battle is actually more real than the day-to-day problems. We need to be prepared with the full armour of God.

Enemy reprisals against our children
Bruce and Annette Rattray

While the spiritual conflict often raged over the advance of the Gospel to unreached areas and over the problems of national believers, there was a growing awareness in Bruce and Annette that the enemy was seeking to defeat the Lord's purposes by infiltrating their family life through sickness, accidents, and rebellion.

'Our son Simon had quite a number of accidents, but the first really serious one was when he was about six years old and fell from his upper bunk bed on to his head and suffered concussion. Bruce was going away that day for meetings, so early in the morning we had a time of prayer. When Bruce sat him on his knee, Simon suddenly began to whimper and was obviously very much afraid. "What's the matter, Mon?" He said, "Don't go away. Don't leave me, Daddy," he cried. "You're getting smaller and smaller."

'Simon obviously had some sort of visual disturbance because he was like this for several days. However, he pleaded with us to let him go down to the river to bathe with the other children, but it was about eight days before we allowed him to go. Unfortunately he started playing with the boys from the school dormitory. One of them elbowed him in the ear quite badly. His ear bled, and when he came home I realised there could be quite a problem because it was on the same side as the concussion.

'A day or two later, when Bruce was due to go off again, Simon still had a lot of watery discharge from his ear. We contacted the hospital about it by radio and they said he would just have to be very quiet, but if it continued he would have to come in to be checked. We were really concerned and Bruce hated leaving.'

Bruce describes his concern. 'I was at Nanga Beloh, about three hours away. Early in the morning the Lord urged me to get away on my own. I sensed a burden to pray. I found the front door of the school open and went in, got down on my knees and began to pray. A tremendous burden of intercession came upon me and I remember praying for Simon with groanings (Romans 8:26, 27). I prayed until the burden finally lifted and the Lord said, "I've heard you." I was surprised when I checked my watch - I had been there over an hour.

'When I arrived home at Merakai that afternoon, I asked Anne, "How's Mon?" She said, "He's about the same." I replied, "He's going to be all right. The Lord led me to intercede for him, so I prayed through." Gradually he got over that and there were no more problems with his ear.'

'Simon had a number of accidents after that for no accountable reason. They were certainly not only because of his over-exuberance. On the last day of a seminar there was a serious situation when he jumped into the river without looking first, and without our permission. He did not see a canoe below him because he launched himself right off the top of the high bank. He managed to land in the water by pushing the canoe away, but it swung back and hit him in the face. He had very bad bruising on his nose, face, and cheek bones, and an enormous gash on his bottom lip. His two front teeth were pushed in with the roots sticking out. It was horrible. He came running up the bank with Ken Jordan, one of our young missionaries, helping him. Simon was saying, "I don't want to die Mummy, I don't want to die." There was blood everywhere. We didn't really know the extent of the damage and had visions of having to call the plane.

'When we cleaned him up I realised that the main thing was the gash that had to be fixed. I didn't have anything for fine internal stitching, so we called the local doctor. Simon was a very emotional child and he was beside himself, but after praying with him he became very quiet. The doctor injected his lip and Simon lay there humming. The doctor couldn't believe it, because he was obviously in a lot of pain. He suddenly said, "Mummy, that stuff is in my mouth." The local anaesthetic was going straight through his lip into his mouth! Eventually the doctor did stitch it. Since then Simon has been able to have plastic surgery to his lip and his fractured nose.

'Even this accident had a spiritual aspect to it. Without help, we wouldn't have been able to carry on and take that last night of the seminar because Simon was really in a bad way. Yet we were able to leave him with Margaret Price. He said, "I'll be all right. Auntie Margaret will look after me." It was really lovely to see the concern of the families, especially the men, when we shared this. Just the fact that we shared our battles and tests and were open with them meant a lot to them.

'There were other accidents. One happened when Simon was twelve. He climbed a tree to retrieve his kite, but in trying to get away from the biting ants, slid too fast down the trunk, cutting his leg within an inch of his groin on a sharp branch. It was a very large, deep cut - a good three or four inches long.

'Having listened to some tapes on spiritual warfare, we realised there was a pattern here - a demonic dimension to it. So we stopped thinking that Simon was "accident-prone" and claimed deliverance from demonic attacks upon him. As we prayed we completely broke that demonic power. From that day to this the pattern has been broken. (And he never ceased to be exuberant!)'

Another factor came to light. Bruce describes the symptoms:
'We noticed that when I was due to go out for an evangelistic trek the boys would

often be impossible, fighting together and arguing for the couple of days before I left. It is strange that we didn't realise that there was something satanic behind it because they weren't usually like that. I remember one day Simon was absolutely impossible. No matter what Paul or anybody else said, he was cantankerous. There was real chaos in the house. It reached such a point that I felt it had gone too far. It didn't matter what I did in the way of remonstrating, it didn't make any difference. In my frustration I suddenly prayed, "In the name of the Lord Jesus Christ I rebuke the devil who is behind this, and command that you leave." Instantly the situation changed and Simon said, "I'm sorry, Dad. I was wrong." It was quite remarkable. It proved to me that in many of these things we experienced there was a demonic element. It stopped immediately.'

Goat attack
Norma Hunt
My goats often got sick, and it dawned on me that it was one way the devil had of attacking me. One day a little female goat died after a short, unexplained illness. Then her twin sister got sick. I felt devastated. I also felt that it was not a normal sickness. As I prayed for her, I ordered the devil and his demons to leave her alone in the name of Jesus.

Immediately the devil answered me, 'You take your hands off my people and I will take my hands off your goats.' I know the devil is not omniscient or omnipresent, but I am sure it was the devil who spoke to me. The experience stunned me, and I had difficulty making my reply, but the Lord is stronger, and enabled me to give my answer: 'I will not take my hands off your people at any cost.' I rushed out to my little goat expecting to see her dying, but she was perfectly well!

Thankfully, it happened only that once.

'Someone prayed': a parable
Richard Shawyer
'The god of this age has blinded the minds of unbelievers, so that they cannot see the light of the gospel of the glory of Christ, who is the image of God' (2 Corinthians 4:4). 'When anyone hears the message about the kingdom and does not understand it, the evil one comes and snatches away what was sown in his heart' (Matt 13:19).

Cheikh listened to the Way of Righteousness tape. He heard the speaker talking in perfect Wolof about how everyone has sinned. Unseen, a demon was sitting comfortably on his right shoulder whispering sweet lies into his ear. 'Sure, everyone makes mistakes. But God is good. You have done lots of   good things. You will be OK, you are not like Souleyman over there who is really bad . . .' The demon chuckled to himself. 'These people are so gullible. Missionaries of the enemy have been here for years, yet not a single person takes in the message of our Enemy. They cannot beat us. How they waste their time!' He saw another demon stronger than himself on Malik's back with his hands over Malik's ears. Malik was listening too, but nothing seemed to be sinking in.

Meanwhile, in Australia, Mary got down on her knees to pray. She began to intercede earnestly that God would bind the forces of evil who are keeping the Wolof blind, and that the light of God's word would shine in their darkness. Suddenly, out there in Senegal, an angel, strong, beautiful, full of light, descended on the demon on Cheikh's shoulder. With one mighty blow the demon went spiralling towards the lake, knocked senseless. Just at that moment Cheikh heard these words on the tape: 'Every one of us is a sinner, and the wages of sin is death. The things we do which are good can never pay this penalty. Every sin will be paid for by death, either by you or by the sacrifice God made . . .'

It was as though a sword pierced his heart, as he began to understand for the first time. 'What will happen to me when I die?' Cheikh asked, his conscience awakened by the Spirit of God. The seed had been planted. There would be many more encounters like this before Cheikh could come to faith, but the work of the Holy Spirit had begun. The demon groggily pulled himself together. 'What happened?' he asked. The angel replied, with a glint in his eye, 'Someone prayed!'

'No one can enter a strong man's house and carry off his possessions unless he first ties up the strong man. Then he can rob his house' (Mark 3:27).

Angels

'Are not all angels ministering spirits sent to serve those who will inherit salvation?' (Hebrews 1:14). 'He will command his angels concerning you, to guard you in all your ways; they will lift you up in their hands, so that you will not strike your foot against a stone. You will tread upon the lion and the cobra . . .' (Psalm 91:11-12). Praise God for the ministry of angels.

Where's the soldier who was guarding you?

Joan Eley was making disciples in eleven village churches scattered across a desert area of Venezuela, centred on Barquisimeto. The churches were growing, and in one village, at least, the brothel and the pub were losing business, and feeling the pinch. The pimp and the publican got together and hired a local assassin to kill Joan on her way home.

There were not many roads in this area, and Joan used to ride her motorbike down the dry river beds, dodging in and out of the boulders. It was simple for the hired killer to trek out of town a couple of kilometres, hide behind one of the big boulders, and wait for Joan to come.

He heard her approaching, but when she came into view, he saw a huge Venezuelan soldier riding pillion behind her, with an AK47 strapped to his back. He faded into the background. Next day, curious, he went to Joan's house. 'Joan, where is the Venezuelan soldier you had on your motorbike last night?' 'What do you mean? I had no soldier on my bike. I never do. Everybody knows I never do.'

We believe it was an angel. They do too, and they didn't mess with Joan after that.

STOPTHINK&DISCUSS

- Discuss the importance of transparency and truthfulness in every aspect of our lives. Discuss the dangers of telling the truth without tact or love. How can we remain truthful and yet avoid the dangers?
- What doubts about your salvation have you had, what caused them, and how did you overcome them?
- Discuss the parable 'Someone prayed'.

9
OFFENSIVE WEAPONS

John Bardsley, Traugott Böker, Trevor Kallmier, Hans Rothenberger

God's purpose for us is a lot more than mere survival. Certainly, he has done everything necessary for our protection, as we have just seen. But as soldiers of the kingdom of light he has purposed that we should make disciples. We are to come against the enemy, restrict his power and set his captives free. For this we have been entrusted with tremendously powerful weapons (2 Corinthians 10:3-6).

Take the sword of the Spirit, which is the word of God (Ephesians 6:17)
The sword of the Spirit is powerful because it is God-breathed. It comes from God. It is authoritative and totally trustworthy and true. Demonic forces are well aware of this, and work hard to make us slack in reading and memorising God's word.

Be careful not to use God's word casually or carelessly. Remember it cuts both ways, so live in obedience to it yourself before you try to get someone else to do so. It is a weapon of defence as well as of attack.

Memorise as much as you can. Set memorisation goals. The word in the book is the sword in its scabbard. The word in your mind is the sword unsheathed ready for action. Jewish boys had to memorise great chunks of the first five books of the Old Testament. Get the word of God into your mind. Jesus used the word three times out of three in opposing the enemy. Scripture memorisation is one of the urgently needed disciplines of the Christian home and the Christian church.

Now I am an adult, memorisation is so much more difficult than when I was a child, but it is not impossible, as Chinese Christians have proved. A young doctor in Edinburgh was so inspired after reading The Heavenly Man that he began to memorise whole chapters like Brother Yun! I managed to learn a paragraph at a WEC children's camp in the summer because all the kids were learning it too, and also because it was set to music! Singing scripture fixes it in your mind a lot more easily! You can buy a CD or two of scripture songs, or you can make up your own song.

Pray in the Spirit on all occasions with all kinds of prayers and requests (Ephesians 6:18)
What is praying in the Spirit? If you have a Spirit-given gift of tongues, that is obviously praying in the Spirit. But what about those of us who don't? Pray for the things the Spirit lays on your hearts. Listen to the Spirit, ask for his guidance. 'The Spirit helps us in our weakness. We do not know what we ought to pray for, but the Spirit himself intercedes for us with groans that words cannot express. And he

who searches our hearts knows the mind of the Spirit, because the Spirit intercedes for the saints in accordance with God's will' (Romans 8:26,27).

What will I pray for today?
John Bardsley

My father was woken one night in 1965 with a feeling that he had to pray for Indonesia. He slipped to his knees beside the bed and prayed for several hours until the burden lifted. In the morning the radio announced there had been a Communist coup in which all but one of the army generals had been killed in their beds. The one who escaped led the army to defeat the Communists, and Indonesia became a strongly anti-Communist nation. 'Lord, make me sensitive to your Spirit, to know what to pray for and when!'

I have already mentioned how I was angry one day as I opened a letter from my friend, the field leader in Senegal. I was WEC Director in his home area, so I was responsible for his pastoral care, and for stirring up enough intercession for him. When is enough? When he starts making progress! He was responsible, among other things, for pastoring the church-planting teams in his country. He wrote, 'The Jola church has been here for 25 years. It has 18 members in two congregations. Neither of the congregations is growing, because the believers are still not completely free from fear of the spirits and cooperation with fetish ceremonies.' That's why I was angry. I was angry with the devil for keeping those people in darkness all that time, when Jesus had died to set them free. I was angry with myself and our chain of WEC prayer groups for failing to equip those teams to plant healthy, holy, multiplying teams among the Jola people.

I called a meeting, and told the local team of a dozen or so about this need. We skipped a meal to fast and pray for the Jola. Next week we did the same, and the week after. Then the team said to me, 'John, what about Japan? There are seventy WEC fields. We can't pray for the Jola every week.' Of course they were right. But God did not let me off the hook. I still pray for the Jola an hour a week.

When it is 'pray for the Jolas' time, I often begin with a simple prayer of worship, and then a request: 'What will I pray for today, Father? Will I pray over some photos? Will I take the latest news? Is there someone particular you want to lay on my heart today?' I expect the Spirit to lead me.

Once when I was in Senegal to see the Jola ministry first hand, two of us visited Himbane, the only married man in his church at that time, one in whom the workers had invested serious time. We caught him with a huge fetish charm on his upper arm, and since he also had his shirt off, he could not hide it! Have you ever seen an African blush? The other worker was so discouraged. He told me, 'If Himbane is still wearing charms after all the discipling I've given him, then I give up on him.' But something caught light in me that day, as I discovered as soon as I arrived home. In my next Jola prayer slot I asked the Lord what to pray for, and he said, 'Himbane'. He said 'Himbane' almost every week for the next nine months! Himbane made it. He is a valuable elder now.

We need to pray for the believers in our area, for all men that they should come to a knowledge of the truth, for an open door for the gospel, for freedom and courage for all preachers. Workers are always in danger, so pray for them with respect to courage (Ephesians 6:19), pride, avarice, lust and other sins. Pray for problems you see wherever you go. Pray for those the Lord lays on your heart. Pray for everyone you promise to pray for. It is not honest to say to a missionary about to leave, 'I'll pray for you', unless you do. If you cannot do it, don't promise.

What does it mean – all kinds of prayers? What kinds of prayers are there? Prayer can be short ('Help!') or long. Prayers can be fasting or feasting. The WEC International Office team has feasting prayer each Friday at coffee time, with a tasty morning tea before some pastoral prayer for each other, then serious intercession for the greatest needs of the week. Prayer can be theological and filled with scripture, or emotional: 'Oh God, please, save that precious girl from that beast who beats her!' Prayers can be silent or audible, depending on where I am and what time it is. There is both public and private prayer. I can be rejoicing in my prayer or broken. I can pray resisting and tearing down prayers, or worshipping and praising prayers.

There are intercessory prayers, the key ideas being responsibility, continuity, intensity and empathy. They exercise claiming faith, and are in the role of a priest. Their objective is God's intervention. Epaphras prayed like this in Colossians 4:12, and the Jerusalem church prayed like this in Acts 12:5.

There are strategic prayers, the key ideas being to wait on God, to be aware, to cooperate with God. They exercise creative faith, and are the role of a Christian soldier. Their objective is the extension of the kingdom. The Antioch church prayed like this in Acts 13:2, and Paul may have been praying like this in Acts 16:9 when he saw the vision of the Macedonian.

There are confrontational prayers. The key ideas are recognition of the enemy, resisting and binding him, reliance on the blood and the name of Christ and the armour he has provided, using authority to eject and deliver. This is conquering faith, as exercised by a king. Its objective is Satan's expulsion. Paul prayed like this in Acts 16:18, and so did the Jerusalem church in Acts 4:24. In the name of Jesus and in dependence on his power oppose the demonic forces and order them to draw back! The authority of these kinds of prayer is not based on the volume of my voice when I pray, but on the finished work of Christ.

There are doctrinal prayers in which I affirm, claim and celebrate the truths of the word of God concerning his attributes, his work of redemption and his promises.

Persistent warfare prayer thwarts attack on infant church
Bruce and Annette Rattray
Bold faith is the kind that refuses to believe enemy lies, or what our senses tell us, but hangs on till victory.

We had established a chain of young churches among the Dayak people of the interior of West Kalimantan. Military and political factors had created a climate which resulted in seven thousand registering officially as Christians under the WEC umbrella. These people were not blessed with a Western education. They were not literate. Their faith was simple, based on what they had heard and memorised. They lived in longhouses, grew rice and sweet potato, and collected spices from the jungle.

When we arrived back in Kalimantan after home assignment the MAF pilot who flew us to our isolated airstrip at Nanga Lebang told us some disturbing news. 'Get up to Merakai as quickly as possible,' he said. 'There are things going on up there that could be very damaging to your work.'

A government-sponsored delegation had arrived to enforce the law that everyone must have an official religion. However, there was a much more sinister element in this than first met the eye. The delegation was stacked with several members of a liberal, backslidden, politically motivated denomination from the more sophisticated coastal city of Pontianak, who claimed to be the church to the Dayaks. These people had informed the other members of the delegation that there was no work being done in the area. There were no pastors and no church buildings. A decision was about to be made to hand the whole area over to this other denomination.

My arrival set the cat among the pigeons. Shocked, some said, 'Where did you come from? How long have you been here?' So I told them. They asked, 'Are there any churches around here?' I said, 'Yes, plenty of churches.' I drew them a map, putting a cross at every place where there was a group, and at every place where there was a worker. When they saw this they became angry with the group that had fed them the wrong information, and they recognised the WEC right of ministry in that area, promising all the help they could. It was close, but God did it!

However, the enemy was not about to give up as easily as that. The leader of this denomination, working through the army commander in charge of the area (who belonged to the same denomination), was in the process of trying to persuade the elders of our congregations to join their denomination instead. He made repeated visits, and offered all kinds of enticements if they would transfer to their organisation. Knowing how little these simple Dayaks had in terms of material goods, and how easily they could be deceived, we could see that these enticements were dangerous. We recognised the unmistakable imprint of that old serpent the devil, who deceives the whole world. A mass movement of all our believing villages into their organisation loomed as a likely possibility.

One morning, a couple of months after all this started, when I was out in the boat praying, I had a real premonition that something bad was going to happen. Then I heard a motorboat approaching. It stopped right alongside my boat. When I looked out it was the leader of this group from Pontianak who had come all the way up, and had brought this other man from Sintang as well. They'd come to visit me. So I invited them up to the house and as soon as we sat down the Lord seemed to say to me, 'They're going to try and trick you with their questions. They are going to make up a report to send to the army commander and governor in Pontianak.'

The Lord gave Annette and me great wisdom. I answered the men honestly enough, but I didn't tell them anything. In the course of our conversation I challenged them: 'Look, what do you think you are doing? You are saying nothing about repentance, a change of life, the new birth or anything like that.' He laughed kind of sneeringly and said, 'We were like you once too. We've backslidden, haw, haw.' I said, 'You admit that you're backslidden, you're not preaching the gospel any more and people are going to hell. And then you laugh about it.' He was embarrassed. As they were about to go I said, 'Don't go before we pray.' He said, 'Well, you pray.' So I prayed and they left.

Later, we took time to pray to the victor of Calvary and the empty tomb. We asked the Lord for a promise on which to take a stand of faith. We settled on Mark 11:23-24, in the context of Jesus cursing the barren fig tree. Jesus promised that if we 'command this mountain to 'be thrown into the sea', and we believe that we have received it, then it will be done! A prayer and praise vigil lasted for over six months, while all the time this other denomination redoubled its efforts, using government officials, subtle enticements, and a smear campaign against a 'foreigner trying to plant a Western church among our Dayak people'.

Early in the morning, often at noon, and sometimes late into the night, I would be in prayer down on our little mission launch. Always my prayer was the same: 'In the name of the Lord Jesus Christ, who by his death, resurrection and ascension has defeated the powers of darkness, I who am seated with him on his throne do command that this mountain of [liberal denomination] be removed and thrown in the sea!' Then I would have a time of praise, thanking the Lord that he had heard me, and that in due time I would receive the answer.

I say it reverently, I troubled the Lord. I was like the widow in Luke 18:3 who bothered the judge, and like the begging friend in Luke 11:5-8 who wanted three loaves of bread and had not the slightest intention of leaving until he had them. I became increasingly bold. Often I would pray: 'Lord, this is for your glory, so you had better do it, because I will not let you rest until you do!' I could tell that such boldness pleased him, as I entered into an increasing intimacy with him.

There were confrontations with the other church on several occasions, but each time, the Holy Spirit gave supernatural wisdom and insight far above anything we naturally had.

Their leader had gone up river to visit one of our most distant groups where the village leader wanted an easier way than the gospel permitted. The man from Pontianak thought this might be the entry point. He sped past our home in his 40 horsepower outboard. Four hours later, I followed him in the slow mission launch, intending to walk across land to cut off a large U bend he was taking. What a day! I got lost several times on the jungle trails, and once fell off a log bridge into the river. I finally arrived, soaked, to the sound of the gong calling the people to the church. The liberal pastor had a surprise that night! There I sat in the congregation, Bible in hand! He almost fell over. So who preached? I did! Full of great joy – in spite of a few grins at the sight of my soaked and shrunken trousers. I think the Lord had a good laugh too!

After the meeting the liberal pastor and some of the village leaders came to speak with me formally. 'Bruce, I plan to stay here a couple of nights to speak to the people. I'm sure you will have no objection to that?' There was nothing I could say in front of the villagers, so I agreed.

Next morning, with Mr Dawi (our leading elder) showing me the way, I set off for another village, to bring them the gospel while I was in the area. Nearing our destination, Dawi was about to return to his rice field, and we paused to pray. Thinking about the previous days events, burdened for the faith of the new believers, we kneeled in the grass beside the muddy path. We did not believe it was God's will that these young believers should have their faith destroyed! The enemy might be whispering that it was all over, that it was too late, that we might as well go home, but we stood on the promise of God. I remember how the anointing of God fell on us to pray. 'In the name of the Lord Jesus Christ, I shut the mouth of Pastor K, so that he will be unable to speak one word which would destroy the faith of those simple village folk.' I prayed with great authority, though I had not consciously planned to pray a prayer like that. I can still see the shocked look on Dawi's face! I myself was shocked – I hadn't intended to pray that way. It was a prayer that God must have given me. I had a good meeting that night, and next morning returned to the village in danger.

Chatting with the constable at the police post, I asked how the meeting had gone the previous night. He burst into laughter. 'You wouldn't believe this,' he chortled. 'They sang a song or two, and invited Pastor K to preach. He walked to the pulpit, looked dazedly round him, opened his mouth, but no sound would come out. So he sat down again. They sang another song, and invited him again. Again he opened his mouth, but could not produce a sound. So he sat down again. They sang yet another song, and this time he stood up and gave a message about rejoicing in the Lord always, and sat down. I tell you, it was really something!' He was so embarrassed he had already left for home before I arrived.

'I saw Satan fall like lightning from heaven. I have given you authority to trample on snakes and scorpions and to overcome all the power of the enemy' (Luke 10:18-19). Hallelujah! Glory to his name! That was not the end of their efforts, however. We maintained our prayer vigil.

Then early one morning the Lord awakened me. 'Find a quiet place. I want to speak to you,' was the direct impression on my spirit. Finding the school empty, I sat on a bench and prayed. 'Lord, what do you want to say?' 'Not by might, nor by power, but by my Spirit' came clearly to me. Knowing it was from Zechariah 4:6, I opened my Bible to check the context. Verse seven leapt from the page: 'What are you, O mighty mountain? Before Zerubbabel you will become level ground.'

'I have heard your prayer,' God said. 'The great mountain has been thrown into the sea. You do not need to pray any longer!' Tears of joy coursed down my face.

The situation worsened, but to the glory of God I can testify that I never once prayed about it again, only praising him for the victory that was already won in the heavenlies. 'Whatever you ask for in prayer, believe that you have received it, and it will be yours' (Mark 11:24).

Some months later, after trying everything possible to gain a foothold, their representative left early in the morning in his outboard-powered canoe. Those months were possibly the most wonderful time of learning the principles of victorious warfare prayer that we ever experienced.

The name of Jesus

When we speak of using the name of Jesus as a weapon, it is not used as a magic formula or mantra. Rather we acknowledge and declare that Jesus Christ has supreme authority over all powers in heaven and earth. His name represents all that he is: his glory and his other attributes. His name represents all that he has done through his death, resurrection and ascension. If we minister in Jesus' name correctly, we are invoking the authority and kingly rule of Christ Jesus into the situation. The name of Jesus will bring people into submission to his Lordship.

- In salvation, 'there is no other name . . . by which we must be saved' (Acts 4:12).
- In justification, 'you were justified in the name of the Lord Jesus Christ' (1 Corinthians 6:11).
- For healing. 'Peter said . . . "in the name of Jesus Christ of Nazareth, walk" (Acts 3:6).
- In preaching, Philip 'preached the good news of the kingdom of God and the name of Jesus Christ' (Acts 8:12).
- In deliverance, Paul said, 'In the name of Jesus Christ I command you to come out of her!' (Acts 16:18).
- In church discipline, Paul pronounced judgement on a man in the name of our Lord Jesus Christ (1 Corinthians 5:3-4).
- The Holy Spirit came in his name: 'The Counsellor, the Holy Spirit, whom the Father will send in my name, will teach you' (John 14:26).
- For thanksgiving, 'always giving thanks to God the Father for everything, in the name of the Lord Jesus Christ' (Ephesians 5:20).
- In prayer, Jesus promised, 'I will do whatever you ask in my name. . . You may ask me for anything in my name, and I will do it' (John 14:13-14).
- When persecuted, the disciples rejoiced that they had been counted worthy of suffering disgrace for the Name (Acts 5:41 and 9:16).
- For every activity, 'do it all in the name of the Lord Jesus Christ' (Colossians 3:17).

Fasting

Do you have a problem? Is there a situation that gets to you, nags at you, hurts you, angers you? That should be enough motivation to make you want to fast. We don't fast until we want something changed. Prayer is dissatisfaction with the status quo. Fasting is serious dissatisfaction with the status quo. 'My heart is blighted and withered like grass; I forget to eat my food. Because of my loud groaning I am reduced to skin and bones' (Psalm 102:4).

'Declare a holy fast; call a sacred assembly. Summon the elders and all who live in the land [or church, or team!] to the house of the LORD your God, and cry out to the LORD' (Joel 1:14). 'Blow the trumpet in Zion, declare a holy fast, call a sacred assembly. Gather the people, consecrate the assembly; bring together the elders, gather the children, those nursing at the breast. Let the bridegroom leave his room and the bride her chamber. [Cancel the honeymoon!] Let the priests, who minister before the LORD, weep between the temple porch and the altar. Let them say "Spare your people, O LORD. Do not make your inheritance an object of scorn, a byword among the nations. Why should they say among the peoples, 'Where is their God?'"' (Joel 2:15-17).

How important does a problem have to be to make people cancel their honeymoon? When God's name is ridiculed and scorned. How soon is that situation coming where you live? This verse touches a chord in me. Do you see the degeneracy? Do you hear the word of Joel 'Declare a holy fast'?

Fasting is fighting, wrestling. Don't expect a walkover. But after the fast, expect barriers to be broken down. The promise stands: 'Your Father, who sees what is done in secret, will reward you' (Matthew 6:18).

Why do people fast?
'I humbled myself with fasting' (Psalm 35:13). 'I wept and chastened my soul with fasting' (Psalm 69:10 KJV).

An Anna-Hannah fast, to birth something new
Hannah fasted because of her infertility. She wanted a new birth. God wanted to birth a new leader. Hannah wept and would not eat; deeply troubled, she told her anguish and grief to God; then she went and ate something (1 Samuel 1 :7-18). Anna never left the temple, but worshipped night and day, fasting and praying. She gave thanks to God and spoke about the child to all who were looking forward to the redemption of Jerusalem (Luke 2:37-38). When I was commissioned to be the International Prayer Coordinator for WEC, I was very conscious of my inability. I went away on a three-day fast to ask for God's touch in this new responsibility.

Fasting for sorrow and bereavement
Abner planned to hand the kingdom over to David. Joab saw Abner as a rival, and killed him. David himself walked behind Abner's bier. The king sang a lament for Abner, and all the people wept over him again. Then they all came and urged David to eat something while it was still day, but David took an oath saying, 'May God deal with me, be it ever so severely, if I taste bread or anything else before the sun sets!' (2 Samuel 3: 35).

Fasting for healing and recovery
David pleaded with God for his child. He fasted and went into his house and spent the nights lying on the ground, and he would not eat any food (2 Samuel 12:16).

Fasting for repentance in the community
Ezra 'ate no food and drank no water, because he continued to mourn over the unfaithfulness of the exiles' (Ezra 10:6). Do you have friends whose hard hearts sadden you? Are there relatives in rebellion against God? How much do you care?

Enough to go without a meal to give more time to pray? In the reign of Jehoiakim, Jeremiah wrote a scroll, and Baruch read it in the temple. A time of fasting before the Lord was proclaimed for all the people in Jerusalem (Jeremiah 36:9). In the days of Nehemiah the Israelites came together 'fasting and wearing sackcloth and having dust on their heads . . . They stood in their places and confessed their sins and the wickedness of their fathers' (Nehemiah 9:1-2). Daniel wrote, 'So I turned to the Lord God and pleaded with him in prayer and petition, in fasting and in sackcloth and ashes. I prayed . . . and confessed . . .' (Daniel 9:3). When Ahab heard the words of the prophet he 'tore his clothes, put on sackcloth and fasted. He lay in sackcloth and went around meekly' (1 Kings 21:27). God encouraged Israel to fast for repentance: 'Return to me with all your heart, with fasting and weeping and mourning' (Joel 2:12).

Fasting for ethnic or national salvation
Do you believe your country is in dire need? How strongly do you feel about it? Strong enough to fast? Strong enough to call others to fast with you? 'Alarmed, Jehoshaphat resolved to enquire of the Lord, and he proclaimed a fast for all Judah' (2 Chronicles 20:3). Ezra was about to set out from captivity in Babylon to go and rebuild the temple in Jerusalem. He writes 'There . . . I proclaimed a fast, so that we might humble ourselves before our God and ask him for a safe journey for us and our children, with all our possessions' (Ezra 8:21). Esther knew her whole nation was in danger of ethnic cleansing. She and her people were fasting with weeping and wailing (Esther 4:3,16).

Fasting to commission an elder or missionary
'While they were worshipping the Lord and fasting, the Holy Spirit said, "Set apart for me Barnabas and Saul for the work to which I have called them." So after they had fasted and prayed, they placed their hands on them and sent them off'(Acts 13:3). 'Paul and Barnabas appointed elders for them in each church and, with prayer and fasting, committed them to the Lord, in whom they had put their trust' (Acts 14:23).

Fasting for spiritual authority
'Then Jesus was led by the Spirit into the desert to be tempted by the devil' (Matthew 4:2). After fasting for forty days and forty nights his body was weak but his spirit was armed.

When is it no use fasting? Jeremiah 14:12
Don't bother fasting if you're ignoring God's commands. 'They seek me daily, they delight to know my ways, they keep the ordinances, but they can't understand why they have fasted without result. On the fasting day they still demand a full day's work; they still take their own relaxation time; they still debate and make strife. They do the sackcloth and ashes bit, but it's not acceptable!' (free summary of Isaiah 58:1-5).

The rest of Isaiah 58 gives a three stage remedy for this failure to listen to what

God wants as prerequisites for his blessing:

Remedy stage 1, social justice: Break unjust chains, free the oppressed, share your food with the hungry, shelter wanderers, clothe the naked, don't turn away! Then your light will dawn, your healing appear, your righteousness shall go before you, the glory of the Lord will follow you, you will have answers to prayer (Isaiah 58:6-9).

Remedy stage 2, political justice and personal identification: Do away with oppressive systems! Satisfy the needs of the oppressed! Do away with malicious talk! When my wife and I spent a year in Indonesia we heard that many beggars made it a business, used old clothes for work, but still had nice clothes at home for going out, and found that eight hours of begging 'work' paid better than eight hours doing anything else. Whenever we were travelling, in no matter what kind of transport, beggars would accost us whenever we stopped. So I memorised an Indonesian phrase: 'Lebih baik bekerja' meaning 'It is better to work!' and I gave them nothing. It was a rough thing to say to someone, and didn't sit well with Isaiah 58. Do away with accusation! Spend yourself for the hungry! Then your light will dawn, God will guide, your needs will be satisfied, he will strengthen you, you will be fruitful and fresh, you will rebuild past ruins (Isaiah 58:9b-12).

Remedy stage 3, a day a week for God: Keep your feet from breaking the Sabbath. Keep from pleasing yourself on my holy day. Honour and delight in God's day. Then you will have joy in the Lord, you will ride on the heights of the land (where he rides!), you will feast on the full inheritance (Isaiah 58:13-14).

Don't bother fasting to make merit, or to earn God's favour, or to bolster your ego. 'I fast twice a week' (Luke 18:12). 'When you fast, do not look sombre . . . to show they are fasting . . . They have received their reward in full. But when you fast, [do your hair and put on your make up] . . . wash your face, so that it will not be obvious to men that you are fasting . . . and your Father, who sees what is done in secret, will reward you (Matthew 6:16-18).

'Let it be done to the Lord, with our minds singly fixed on him. Let our intention be this and this alone, to glorify our Father in heaven, to express sorrow and shame for our sins, to wait for an increase of purifying grace, to avert the wrath of God, to obtain all the precious promises he has made to us in Jesus Christ. Let us beware of fancying that we deserve anything from God because we fast. Fasting is only a way which God has ordained by which we wait for his undeserved mercy, and in which, without any desert of ours, he has promised freely to give us his blessing' (John Wesley).

Don't fast if it's a celebration! '"How is it that we and the Pharisees fast, but your disciples do not fast?" "How can the guests of the bridegroom mourn?"' (Matthew 9:14). Paul lists fasting as one of his privations: In labours, watchings, fastings (2 Corinthians 11:27 KJV).

How should I fast?

The shortest fast is to skip one meal: It's good. It gives extra time to pray. Breakfast is easy, because not many of us have an organised family breakfast, but it's rushed anyway, so it doesn't give much more time to pray. If you normally eat lunch in a canteen or cafeteria at work, then that is an ideal meal to fast. People will not miss you, and you have a significant time to get down to intercession.

You could fast till sundown. This is how Muslims fast. David fasted for Abner that way (2 Samuel 3:35); 'Then all the Israelites, the whole army, went up to Bethel, and there they sat weeping before the LORD. They fasted that day until evening and presented burnt offerings and fellowship offerings to the LORD.' (Judges 20:26). 'They mourned and wept and fasted till evening for Saul and his son Jonathan (2 Samuel 1:12).

You could fast for some days, as Nehemiah did (1:4). You could fast seven days, as David did with all Israel when they buried Saul and Jonathan (1 Chronicles 10:12). Maybe you could even fast two weeks. Paul reminded the sailors that they had continued fasting fourteen days in the storm, and now needed strength (Acts 27:33).If you fast fourteen days, you may feel physically weak too.

I wouldn't try fasting for forty days unless I had already succeeded at some shorter fasts first! Professor Zachariah Fomum of the University of Yaounde, Cameroon, has led teams of people to fast forty days for the downfall of Communism, and for the downfall of Islam. Dick Eastman of Every Home for Christ has twice fasted forty days, and he tells the story of his second fast in the book *Heights of Delight*.

Fasting makes you physically weak and cold: 'My knees give way from fasting' (Psalm 109:24). 'They have already been with me three days and have nothing to eat. I do not want to send them away hungry, or they may collapse on the way' (Matthew 15:32). Fasting gives you bad breath. You still have to clean your teeth just as much.

I don't recommend dry fasting, even though it is biblical. Muslims fast from drinking as well as eating. But fasting from water can endanger your health. Fasting from food while drinking water or juice is very beneficial physically as well was spiritually.

If you have to eat for medical reasons, you can fast in other ways. The king passed the night fasting, and without entertainment (Daniel 6:18). Fasting from television could give some excellent extra time to pray. Daniel fasted from choice food, (meat and wine), but you can make up your own mind what that would mean for you (Daniel 10:3).

Fast together. Unity strengthens a fast

The people came together from every town. 'All the men of Judah, with their wives and children and little ones, stood there before the LORD' (2 Chronicles 20:4, 13). 'A time of fasting before the LORD was proclaimed for all the people in Jerusalem and those who had come from the towns of Judah' (Jeremiah 36:9). 'Gather the people, consecrate the assembly: bring together the elders, gather the children, those nursing at the breast. Let the bridegroom leave his room and the bride her chamber' (Joel 2:16). The unity of the family, the home group, the church, the churches of a city or a county or a nation has a dramatic effect on the effectiveness of prayer. See the chapter on unity.

One city in Australia has several groups, all separately trying to organise city-wide prayer. We need humility to work together, don't we? Humility to admit someone else thought of it first, or to accept a plan that is not exactly the same vision as mine, but to recognise that God is in it. The churches of London have divided the city into segments reaching out as far as the M25 ring road. Each segment has churches committed to organising united prayer. One Satanist group is moving its headquarters from London to Austria, complaining that there are too many prayer groups in London. Let us pray for Austria!

Destroying demonic artefacts is another weapon of attack

Sometimes when commanding demons to leave their victim, we strike opposition. They don't go. There are several possible reasons. There may be a foothold not dealt with. There may be no authority today in the person commanding. Or there may be something belonging to the demon still among the victim's possessions. Some workers noticed unusual ineffectiveness in setting a woman free. They asked the spirit, 'Why won't you leave when we command you in the name of Jesus who defeated you?' The spirit replied, 'She has something of mine.' So they asked the woman, 'What is there in your possession?' She thought for a minute, and the Lord reminded her of something. She ran into the house and brought it out. They destroyed it, and the spirit left.

What does the Bible teach?
The first commandment states that there is one God only (Deuteronomy 5:7-8). He has no rivals (Exodus 20:3-5). He is Spirit. Those who worship him must worship in spirit and in truth (John 4:24). Part of worshipping in spirit is having no image or likeness of any visible thing to represent the invisible God (Deuteronomy 4:15-19). It is ridiculous to make something and then worship it (Isaiah 44:12-20; 46:5-10). We know that an idol is nothing (1 Corinthians 8:4-6). At the same time, sacrifice to idols is sacrifice to demons (1 Corinthians 10:19-21). If you know food has been offered to idols, don't eat it (1 Corinthians 10:28-32).

'You shall burn the carved images of their gods with fire; you shall not covet the silver or gold that is on them, nor take it for yourselves, lest you be snared by it; for it is an abomination to the LORD your God. Nor shall you bring an abomination into your house, lest you be doomed to destruction like it. You shall utterly detest it and utterly abhor it, for it is an accursed thing (Deuteronomy 7:25-26 NKJV). In Ephesus the new converts burned sorcery scrolls. We should destroy anything that gives a demon influence in our lives (Acts 19:19).

Agenda for a burning
An ex-Buddhist family wanted to smash their 'Goddess of Mercy' and burn their red paper charms. We set out what we would do.
1. We will pray for you.
2. You should pray to God, telling him he is the only God, and he is Lord and Master in your life. Tell him you do not believe in good luck, other gods, or praying to anyone but him any more, a loving Father who cares and provides.

3. Then we will take the idol and the charm into the garden. You should strike the match to burn what will burn. And you should strike the first blow to smash china or stone images. If you cannot break an image yourself, we can then help. This destroys the rights of its demon to visit your home, or influence your life. You must break it so it can never be used again to deceive anyone.
4. You should then speak to any demon which may have had access to your home through what you used to do. Tell it that you belong to God, the only God, and that you want nothing more to do with it. Tell it in the name of Jesus to stay out of your life from now on forever. You must demonstrate you no longer fear it or respect it.
5. Then we will pray to command these spirits to leave. You will experience freedom you have not had before.

These scriptures were given to the family as scriptures they could use against the enemy:

- 'By embracing death, taking it into himself, he destroyed the Devil's hold on death and freed all who cower through life, scared to death of death' (Hebrews 2:14, The Message).
- 'Having disarmed the powers and authorities, (Jesus) made a public spectacle of them, triumphing over them by the cross' (Colossians 2:15).
- 'Jesus Christ . . . is at God's right hand – with angels, authorities and powers in submission to him' (1 Peter 3:22).
- 'I have given you authority . . . to overcome all the power of the enemy' (Luke 10:19).
- 'Be self-controlled and alert. Your enemy the devil prowls around like a roaring lion looking for someone to devour. Resist him, standing firm in the faith' (1 Peter 5:8-9).
- 'Submit yourselves, then, to God. Resist the devil, and he will flee from you' (James 4:7).
- 'Put on the full armour of God so that you can take your stand against the devil's schemes' (Ephesians 6:11).
- 'The weapons we fight with . . . have divine power to demolish strongholds. We demolish arguments and every pretension that sets itself up against the knowledge of God' (2 Corinthians 10:4-5).

It happened at Easter camp
Bhim and Shirley Singh

It was very encouraging to see the committee at work for the camp, arranging accommodation, catering and transport, working out the programme for the weekend and the baptism service. Whenever they needed advice, they would ask us. We were pleased at their maturity in handling responsibility. Many had been fasting and praying for God to move in this special weekend. Little did we know what we were getting into.

The accommodation that had been recommended to us belonged to the ex-president, Ratu P. Ganilau. It was a huge, modern home with an ensuite to every room.

We started with praise and worship and the word, focusing our thoughts on the death of Christ. At the end, Bhim made an appeal for any to come for prayer. To our surprise, there were manifestations of evil spirits in some who came forward. We had not expected that, and prayed till late that night for deliverance. For some reason it wasn't easy, and we were involved in a spiritual battle that left us exhausted.

That night we waited on God for wisdom and guidance. We called for an optional fasting time next day, and many fasted after seeing the reality of the spiritual warfare we were in.

Next day there were manifestations during our worship time. It seemed spirits were jumping from one to another among our young people. Those who fell and started manifesting were carried away to nearby rooms and were prayed for while the session continued. Two girls who were due to be baptised that day were Zaneta, from a Christian background, and Grace, from a Hindu background whose mother had committed suicide. Both girls were unconscious, struggling with what was inside them. When they were conscious they could not understand why this was happening to them, and pleaded with God to help them.

In our evening session many were affected. We all felt so helpless. For most of them from our church this was their first experience of something like this. All they could do was cry out to God. That was a very long night. The children saw it all and many were frightened. We had to reassure them that Jesus is all-powerful. The elders decided to take turns in keeping all-night vigil, since some girls were still unconscious and we didn't want any aggressive manifestations.

We learned from the caretaker that a lot of Fijian ceremonies had taken place in this particular location, and that once, when the President came there, he was led by two sharks which are believed to be his gods. We were told they had seen the Fijian god coming out of the small river nearby and walking towards the house. One girl saw a Fijian man coming to her with a pillow on which was a bowl of yagona, the Fijian national beer, often used in traditional ceremonies and witchcraft. It made sense when we heard all of this. We were on the devil's territory. He couldn't stand the power and presence of God in our worship. So he stirred up all those who were his and tried to put up a fight. We are thankful that it was revealed to us. We could now deal with the root of the problem and knew we could not take their walk with God for granted.

In the morning we had planned a sunrise service. We decided to continue our fast and to claim protection. In all God's wisdom we felt the need to ask the campers what they had with them that didn't belong to God. There were all sorts of things! There was a T-shirt with the dragon on it, books, tapes, pictures with evil drawings. It was amazing to see how the evil spirits reacted when those things were burnt. They screamed and seemed to want to throw themselves into the fire. Some would refuse to go or say they would take the people concerned with them. They couldn't stand when we sang about the Lord Jesus' power and his precious blood. It was quite an encounter.

The baptism went fine, with three baptisms. Zaneta and Grace were unable to be baptised because they were 'out' all the time. After the baptism service they came to their senses and were sad to know they were not able to be baptised this time. One Indian girl who was baptised had been freed from three Hindu spirits on the Saturday night. She literally saw them leaving her.

On Monday we decided to conclude our weekend with praise and testimony. One by one the campers came forward. To our dismay, some fell backwards while they were sharing. Grace came forward. While sharing, she felt weak and was about to fall, but we prayed there and then. She struggled with the spirits trying to stop her from testifying. Many were surprised to discover they had something hiding inside them even though they had been Christians for a couple of years.

We are all still learning, but we know that we all left the camp touched and changed by God in a miraculous way. Some of our youths stood, giving their lives to God. Others came confessing sins before the whole church, pleading for forgiveness. I said to Bhim, 'This is like a small revival!'

We got busy to follow up what had begun at camp. Those who were affected are still in need of deliverance, as they had attacks even at home. So we called for a 40-day chain prayer with fasting for the whole church. Many had never fasted, and many shared how they were praying and reading the Bibles as never before. When God moves, no one can withstand it. We will break our fast at Pentecost with communion and claim victory and healing for those who need God's special touch. Zaneta has asked if she can be baptised then.

Working for justice is a weapon we are commanded to use

We Christians need to model God's justice for all in a world of selfishness and corruption. There is an enormous amount of scripture about justice: 'The LORD works righteousness and justice for all the oppressed' (Psalm 103:6). 'Woe to those who make unjust laws, to those who issue oppressive decrees, to deprive the poor of their rights and withhold justice from the oppressed of my people, making widows their prey and robbing the fatherless. What will you do on the day of reckoning?' (Isaiah 10:1-3).

Part of spiritual warfare is trying to help the third world out of poverty. This may be by creating opportunities for micro-loans to get someone launched into business, or by buying Fair Trade products. Part of spiritual warfare is pleading for the rights of believers in prison for their faith, writing to governments about attacks on Christians and churches, smuggling Bibles where they are banned, lobbying parliaments to legislate in biblical ways about abortion, homosexuality, rights to proclaim the good news and many other issues that concern the church. 'If you do away with the yoke of oppression, with the pointing finger and malicious talk, and if you spend yourselves on behalf of the hungry, and satisfy the needs of the oppressed, then your light will rise in the darkness, and your night will become like the noonday. The LORD will guide you always; he will satisfy your needs in a sun-scorched land' (Isaiah 58:9-11).

Micro-loans are a brilliant way of helping a small group, often women, to become breadwinners. The first one gets the money for her project, and is urged to repay it quickly so the second one can have it, and so on round the circle. The friendship loyalty helps each member to be faithful in repayments.

There are so many pitfalls in this area. So much dependency is created. So much irresponsible sponsorship occurs where the person who receives the money has no accountability to anyone living close by who can check up on them. But we can learn by our mistakes. It should not make us so disillusioned that we fail to obey the scripture any more.

In the Reformed tradition, powers (the powers that be) are seen as social structures, not personal spirits. These social structures need to be transformed through the involvement of believers. Brilliant examples are the abolition of slavery through the work of Wilberforce and Clarkson, the improvement of nursing by Florence Nightingale, and of prisons by John Howard.

Political powers can be influenced by spiritual powers. When Catherine de Medici and Henri Duke of Guise organised the massacre of the Huguenots on St Bartholomew's Day in 1572, when Japanese Emperor Hideyoshi ordered the massacre of every Christian in 1638, do you think Satan was not encouraging it? When the age of consent for homosexuality is lowered from 18 to 16, leaving a whole swathe of the population of a country open to abuse legally, are not the devil and his hordes behind it?

In our struggle for justice, there is another limit to the activities a Christian can participate in. Try to be gentle in bringing justice. 'Here is my Servant whom I uphold, my Chosen one in whom I delight; I will put my Spirit on him and he will bring justice to the nations. He will not shout or cry out, or raise his voice in the streets. A bruised reed he will not break, and a smouldering wick he will not snuff out. In faithfulness he will bring forth justice; he will not fail or be discouraged till he establishes justice on the earth' (Isaiah 42:1-4). If we are to bring justice biblically, then, we may feel free to lobby parliament, but not to bomb an abortion clinic. We may feel free to march in protest about something, but not to engage in acts of destructive civil disobedience to stress our point.

Marching for justice
John Bardsley

I marched in a procession against the legalisation of homosexuality in Perth, Western Australia. I painted my own placard, which said 'God loves Gays' on one side, and on the back 'enough to change them'. I was standing on the steps of Parliament House when the TV cameras arrived, and I happened to notice them focus on my placard. So I let them have side one for several seconds before flipping it quickly to side two. They didn't want side two, and moved away immediately. However my students at Bible School told me, 'It's nice to see a lecturer who practises what he preaches.'

My daughter has encouraged our whole family to buy Fair Trade coffee, tea, chocolate and bananas. They are all excellent, and are becoming much more widespread in regular supermarkets. Ask your supermarket to stock them.

Justice has been a very neglected area. We evangelicals have tended to leave it to the liberals. We cannot afford to do so. It is hugely important in the Bible. For that reason, it is exciting to see the younger generation of evangelicals more active in this area.

Justice for children at risk
Chris Hund

We have seen so many suffering children in India. It breaks our hearts. One little girl in particular has made a deep impression on us. We found her close to the Taj Mahal in Agra. There she was, no more than four or five years old, carrying her baby sister. She did not beg, she just stood there and watched. No parents around, no one to care for her. The tormented expression on her face did not disappear for a moment, not even when she was offered some food or when one of our workers tried to communicate with her. This child was completely numbed and traumatized. We can only guess what she has suffered. Daily we look at her troubled little face on our desktop screen and pray: 'Lord, have mercy.'

The position of the girl child in particular is an issue of major concern. There is a decreasing number of girls in the population. Female infanticide has greatly increased since ultrasound tests have become widely available. Girls are being discriminated against in areas like health care and education and are being exploited at large. Because of the lack of girls in society, they are trafficked from other countries to become brides for the young men of India. Please pray with us for intervention in this terrible situation.

The church we work with has already developed five projects: two schools for poor/slum children, a home for boys with HIV/AIDS, a drop-in centre for street children, and they are setting up a day centre for special needs children (physically and mentally challenged etc). They will also work on developing a holistic club program for one of the slums. This will be a pilot program and a reproducible model for other churches. We always work holistically with the children. This means child development programs where the children will be nurtured spiritually, emotionally and physically.

In the Alpha course, Nicky Gumbel tells of a huge storm which swept hundreds of thousands of starfish up onto the beach. A boy was picking them up and throwing them back into the water, one by one. A man walking by said, 'Oh, give it up, son. Can't you see how many there are? You can never throw them all back, so what difference can you make?' The boy picked up another one and threw it in. 'It made a difference for that one,' he said.

In a world of poverty, war and injustice, you can't do everything, but you can do something. And it will make a difference to that one. I was telling this story in an Alpha course where one participant struggled with self-acceptance because of her traumatic background. She took that story away with her, and reminded me of it six months later. She was so grateful that we were willing to try to rescue her.

STOPTHINK&DISCUSS

- Share your experiences in fasting, reasons why you fasted, and possible reasons for a future fast.
- Discuss how best to use scripture in spiritual warfare.
- Discuss the most effective ways to work for justice.
- Why do we need to destroy artefacts to gain freedom?
- What principles of prayer did Bruce learn from his experience of the poaching preacher?

10
INTERCESSION, THE CENTRAL CORE OF SPIRITUAL WAR

Stewart Dinnen, Brian Woodford, John Bardsley

Characteristics of an intercessor
Strategic praying

The very word 'strategic' comes from the Greek word for soldier, *stratiotes*. Ephesians 5:15-17 tells us that we are to live carefully as wise people, seeking to know what the will of the Lord is. Many of us ignore this simple command when we come to pray. Acts 13:1-3 and Acts 18:9-11 indicate that part of prayer is to be a discovery of what God's will is. In many ordinary situations there will be no doubt what this is. Often in deciding on a particular approach to some advance of the gospel, it is essential first to reach a point of assurance on how to proceed in prayer. There appears to be a sequence of steps something like this:

Awareness, burden, concern
Discussion
Waiting on God
Agreement
Praying through
Praise
Declaration

In his small booklet *Touching the Invisible* Norman Grubb describes the early days of WEC in London, to explain how crucial it is to wait on God to discover his will.

'It had been our custom to divide the prayer meeting into two parts, reading the scriptures with a few comments, and then open prayer. But much of our praying, though sincere, was without strong assurance, because so often we were not sure if our requests were God's will. Often we rose from our knees as uncertain as before we prayed.

'We began to observe a different emphasis in the prayer lives of Bible people. They first discovered whether their prayer was God's will. When they were sure about that point, they prayed, received by faith, persisted, declared things to come, with all the authority of God himself. Elijah turned up and announced, 'As the Lord God lives, there will not be dew or rain until I say so.' James tells us this was effective praying. We were struck by the contrast between Hezekiah's ineffective prayer, 'It may be that the Lord will hear,' and Isaiah's bold answer, 'This is what the Lord says: "... I will have him cut down"' (Isaiah 37:4-7).

'So it became more and more impressed on us that effective praying must be guided praying; that the first essential was not to pray but to know what to pray for. On this basis our prayer meeting took a new form. Guidance must be found. We must go to our knees only when we know from God what we want. To get this guidance, time limits had to go.'

The second and third models to show us our function in the heavenlies are found in 1 Peter 2:9 where we are described as a royal priesthood, King-Priests. Priests to worship, Kings to rule. Both of these roles function through prayer.

Norman Grubb continues: 'Prayer is the product of our union with Christ. He in us is the Pray-er. Quietly recognising the Real One with us, we sort out what warms or stirs our hearts with a sense of definite need or challenge. Now we are ready to pray. One fact seems to stand our from the lives of Bible characters. However they might start their prayer, it ends in faith. They are not called men of prayer, but men of faith, though recognising that their exploits of faith have a background of agonising in prayer. Prayer meetings that are merely asking sessions are dead things, but when they are believing sessions there is adventure, hope, and life as faith is corporately developed.'

Encounter praying, the role of a king

Royalty has authority. Encounter praying is facing the issue of confrontation. The believer becomes aware that Satan or one of his agents is exercising power over a person or situation. The believer then asserts his authority in Christ to limit or eject those forces of darkness, in order to release the individual or group. There are several phases:

- Rely on God-given resources – the blood of Christ (Revelation 12:11), the name of Jesus (John 14:13-14, 15:16, 16:23-24), the Christian's armour (Ephesians 6:10-18), overcoming faith (1 John 5:4).
- Recognise Satanic activity. See 'Know your enemy' for a full list.
- Resist Satanic activity. See James 4:6-7, 1 Peter 5:9 and Matthew 12:29.
- Rebuke, eject and release. See Mark 1:25, 9:25; Luke 13:11-16; Acts 10:38, 16:18.

The role of a priest

The essential qualities of a priest are found in 1 Peter 2:5,9. They are his identification with humans because he too is a human, his intimacy with God, and his function as a 'go-between' (the meaning of 'inter-cessor') between sinful mortals and holy God. One of the great truths of the Protestant Reformation was its rediscovery of the priesthood of all believers. As Christians we are meant to identify with people in their need, be close to God to understand his purpose for them, and pray it into reality.

Intercession is a key activity in spiritual warfare. True intercession is intensely personal, and comes as a commission from God to act as a responsible 'go-between' for some situation, person or group.

1. The feature that marks off the intercessor from all other praying people is that he or she accepts responsibility, carrying it until God removes it. The life of Samuel gives us unique insights into the intercessory role. At Shiloh God 'revealed himself to Samuel through his word. And Samuel's word came to all Israel' (1 Samuel 3:21-4:1). The strength of the commission becomes apparent

in 1 Samuel 7:5 when Samuel says, 'Assemble all Israel . . . and I will intercede with the LORD for you.' When the enemy gathers, the nation of Israel recognises Samuel's ministry and begs him, 'Do not stop crying to the LORD our God for us' (7:8). Samuel recognises it would be sin if he did: 'Far be it from me that I should sin against the LORD by failing to pray for you' (12:23).

2. Another characteristic of an intercessor is empathy, the ability to enter into the feelings and thoughts of someone in their time of need. Moses and Paul both exemplified this. Each was prepared to give up life itself if their prayer could be answered that way (Exodus 32:32; Romans 9:3).

2. Continuity is an indication of true intercession. An intercessor recognises that the commission has to be carried until the Lord removes it.

4. There is long-term endurance. We have a picture of this in Exodus 17:8-13 when Moses was interceding for Israel. When his arms were up, Israel won. When he grew tired and his arms were lowered, Amalek won. So he needed helpers to keep up the continuity.

5. Authority. The true intercessor knows he is cooperating with God and that he can pray with the delegated authority of Christ himself. See the authority section.

6. Intensity. The intercessor often experiences an intensity of desire regarding the object of his praying. Epaphras is described as wrestling in prayer (Colossians 4:12). The Greek word is *agonizomai*, from which we get our English word 'agonize'. The same root is used in the word chosen to describe the depth of Christ's prayer in Gethsemane: agonia, anguish or agony, sweating blood (Luke 22:44).

7. Finally, there is accountability. The teaching of Hebrews 13:17 seems to indicate that the leaders, as praying men, were accountable to the Lord for the condition of the souls of their people. Jesus is the perfect intercessor and actually becomes accountable for bearing our sin. He 'became sin for us' (2 Corinthians 5:21).

Intercessors make sure they discover detailed knowledge of the situation. They take extended times to wrestle in prayer. They have a joyful experience of the presence and power of God. They have a deep understanding of spiritual issues. They are sensitive to needs, and show concern. They accept responsibility, and are willing for the intensity of the battle, and to continue until the answer comes. They have authority in the Spirit. There is a holy anger, a righteous indignation that the enemy should so usurp the position that belongs to Christ. Remember young David when he first heard Goliath roar his defiance? 'Who is this uncircumcised Philistine that he should defy the armies of the living God?' (1 Samuel 17:26).

Praying God's will

God is not a genie in a bottle. Prayer is not getting God on my side. Prayer is turning to my Maker and learning to think his thoughts. Prayer is not bringing God into my plans to solve my problems, but bringing me into God's plans to fulfil his purposes.

Prayer is less about talking and more about listening. 'While they were worshipping the Lord and fasting, the Holy Spirit said . . .' (Acts 13:1). Ephesians 2:6 describes believers as raised with Christ and seated with him on his throne. If we check Ephesians 1:19-22 we discover that throne is where Christ reigns with the Father, far above any and every other power of any kind, celestial, terrestrial or infernal. Imagine yourself, a tiny person, seated beside the immensity of the Father and the Son, tuning in to their conversations, listening to their strategy discussions, discerning what they intend to do, and then commanding that it be done on earth. So the essence of prayer is abiding. The key gift for answered prayer is discernment. 'Understand what the Lord's will is' (Ephesians 5:17). I must be thinking his own thoughts back to him. I must be praying his will. 'If you remain in me and my words remain in you, ask whatever you wish, and it will be given you' (John 15:7). Prayer is not overcoming God's reluctance, but overcoming the reluctance of his enemies.

War in Chad
John Bardsley
Dario Noonan and his family were WECers in Chad, caught up in a war. One night their town was attacked. They wrote, 'We dressed the kids, got our money and passports and a jerry can of water, and lay down on the bathroom floor, watching the machine gun fire whistling past the window. But we lived.' In the morning Dario went down town to find out who had won, so he knew which flag to hoist. Next furlough, as he told this story, a woman said, 'One night I had a fearful burden to pray for some place called Chad. I didn't even know where it was.' As they compared diaries, they discovered she had prayed on the very night they were in danger. How close we need to be, to hear God when he wants someone to intercede.

Union with Christ ascended
What possible present significance comes out of the fact that we are one with Christ who has not only risen, but ascended to heaven? Why are we with him there? What does it mean to be seated there in the heavenlies? Where are 'the heavenlies'? Not only are 'the heavenlies' where Christ and his saints reign (Ephesians 1:20; 2:6), but also where the church is God's demonstration model to the spirit world (Ephesians 3:10), and where the spiritual forces of evil attack believers (Ephesians 6:12). Therefore this reigning Christ, far above all principalities and powers, is enthroned just where we are – in our circumstances, in our situations of need and apparent satanic mastery. And why does he reign? And why are we reigning with him? Because he is wholly occupied in making his saving grace known to the world, and in adding to the church daily those who are being saved. This is our praying ground. We pray, not as beggars at a great distance from him, separated from him. Prayer is sharing his mind about a situation, and our tongues are his mouthpiece to speak the word of faith.

Soldier, king, priest

Three models are used in the New Testament to convey to us our function in the heavenlies. The first is seen in Ephesians 6:12-18 where we are soldiers with spiritual armour, equipped for spiritual conflict. This is confirmed in 2 Timothy 2:3-4. The characteristics of the soldier are given: detachment ('No one serving as a soldier gets involved in civilian affairs'); direction ('he wants to please his commanding officer') and discipline ('endure hardship').

Prayer is the battleground. That is why Paul says, 'pray ... on all occasions with all kinds of prayers and requests. Always keep on praying for all the saints.' The New Testament gives the highest priority to prayer. 1 Thessalonians 5:17 instructs us to pray continually, and in 1 Timothy 2:1 Paul urges us, 'first of all, that requests, prayers, intercession and thanksgiving be made for everyone.' In Luke 18:1-5 Jesus told his disciples a parable to show them that they should always pray and not give up.

Put our faith in prayer? What is faith?

A climate of faith
John Whittle

I was injected into the challenging stream of London headquarters in 1937 when I was 28 years old. I became the first deputation secretary after the death of CT Studd. The burning challenge and spiritual illumination of those vital years enlarged my whole concept of how the resources of God were to be applied by us in the daring name and task of WEC - God who 'calls things that are not as though they were' (Romans 4.17).

What saved the infant WEC from extinction after the death of CT? What brought it to be a recognised power for the extension of the gospel? What enabled it to open country after country in the teeth of a world war with a steady flow of candidates that came to us, drawn by that climate of faith they sensed?

Many would say it was prayer, and that would be true if they meant the prayer of faith. Prayer is a preliminary act, a consultative period, which becomes effective when it culminates in an inner act of faith, and an outward declaration of having received the resources of God. Without that, prayer is incomplete. The point of need before us when we pray must never eclipse the present supply of God to meet it. The power is available, but must have the needed bridge of faith (Mark 11.23-24). There is a tide of prayer today. What we need is a tide of believing meetings that bring us to current possession and praise for the reality of God at work. The word is not 'pray to this mountain' but 'SAY to this mountain "Be removed!"'

We move from the act of asking to the act of receiving. This completes true prayer, the prayer of faith. Miss this, and our prayer meetings languish. Jesus did not ask, 'Where is your prayer?' but 'Where is your faith?' Waiting on God is where we Evangelical activists fall down. The importance of silence and hearing God's voice is the only way to prepare for the declarations of faith. The vast amount of our speaking should be replaced with waiting on God in a consultative attitude. The purpose of the verbal information we give to God is only to build us up to the point of faith where we take his supplies.

Only once that I recall, did Jesus say 'If it be your will,' and then how rapidly he moved on to acceptance of 'My Father's cup'. He passed from asking to receiving – even the cup of suffering. Faith is for suffering as well as for emancipation from need. Hebrews 11 is not 'Prayer is the substance of things hoped for' but faith is that substance. This is the victory that overcomes the world, even our prayer? No – our faith. Your prayer has saved you? No – your faith.

If union with Christ is a reality, then our prayers are his prayers too. Without this union our whole life becomes hit and miss. Down through 54 years I have found this to be the real cutting edge in the life of completed prayer. We are intended to exercise a ministry of having, not 'going to have'. Aspiration, longing and asking are purely preliminaries to the inner action and reception of faith.

Faith for answers? Some definitions of faith
When I started praying for the Jolas, I was asking God, begging God, imploring God to teach me how to get answers. I wanted faith for answers. I have just been reading Hebrews 11, and am glad faith is mentioned in other portions of scripture as well as Hebrews 11, because the definitions of faith I have found here are not so much about getting answers.

1. Faith is confidence in the Invisible God, no matter what (Hebrews 11:1-7, 27-28).
'Now faith is being sure of what we hope for and certain of what we do not see. This is what the ancients were commended for. By faith we understand that the universe was formed at God's command, so that what is seen was not made out of what was visible' (1-3).
'And without faith it is impossible to please God, because anyone who comes to him must believe that he exists and that he rewards those who earnestly seek him. By faith Noah, when warned about things not yet seen, in holy fear built an ark to save his family' (6-7).
'He endured as seeing him who is invisible' (27 KJV).
'By faith he kept the Passover and the sprinkling of the blood, so that the destroyer of the firstborn [another one of the things not seen!] might not touch the firstborn of Israel' (28).

2. Faith is confidence in the God who promised, no matter when that promise reaches fulfilment (Hebrews 11: 11-13, 20-22).
By faith Abraham, even though he was past age – and Sarah herself was barren – was enabled to become a father because he considered him faithful who had made the promise. 'And so from this one man, and he as good as dead, came descendants as numerous as the stars in the sky and as countless as the sand on the seashore. All these people were still living by faith when they died. They did not receive the things promised; they only saw them and welcomed them from a distance. And they admitted that they were aliens and strangers on earth' (12-13).

'By faith Isaac blessed Jacob and Esau in regard to their future. By faith Jacob, when he was dying, blessed each of Joseph's sons, and worshipped as he leaned on the top of his staff. By faith Joseph, when his end was near, spoke about the exodus of the Israelites from Egypt and gave instructions about his bones' (20-22). Believing prayer is not so much about screwing up my faith as it about persistence until God's time; confidence in God even if his time is not now. He sees the whole sweep of history as now.

3. Faith is living in time but drawing on the resources of the world to come (Hebrews 11: 17-21).

Abraham reasoned that God could raise the dead. By faith Jacob blessed each of Joseph's sons. He spoke incisive words of prophecy that were penetrating and showed discernment as well as confidence for the future.

4. Faith is loyalty to the one true God, whether it's popular or not, whether he answers or not (Hebrews 11:29-38).

At first I thought, 'At last! Answers by faith!' And there are some. At the Red Sea they prayed and God did a miracle! At Jericho they prayed and God destroyed the city walls! Victory! There are miracles of protection, salvation, and deliverance! This is the stuff I was expecting! Gideon, Barak, Samson, Jephthah, David and Samuel were loyal to God through good times and bad, to conquer kingdoms, enforce justice, receive promises, win strength out of weakness, escape the edge of the sword, to become mighty in war, to put foreign armies to flight. For Daniel, God shut the mouths of lions. For Shadrach and his friends, God quenched raging fire. At the prayer of Elisha, the Shunamite received her dead lad back to life again. But now look at the second half of verse 35. 'Others were tortured and refused to be released.' Rahab chose the true God even though it meant treason to her people.

Challenges in Turkey
John Bardsley

Simon's grandfather and the Agha (village chief) had been friends since childhood. They lived in the Kurdish area of south-eastern Turkey. In 1914 the Agha was under pressure from Muslims higher up to Islamize the village. The Agha commanded his son to shoot Simon's grandfather because he was a Christian and refused to change. His son refused to shoot this friend, so the Agha himself shot him. From that time on Simon's relatives called themselves Muslims, but still told stories about grandfather and Christianity. Simon determined to find out more. At the age of 17 he got hold of a Turkish Bible, but his shepherd-boy Turkish was not good enough, and he could not read it. Later he moved to Istanbul, where he studied the Bible in Turkish and became a leader in a local church. Then he found books in his mother tongue, Kurmanji Kurdish, that were banned in Turkey. He found Luke's gospel in Kurmanji and loved it. Since 1993 he has been translating the whole Bible for his people.

Others suffered mocking, scourging, chains and imprisonment. They were stoned, sawn in two, stabbed; destitute, afflicted, ill-treated, and lived in caves.

But they were well attested by their faith! Faith is not about circumstances, but about your relationship with your Maker!

Bold faith hangs on
Bruce Rattray

Bold faith refuses to believe the enemy's lies, or what our senses tell us, but hangs on until the victory is won! Our Lord only taught about prayer twice (Luke 11:1-13 and Luke 18:1-8), and on both occasions he told a parable which graphically emphasised that persistent prayer refuses to take 'No' for an answer.

When I was a missionary candidate in Sydney, Australia, the Lord spoke direct to my spirit: 'I am going to bring you into contact with a man who has an evil spirit. I want you to cast it out of him.' I had very little experience of deliverance in those days. Several days later a prayer group leader phoned to ask if I would come and minister to Gordon, his fellow preacher, who was in a desperate condition spiritually. 'This is the man I told you about,' the Lord said.

His problem began when a voice he assumed was the Lord told him he had committed the unpardonable sin. Since that time he had lost his assurance of salvation and was often strongly urged to take his own life. Counselling had not helped him. We began to pray for his healing, then, mindful of God's word to me, I commanded the evil spirit to come out of him. Nothing happened! On the way home and for several days, Satan taunted me: 'Ha! It didn't work, did it!' However, deep in my spirit, although my faith was tiny, I did keep on believing.

Several days later I was called to the phone. 'Gordon here, the one you prayed for three days ago. I'm free! I'm out preaching again! Oh, hallelujah!' Gordon became one of our most faithful supporters. It was an important lesson to me, one that I was to remember many times later, in situations much more difficult.

Five fighting words in prayer

According to Acts 26:18, our purpose is to open people's eyes and to turn them from darkness to light, and from the power of Satan to God. We are commanded to pray like this, and promised answers when we do. Look for the command and the promise in each of the scriptures below:

1. SUBMIT to God. RESIST the devil, and he will flee from you (James 4:7-8)

What does it mean, practically, to submit to God? It means he has control of my life, and I can now look into my attitudes and find no rebellion against his ways or the leaders he has put over me. This command to resist the devil comes with no 'how-to' instructions. There is no formula. If my will is actively set in a godly direction instead of in the direction of the devil's will, that is resisting. If I state my resistance, that's important.

Spiritual warfare
John Bardsley

Soon after I began to pray for the Jolas, our youngest daughter had a nightmare. I thought perhaps she had eaten something that disagreed with her, or that she had watched some scary television with her older sisters. It took me half an hour to pacify her, but finally she drifted back to sleep. The next night it happened again. I put her on the toilet in case that was the problem, spent another half-hour walking up and down, and at last she slept. When it happened the third night in a row, I began to suspect something. This was 1986. I knew nothing of spiritual warfare at that time, but I was about to get my first lesson.

I thought, 'If this goes on, I will sleep in and miss my Quiet Time in the morning. Who would be happy if I missed my QT? Aha! I wonder if this is the devil?' I decided to find out. I put her back in bed, still utterly miserable, frightened, definitely not at rest. I tucked her blankets round her. Then I stood in the bedroom and said, 'Satan, in case this is you, I tell you we do not belong to you any more. We are bought with the precious blood of Christ, and transferred from the dominion of darkness into the kingdom of God's dear Son. So you have no right to come in here, and in Jesus' name I command you to leave.'

The result was instantaneous. She shut her eyes, and I saw her taut little body relax into sleep. I was so surprised I sat down. So it had been just an ugly demon sent to frighten her! I thought to myself, 'Great! My prayers must be making some impact then, if they send a scary monster from West Africa to try and get revenge.' But the best result was that I learned this verse works! The Bible is practical! You can do it, and it works!

2. STAND!

'Our struggle is not against flesh and blood, but against the rulers, against the authorities, against the powers of this dark world and against the spiritual forces of evil in the heavenly realms. Therefore put on the full armour of God, so that when the day of evil comes, you may be able to stand your ground. . . . Stand firm then . . . ' The command to stand occurs five times in these few verses in Ephesians 6:12-14. This is easier to comprehend, because we all talk about making a stand.

Marcel makes a stand
John Bardsley

Marcel, a Jola from Senegal, was converted as a ten year-old lad. Then his animist parents forbade him to come any more to meetings or visit the missionaries. While he was a teenager, his father died. The worst of it was, he died in the middle of rebuilding their mud house. Mud houses have to be rebuilt every fifteen years or so, because of termites. His father had already dismantled the family fetish from the old house, but had not yet rebuilt it in the new one. The family called a meeting. 'Marcel, we appoint you to be the priest of the fetish for our family, and your first job is to rebuild the fetish in the new house.'

'Sorry, I'm a Christian. I can't do that.'

'But we're not Christians, and you know that if you don't do it, the spirits will be angry, and some of us might get sick or even die. You don't want that to happen, do you?'

'Well, you can be Christians too.'

'We don't want to be Christians! We want to follow the way of our fathers! Now here are the bits of the fetish. Go do what you're told!'

For us in the West, telling a fifteen-year-old to obey is a bit risky, but anyone from Asia or Africa will understand the extreme pressure Marcel was under as they handed him a plastic bag filled with bits of stick, feathers, stone and dried mud. It was so ordinary looking, but so filled with dread. He handed it to his uncle, saying, 'Uncle, you are my father's brother, and you are the oldest man in the family now. You decide what to do with it, but I cannot have anything to do with it.' His uncle replied, 'I don't want it either.' He knew that the priest of the fetish was sometimes the first to suffer if the spirits were angry. He put it outside on the roof of their lean-to kitchen shed. That night a strong wind sprang up and the bag of bits blew down. Some were broken. Those bits would be no longer be any good for a fetish. So Marcel was free, and went on to become a gifted evangelist and elder in the church.

He made a stand. It's like telling the devil, 'This far and no further.' It's like planting the flag in a battlefield to say, 'This is ours.'

'We will serve the Lord'
John Bardsley

Roger was a teenager in a family where his mother was a witch and his older sister her assistant. They had charms over every door and window in the house to ward off evil spirits. Every door except one, that is – Roger's bedroom. Over Roger's bedroom door was a calendar text saying: 'As for me and my house, we will serve the Lord.' He made a stand in the area under his control.

3. BIND and LOOSE

In Matthew 16:19 we find an important passage which relates to our mandate as Christians: 'Whatever you bind on earth will be bound in heaven, and whatever you loose on earth will be loosed in heaven.' Jesus said in Matthew 12:30, 'How can anyone enter a strong man's house and carry off his possessions unless he first ties up the strong man? Then he can rob his house.' Who is the strong man Jesus is talking about? Satan. Who wants to rob Satan's house? We do.

So Jesus has entrusted to us the authority of his kingdom, in order for us to tether or nullify the forces that are resisting the expansion of God's kingdom on earth. 1 John 3:8 says that Jesus came to destroy (bring to nought) the works of the devil. That task has now been entrusted to the church until Jesus returns in his kingly glory. We are to break the power of the enemy in the various situations of our world where we see it expressed. This is perfectly in line with the prayer Jesus taught his disciples: 'Your kingdom come! Your will be done on earth as it is in heaven' (Matthew 6:10).

'Whatever you loose on earth will be loosed in heaven.' What do we want to

HE GIVES US AUTHORITY

loose? We want the prisoners from Satan's dungeon, blinded and enslaved by sin. 'The god of this age has blinded the minds of unbelievers' (2 Corinthians 4:4).

We want to free from bondage, oppression, or infirmity of any kind those who have been afflicted or enslaved by the devil. It is important to remember the victory has already been won by Christ. We don't loose people from Satan's power ourselves. Rather we proclaim and apply the loosing power of Christ over a situation where the enemy has not yet admitted his defeat.

So, in Jesus' name we are able to release people from the power of Satan. This is a great privilege and tremendous responsibility that Christ has entrusted to all his people in the church.

Some areas where we can be used by God to 'bind' things on earth:
● False religions that are holding people under the power of the enemy
● Demonic spirits that have direct influence or control in people's lives
● Social and political structures that oppress people and prevent them from being free as God desires

Some ways in which we can be used by God to 'loose' things on earth:
● Declaring the gospel and ministering to people, setting them free from the bondage of sin (Romans 5:12-17, 6:20-22; Galatians 4:3-7)
● By prayer setting people free from physical and psychological sickness if it is an affliction of the enemy (Luke 13:15-16)
● By prayer and ministry setting people free from demonic powers in their lives
● By prayer and practical ministry restoring broken relationships and releasing people from injustice and oppressive structures.

Defending the Lord's reputation
John Bardsley

There were three believers in an animist village in Senegal. Pierre and Mame were married and Phil, the expatriate worker, hoped they would be elders in the future church. Roger was still a teenager, but very keen for Jesus. Phil and his wife Elspeth built a house in the village. The people were fascinated as they watched the workmen. There were no charms laid in the foundations, by express command of the owner. There were no charms built into the walls, above windows or doors. There were none hidden in the roof, or in the toilet. There was no bottle buried outside the front door to catch any spirits who might want to enter. This was a house without charms, unprotected! They waited for Phil and Elspeth to get sick. Not that year. Phil and Elspeth were fine. The villagers thought, 'Maybe it doesn't work for foreigners.'

The next year Phil and Elspeth were to be away, so they invited Pierre and Mame to live in their house. The villagers waited for one of them to get sick, and they were not disappointed. Mame developed a huge swollen jaw. Roger said, 'That is the kind of sickness our family fetish would cause if it were angry.'

By this time I was an advocate for the Jola people, with a modest mailing list of 60 addresses of people pledged to pray an hour a week for the Jolas. I was deeply concerned. If God did not heal Mame's jaw, the whole village would believe that their fetish was stronger than the God of all the earth! It wasn't on! It must be stopped! The glory and honour of the Lord was at stake! I put out the news to the team, and got on my knees to the Father. 'Lord, you need to defend your reputation out there! Please heal Mame now! In Jesus' name I bind Satan from touching her. She is bought with the blood of Christ!' Mame recovered, praise God.

4. DEMOLISH strongholds

'For though we live in the world, we do not wage war as the world does. The weapons we fight with are not the weapons of the world. On the contrary, they have divine power to demolish strongholds. We demolish arguments and every pretension that sets itself up against the knowledge of God, and we take captive every thought to make it obedient to Christ' (2 Corinthians 10:3-5).

How does the world fight? If it's war, there are guns, grenades, rockets, bombs and tanks. If it's parliament or business, they may use character assassination, deceit, gossip, stabbing in the back, leaking documents. We use none of those weapons. What weapons do we use? The verse doesn't say! But it does say how powerful they are! We have already listed our weapons in the previous chapters, and the main one is prayer. 'Every prayer a powerful weapon, strongholds come tumbling down.' (Petra)

What is a stronghold? See Chapter Four. A stronghold is part of the life of an individual, family, town or country in which the devil has been getting his own way, based on lies he has tricked people into believing. A stronghold is based on arguments – considered, carefully crafted presentations of lies; and pretensions – proud, arrogant, pretended power, something that looks impregnable, set up to oppose the spread of the gospel.

How do we demolish a stronghold? We teach truth to combat the lies; systematic, well-reasoned truth, with evidence from archaeology and history, science and the Bible. We pray against the impregnable-looking power base in the name of Jesus.

Prayer against festishes
John Bardsley

The town of Oussouye in Senegal had a population of about 2000, divided into five villages. A French anthropologist lived there for two years, doing research into their religion, and they allowed him to map their fetishes. He discovered that there were five levels of fetishes, from those with authority over one family right up to Jangyangyande and four others which had authority over the whole plateau. In all, there were 200 fetishes for a population of 2000! Horrendous! Each one demanded its sacrifices and oblations, and had to be propitiated and appeased. Sometimes I would pray against those five main fetishes by name, asking that God would pull the veil off people's minds so they would realise how cruel, hate-filled and evil these fetishes were. I would pray that their curses would fail, that their authority would wane, their sacrifices be neglected, their initiations disregarded. Sometimes I would pray against some of the smaller fetishes, area by area, asking that families, compounds, districts and clans might be set free. I don't believe we have to know their names before we can pray against them, but it was interesting to have the names as a focus for my aggressive attack on their strongholds. May the Lord guide you into even more insights into this wonderful weapon.

To demolish a building, one man can take a sledge hammer, cold chisel and crowbar, and take it apart a brick at a time. Or he can take a half-tonne iron ball swinging from an enormous crane, and reduce it to rubble in half an hour. If I am praying on my own, I feel like the man with the hammer and crowbar. If there are 60 of us praying consistently, I feel like a member of a team, each with a crowbar. If there are a million people praying, I imagine God has wheeled in the crane with the swinging steel ball, for a demolition blow. It is good not to do battle alone.

5. OVERCOME!
'For the accuser of our brothers . . . has been hurled down. They overcame him by the blood of the Lamb, and by the word of their testimony; they did not love their lives so much as to shrink from death' (Revelation 12:10-11).

Three factors are listed here that enabled the saints to overcome the accuser. The first one is the most important: the blood of the Lamb. See Chapter Four 'Personal Preparation' for detail. 'His powerful blood did once atone, and now it pleads before the throne' (Isaac Watts).

The second factor is the word of their testimony. When Jesus was on the way to the cross he said, 'The prince of this world is coming. He has no hold on me' (John 14:30). That is a wonderful testimony, but it is one that we all can give. His powerful blood was shed for each of us. As we walk into the light, and confess our sins openly and completely, the blood washes them away so that we are forgiven and cleaned up (1 John 1:7,9). Then we can honestly say 'The prince of this world is coming, but he has nothing in me.'

The third factor is a tough one. They did not love their lives, or shrink from death. This is the kind of attitude the early believers had when the Sanhedrin in Jerusalem told them to shut up about Jesus or face the consequences. 'We cannot help speaking' (Acts 4:20). 'Now, Lord, consider their threats and enable your servants to speak your word with great boldness' (Acts 4:29).

Every mission and every national church has its share of martyrs. This era, for all its professed tolerance, has created more martyrs than any other, and we are promised many more as we hold out the word of life to a crooked and depraved generation. We will be hated by all peoples for his sake, and already we are hated by many. Our Chinese brothers have shown us amazing examples of this kind of overcoming. They praise God for enough persecution to make them grow, but not so much as to stamp them out.

Pray scripture for someone
Pray Paul's prayers, the promises of scripture, the truths of Romans 8, into someone's life. The word can penetrate, cleanse, charge, cut away Satan's grip on

a life. Ask someone to pray scripture for you.

Go prayer walking

Take prayer walks round your area. Why? As far as I know, prayer is not more powerful in one place than another. I can pray effectively for anywhere in the world, staying at home. So why spend money to visit a place and then walk round and pray? It does not even have a biblical precedent. We cannot claim the silent marching around Jericho for six days as a prayer walk, though I am sure some of them were praying! So what is the one huge advantage of going there, walking the land and praying? It leads to more informed praying, because you see what some of the problems are. It leads to localised praying – claiming the territory you walk on: 'I will give you every place where you set your foot . . .' (Joshua 1:3).

Church prayer walk

One night Gold Hill Baptist church in England asked all its home groups not to meet at home, but to divide their area between them, and prayer-walk the streets. The leaders suggested we walk in pairs or groups of three, praying quietly at normal conversational level, and keeping our eyes open for clues to help us to pray accurately. One house in our street had a horse shoe over the door, so we prayed for the superstitious people there. Another home had stone lions on the gateposts – nothing strange about that. But these stone lions had their tongues painted red, and I had the feeling it was evil. We prayed against forces of darkness and evil deeds. The next day I had a phone call, and a voice I did not know asked, 'I have three spiritualist books here in the house, and I would like to destroy them but have nowhere I can light a fire. Could you help me?' 'With pleasure,' I replied. I am always keen to help someone destroy anything that might impede their prayers. 'I can burn them here. Where do you live?' She named the street we had prayed in the night before! 'How did you get my name?' I asked. 'Oh, I have a friend who has heard of you.'

Seeing it was a woman, I asked a lady from the office to come with me, and the two of us drove the two miles to her home. She gave us the books. We had a cup of tea together. She happened to mention that the people in big house opposite ran a pornographic video distribution centre. That was the house with the stone lions! That same day, a lady from another street popped into the church office, and said, 'I'm just curious. What do you people believe in here?' And the administrator led her to Jesus right there.

Margaret and the biker engineer
John Bardsley

My wife Margaret felt an urge to walk and pray for the shopping centre in our tiny village. She felt she should walk round the block praying for each shop and for each home above the shops. She was to do it once a week until the Lord told her to stop. She did not want me to go with her. She has a gift of being inconspicuous, and that gift is conspicuously absent in me! But once I did follow her, just to see what she did. There she was, with her bag over her arm, pausing in front of shop windows and looking in, then moving on. It looked so utterly natural, nobody would know she was praying.

She prayed for the church coffee shop, which was there in the street. Above it was a flat occupied by Ian, a young engineer who had just begun coming to church. He rode a motor bike, and so did one of our daughters, so the two of them were often seen at our place. Margaret prayed for Ian each week in the course of her journey around the block. One day I had been yarning with Ian over a coffee in our kitchen, telling him how I had got free from my compulsion to sin. He didn't respond that day, but after Margaret started prayer walking his block, he rang me to say, 'I need to get free from a compulsion like that! Can I come and see you?' So we had a delightful half hour on a tree stump in the garden while he renounced the entry point of his demons and was set free.

Pray in the heights: places of power for good or evil

If there is any special kind of praying that has abundant support in scripture, it is praying in the heights. I see no reason why a height is better than a valley, but the Bible says differently. The Bible is full of praying in high places. Here are some examples.

'Balaam said to Balak: "Stay here . . . while I go aside. Perhaps the Lord will come to meet with me." . . . Then he went off to a barren height. God met with him' (Numbers 23:3-4). 'The Lord alone led him . . . he made him ride on the heights of the land' (Deuteronomy 32:12-13). 'Then you will find your joy in the Lord, and I will cause you to ride on the heights of the land' (Isaiah 58:14). 'Your enemies will cower before you, and you will trample down their high places' (Deuteronomy 33:29). 'He makes my feet like the feet of a deer; he enables me to stand on the heights' (Psalm 18:33). 'The Sovereign LORD is my strength; he makes my feet like the feet of a deer, he enables me to go on the heights' (Habakkuk 3:19). Isaiah 33:15-16 speaks of the one who walks righteously and rejects extortion, bribes and murder as the one who will live in the heights, whose refuge will be the mountain fortress.

'He who . . . treads the high places of the earth, the LORD God Almighty is his name' (Amos 4:13). 'Look! The LORD is coming from his dwelling-place; he comes down and treads the high places of the earth' (Micah 1:3). In Exodus 3:1 we read that Moses came to the mountain of God, and in verse 12 God promised him, 'You will worship God on this mountain' (Exodus 3:12). 'Then Moses went up to God, and the LORD called to him from the mountain' (Exodus 19:3). 'Come, let us go up to the mountain of the LORD' (Isaiah 2:3). 'The glory of the LORD settled on Mount Sinai' (Exodus 24:16). When Elijah reached Horeb, the mountain of God, 'the LORD said, "Go out and stand on the mountain in the presence of the LORD"' (1 Kings 19:8,11).

From the hill tops
John Bardsley

In the 1960s a WEC team went to a traditional city in Spain. The place was hard. The team had a serious disagreement, split, and went home. In the 1970s, a second team went to Cuenca. They prayed and worked together, and gradually saw a small fellowship begin to emerge. Then that small fellowship was torn apart by jealousy and hatred, and the team was so discouraged it too left for greener pastures. A decade later, Juan and Barbara Torres felt the call from God to make disciples in Cuenca. But they knew the history and said 'We feel called to Cuenca. Will the whole team come with us for a day of prayer for Cuenca?' So the whole team went and prayed in the heights over Cuenca, where there are some dramatic cliff-top dwellings overlooking the city that have become a tourist attraction. Juan and Barbara began selling and lending books and tapes door to door, and running a family programme in a park near their home. A few people were born again, and a church began to meet in the garage of their flat. Then the Betel drug rehabilitation ministry opened a house in Cuenca, and born-again ex-addicts began to strengthen the church. Now the church is under its own leadership.

A similar story occurred in France. Matt and Margaret Paton were trying to move to Lens, a village near Clermont-Ferrand in the central plateau, to start a church. At first they could not even rent a flat! 'Sorry, I just let it to someone else . . .' After several refusals, they managed to sign an agreement with one landlord who then rang and cancelled it! They went to enrol their boys in school, but each school in turn said, 'Sorry, we are already over quota, and can take no more.' Matt and Margaret called their team leaders, and the whole French team came to Lens for a day of prayer. They went up on a hill outside the town to see it all from on high, and claimed it for Jesus. Then Matt and Margaret went back to one of those same schools, and it accepted the boys. They managed to sign an agreement on a flat, and move in. And now there is a church in Lens.

STOPTHINK&DISCUSS
- What definitions of faith you can find in Hebrews 11? Can you get a different definition from each of these passages: Hebrews 11:1-7, 27-28; 11-13, 20-22; 11: 17-21 & 11:29-38?
- Submit and resist! Stand! Bind! Loose! Demolish strongholds! Overcome! These are biblical words, but God has not spelled out in detail how we are to put them into practice. Discuss why you think this is. Discuss a meaning for each of them with which you are comfortable in the light of scripture, and use them in your struggle.
- Have you ever taken a prayer walk? Have you ever gone up on a hill to pray? Have you ever looked up verses of scripture to pray for someone? Try it, with a friend or two, then discuss how you felt and what happened as a result.

11
HOW PEOPLE HAVE USED WARFARE PRAYER

John Bardsley

The full story of a famous chapter

Most people are familiar with the story of King Jehoshaphat and the attack on Jerusalem in 2 Chronicles 20. Many have heard the famous verse, 'As they began to sing and praise, the LORD set ambushes against the enemy.' But there is a lot more to it: may we begin at the beginning?

In verses 1-2 Jehoshaphat discovered the problem: 'A vast army is coming against you!' He knew this army was too big for him. Alarmed, he called the whole population to prayer and fasting. Verses 3-4 record that the whole of Jerusalem was fasting in unity; verse 13 indicates that everyone was there, young and old, rich and poor.

Jehoshaphat prayed a wonderful prayer in verses 5-12, a prayer of intercession. He began by reminding Israel who God is. Verse 6 says, 'LORD . . . you rule all the kingdoms of the nations.' As we said at the beginning of this book, such a confession of faith is essential before we take on the enemy. We need to know with absolute faith that God is king.

Jehoshaphat went on to claim one of the promises of God. Verse 7 records that God gave them this land. If God has given you a baby, a vehicle, a ministry in a country, suburb, or ethnic group, you too can remind him of his promise in threatening times. Claiming the promises is a huge boost to faith, and in verses 8-9 Jehoshaphat goes on to say, 'If calamity comes upon us . . . we will cry to you in our distress, and you will hear us and save us.'

Then Jehoshaphat reminded God in verses 10-11 that he had not allowed them to raid the territory of their enemies, but now theses enemies were raiding them. God likes us to be specific, and to describe the problem in detail. If you need a house, list what kind of house! Specific answers to specific prayers prove that God is a loving father who is interested in the minutiae of our lives. It's amazing when we consider how many of us there are!

Verse 12 is another famous text: 'We do not know what to do, but our eyes are on you.' When we are still struggling in our own strength or grit, wisdom or determination, God waits. But when we admit we do not have what it takes, it is time for God to move.

God spoke to Jahaziel, a Levite, perhaps a member of the choir, or one of the men who cleaned the ashes out of the altar or looked after the tithes and offerings and distributed them to his fellow Levites. We read this man's name only here. He was not famous. He was not a regular prophet. But this once, he heard from God, and spoke boldly to encourage the king. Verses 14-17 record God's response, through the mouth of this unknown Levite, to this wonderful prayer that began with worship, claimed promises, listed specifics, all in the context of fasting. 'God will fight for us!' he promised. 'We will not fight. We must trust, stand, and see what God will do.'

Jehoshaphat's faith latched onto this wonderful promise immediately. He did not need to be told twice. In gratitude he bowed to worship and praise the God of heaven (18-19) in faith for the morrow. I am sure he even slept well, and the next day he proved his faith by placing the band and the choir at the front, with the army behind them. He was not expecting to fight (20-21).

As they praised, God set the enemy in-fighting until they destroyed themselves (22-24). 'As they praised' records the timing of God's move, not the whole reason for it. There was more behind this victory than praise, wonderful as praise certainly is. There was fasting in unity. There was worship of God as the ultimate power. There was claiming the promises, and spelling out specific needs. There was a prophecy on which to base faith, and a heart response of joyous believing faith, declared in word and demonstrated in deed. There was a lot behind that worship, and that victory.

After they watched the enemy destroy itself, they gathered the loot, and returned with even more praise to their homes (25-28). And the fear of God fell on all surrounding nations (29), a fitting response to an awesome deliverance by a wonderful heavenly Father.

Gates of Chiangmai
Dave Macmillan

At the end of a prayer walk around the ancient walls and gates of Chiangmai, our small group stood at the final gate asking the Father of Compassion to shake the city's ancient spiritual foundations.

Entrenched religious belief systems have affected generation after generation throughout the city's 700-year history. Occult practitioners have been authorised to lead the city into covenants and oaths with 'gods' and 'ruling spirits'. The city lives on a foundation of spiritual marriage and obligation to demonic powers. If there is to be a harvest and transformation that impacts the city's spiritual foundations, spiritual warfare is unavoidable.

In our prayer sessions over the past months there has been a recurring theme: arousing the Lamb's dangerous priesthood. He paid the extreme price to raise up an order of warrior-priests clothed in the same zeal he wears. The Lamb died for a practising, militant priesthood, not a ceremonial one. We live to extend the Kingdom through worship that is both passionate and aggressive. There's a quality of holy violence in the way we press into worship, convinced that the Lamb's praises can sever the artery of Satan's historic hold on a city, and silence his current nerve centre in the land. The 'royal priesthood' company here is relatively small, but it has heaven's full backing to affect the future of the city. Won't you join us in praying that Chiangmai's amazing kingdom of redeemed ones would live fully as priests of God; uninterested in mediocre praise rituals and performance hype; devoted to selfless, whole-hearted extravagant worship that exalts JESUS as the only legitimate spiritual foundation for this city's future?

A church in Peronne
Matt and Margaret Paton

At first the problems in Peronne had often been within – Christians without a vision discouraging the effort: 'There are no funds available'; 'The papers for a public building are very slow in coming'; 'Our architect is not allowed to present plans any more'. Our only hope and strength has been to call the Christians to daily prayer. The new little church building exists. The Lord sent a wonderful team from Devon, during one hot summer. The finances came in. The architect found someone else to sign his plans. The official papers did come through.

Not long ago the Peronne Archaeological Society wrote the history of the town. How surprised we were to read that in the year 646 an Irish missionary brought the gospel to Peronne. His name was Fursy. He was buried on a hill, and the street was named after him. Our little church stands on that hill in St Fursy Street, Peronne!

You are my battleaxe and weapons of war
Denise Christie, Colombia

A keen young pastor had planned a bold evangelistic event in a city theatre in Manizales. Pausing to wipe away her tears, the young pastor's wife handed me a fax from the government security agency. It warned that a militant satanic sect called 'Wolves against Christ' had vowed to murder the next evangelist who dared to preach in their city of Manizales.

That it was no idle threat had been confirmed by the assassination of a Catholic priest one month earlier during Holy Week. Never faltering, the young woman said to me, 'Denise, when you are called you are called. I must go. If any thing should happen, please look out for my children and help the church.'

Sobered by the urgency of the challenge, the church leaders invited me to join them in prayer. What a glorious time of warfare we had. One brother knew by a word of knowledge that the enemy's strategy was going to be to cut off the power and take advantage of the darkness and confusion to kill the pastor. Thank God for the era of cell phones! Immediately they rang the theatre, and someone was posted permanently alongside the fuse boxes. Other members of the group received encouraging prophetic promises.

The crusade in Manizales was a glorious success. The Lord ripped open the heavens and came down. His name was made notorious to his enemies. Signs and wonders were done in his everlasting name. The Satanists were rendered powerless.

I heard the voice of the Lord stating, 'You are my battle-axe and weapons of war.' Every intercessor, whether a grandmother like myself or a young person, is God's battleaxe and weapons of war. Every Christian who believes in the power of prayer, and is prepared to come to God's work in the battle against the mighty, is valuable to God. As small and insignificant as they may be in their own eyes, their prayers break down the powers of darkness in the nations. Kingdoms are destroyed through the prayers of ordinary people like you and me.

Bless the Lord, we don't require diplomas in theology, nor years of intensive training to become God's battleaxe and weapons of war. It simply requires hearts that weep over lost nations; hearts full of faith that will dare to ask for the nations as our inheritance and the ends of the earth for our possession; hearts that know beyond a shadow of doubt in whom we have believed, and are convinced that he is able to do exceedingly and abundantly above all we ask or think; hearts that are convinced that he will be very gracious to us.

Thousands of warriors

In 1985 the Lord assured me that he would raise up an army with the same characteristics as King David's army: 'prepared and ready for battle, with every kind of weapon' – men and women whose hearts are united with God's own heart; friends of the Holy Spirit, helpers in the war. My late husband and I made 22 visits to different nations throughout Central and South America and saw God raise up thousands of warriors. At first glance they were students, labourers, housewives or professionals. Yet in God's eyes each individual was his battleaxe and weapons of war.

That is why the walls of superstition, which for generations have surrounded these Latin nations, are falling down flat. It is in response to the faith and love of these helpers in the war. Begin to see yourself as the Lord sees you. It is a glorious thing to go to war for the nations. It can be done as you walk the streets or travel on the bus or train; it can be done within the confines of your own home, as you work in the kitchen, mind the children or work in the office. You can prophesy words of life to the dry bones of your land. Ask the Holy Spirit to blow on the dry bones. Abandon yourself completely to the Lord. Allow Him to destroy, through your prayers and supplications, every fortress of darkness in your family, town and city. Then choose the nations that you desire for your inheritance. Choose carefully, choose well. Look out for the darkest and neediest, and focus your battery of prayers on their cities and idols, reclaiming them through prophetic promises of the Word of God.

Remember, the walls of Jericho will only yield to faith. Take active possession of these lands and their cities in the name of Jesus. Drive out the giants. Be sure and use the sword of the Spirit to root out, pull down, destroy, to throw down the principalities and powers. Stand on the Lord's promise in Haggai 2:22: 'I will overturn royal thrones and shatter the power of the foreign kingdoms.' Take possession!

Intercessor for evangelistic crusades in eight cities . . .

The Holy Spirit gave a bold, ambitious strategy to pastors and leaders in the Colombian revival movement. 'Mobilize a team of 50 people, hold evangelistic crusades in eight principal cities of the coastal region. Minister to all the leaders and pastors throughout the area. Let revival fires burn. Go to war and take possession in each department.' After 33 years in Colombia I longed to participate in this offensive against the gates of hell. One thing hindered me. I didn't have a penny to my name. Lack of visible finances should never hold back the advance of God's Kingdom. Another seemingly wise consideration: 'Would a grandmother, nearly sixty, be able to withstand the intense tropical heat?' God quickened a promise to me from the book of Zechariah: 'I will strengthen them in the LORD and in his name they will walk' (10:12).

Monteria was the first city, a city under siege, totally surrounded by oppressive communist terrorist forces. It was not a hard task to identify those men and women called, faithful and chosen. The Holy Spirit came on them like fire; they were overcome by the presence of the glory of God. Little conversation took place during the tense one-hour drive to the next city. All were concentrating on effectual fervent prayer. At any moment we could have been kidnapped by guerrilla troops. (During the past four years some 30 Colombian pastors and six missionaries had been found worthy to seal their testimony with their blood).

On the very first night of the evangelistic crusade in the sports stadium, as we worshipped the Lord, his glory began to descend. Wave upon wave inundated and enveloped the entire sports stadium. Each successive visitation brought an increased intensity, until young and old were on their knees weeping, totally broken before the majesty of the Almighty. I recall wishing that I could hide beneath the floor boards. Just ten minutes, yet it seemed like an eternity.

As the end of the journey neared, heat and late nights took their toll of me. A heavy chest cold made me miserable. My feet broke out in weeping sores due to a fungus infection. My toothpaste came to an end, I was down to washing my dentures with soap. I knew deliverance must be near. Sure enough, as we gathered in fellowship around the table, the visiting pastor exclaimed. 'I see the Lord laying a banquet table with special food: it is to strengthen bones.' Hallelujah, just what this granny needed. The Lord totally restored me. At the close of the eight-city tour most of the young people were worn out, not so grandma. The ever-faithful Lord amply fulfilled his promise to strengthen me. All my needs were supplied including the longed-for toothpaste.

Take possession

The word God gave for 1999 was 'Take possession of the land.' My faith began to rise as I studied the scriptural principles for taking over the land of Canaan. My enthusiasm grew as I delved into the prophetic word and discovered the recurring theme of taking hold of our possessions in these last days.

For me, Colombia is my Canaan, the land of my inheritance. India, Africa, the Muslim nations could well become the lands of your inheritance. Remember, possession is a costly business. A just price must be paid by the intercessor. You cannot gain possession on the cheap.

May the Holy Spirit quicken to you the word in Jeremiah 32:7: 'Buy my field . . . it is your right and duty to buy it.' How much to redeem Calcutta? Benares? Delhi? Who will buy the rights to Mecca? Riyadh? or Cairo? The Lord encouraged Jeremiah by saying, 'I am the LORD the God of all mankind. Is any thing too hard for me?' (verse 27).

The kind of love that lays down its own life for its friends is a valuable currency in God's kingdom. My late husband took possession of the drug addict district in Santa Fe de Bogotá. We opened a school, an oasis of love for the children of the prostitutes, thieves, murderers and drug addicts. One day terrorists broke into our home, stole all our possessions and threatened to murder our family. My husband retaliated by building a second school to bless the children of this ex-terrorist movement high on the bleak, barren mountains which surround our beautiful city of Bogotá. Then, diagnosed with an incurable cancer, he literally laid down his life for his little friends.

Who will love the Muslim nations enough to lay down their lives in prayer for them? Love and faith will work wonders. Abraham paid a just price, a worthy price to obtain a burial place for his beloved Sarah. He insisted on paying as much money as it was worth to take possession. How much is Africa worth? What will you pay for India? What will you give to buy the field of the Muslim nations? To take possession? King David made a regal decision, when he said, 'I will not sacrifice to the LORD burnt offerings that cost me nothing' (2 Samuel 24:24). True, the right of redemption is ours; but it is costly, very costly. Yet the present sufferings cannot be compared with the glory that shall be revealed amongst the nations.

For our ninth women's congress, I envisioned the Lord setting women's hearts afire – the way Samson ignited the foxes' tails, then set them loose to cause havoc in the enemy's camp. Instead, I slipped on a pineapple skin, sustained a double fracture, and was an invalid for two months. God sent Sonya. She became my friend, my nurse, my secretary and companion-in-arms. Earthworks cut off the telephone of the secretary of the committee, but we managed. A new member of the committee offered to do all the advertising, then failed to produce any of it. Sonya organized an efficient voluntary team, who at times worked right through the night. There was rivalry over our venue – a 3000-seat warehouse in one denomination, or a 2000-seat church in another? The Christian radio station refused to announce our event unless they approved the theological stance of the venue. But at last, it was all done. '"Not by might, nor by power, but by my Spirit," says the LORD Almighty.' My personal goal of faith was realised by God's grace. Just two months after my accident, I was able to stand and translate in every service of the congress. All things are possible to those who believe.

How my heart sang when the 2000 women who attended selected 40 promises to intercede 40 days for Colombia. No wonder the opposition was so fierce! 2000 warriors rose up to pray and take possession of the gates of this wonderful country and her dear people.

Women's congresses – training warriors
'Denise, I brought you on this journey to witness the effect of the women's congresses throughout the land.'
Back in 1992 a group of twenty dedicated Colombian pastors' wives and myself had discovered that we shared the same burden and vision for the restoration of

our women. So many pastors' wives were consumed by bitterness and resentment. Constant criticism and rejection from their congregations had crushed their spirits. Many were totally unprepared for the demands of the ministry, unaware of the grim realities of spiritual warfare. We were inspired by the verse: 'The Lord gave the word: great was the company of those that published it' (Psalm 68:11 KJV). Our vision encompassed a multitude of women equipped to proclaim the word of God with prophetic anointing; women to help gather in the last great harvest, working in harmony and unity alongside the leaders; women to pray and to intercede. Our goal was brave women prepared for war; wise women to help build up the church of God; women girded with strength for the battle.

We began an annual congress for women. In each congress the Lord has given a theme. 'Awake, awake, put on strength!' was the first challenge. 'Tread down strength, march with power'; 'Arise, shine for your light has come'; 'Launch out into the deep', to name just a few. Each year, prior to the main gatherings, we have celebrated Operation Esther: three days of united prayer and fasting, believing God to open a door of hope for all Colombian women. How God has honoured our faith and prayers, far above all we could have asked or thought.

Training counsellors
Denise Christie

'We have come into the kingdom for such a time as this. Every Esther must don her royal garments, approach the throne room fearlessly, and touch the royal sceptre of the King of Kings on behalf of the nations.' I had heard the Lord say to me in 1990, as we arrived in Guatemala to train Christian counsellors: 'What is your request? What is your petition?' Carefully formulate your request for the salvation of the nations. Wait on the Holy Spirit until you acquire the necessary clarity in your petition.

'Light for those in darkness and in the shadow of death.' This was my petition for Colombia in 1997. In 1990 I had participated in the excitement of training thousands of counsellors in Guatemala, San Salvador, Nicaragua and Argentina to gather in the harvest of souls. Now my heart longed for a similar blessing in the land of my inheritance. Only one thing stood in the way: no finance available. I love the phrase, 'Faith laughs at the impossible and cries it shall be done.' The Lord can save with many and he can save with just a few who truly believe him. My team members were all young, yet they were 'all or nothing' people. Remember the catchy song, 'With me it's all or nothing'? Is it all or nothing with you? God can do something with 'all or nothing' people.

Arthur was returning from an intense day training counsellors in the tropical city of Neiva. Suddenly in a vision he saw a terrorist chief with his face disguised by a red kerchief. The Holy Spirit alerted him that his bus was about to be detained and the passengers would be robbed. Just 30 minutes later, around midnight, the vision became a harsh reality. Again the Lord urged Arthur to take authority, because the terrorists planned to board the bus. (This is a common event, and often the terrorists later abandon and burn the bus.) Every passenger except

Arthur was robbed. Inexplicably (for those who ignore the power of prayer), the terrorists allowed everyone to continue on their journey.

Milena was attending to her daily office duties in the nearby commercial centre, when a man grabbed her arm in a vice-like grip and propelled her down the street. Unaware at first of her danger, Milena witnessed to him of the reality of her faith in Jesus Christ. As the pressure of his grip intensified, this dear lassie prayed as never before, wrenched herself free and raced into the traffic. Cars and buses honked wildly, but she escaped, thank God! Adventures are daily bread when you live abandoned totally to God and his purposes .

That same year, due to the bumbling of a young lawyer hooked on drugs, I found myself enmeshed in serious legal proceedings and couldn't even attend the first series of training. Thank God we had behind us a whole year of serious prayer and warfare for our cities. Every Thursday morning work came to a standstill and phones were unplugged while we devoted ourselves to seeking the Lord. My petition was granted beyond my wildest dreams.

Evangelism training

One morning the Lord awakened me at 2:30 saying, 'I want you to contact my unknown apostles in this city, those who have dedicated 10 or 15 years to rescue the drug addicts, prostitutes, homosexuals, lesbians, abandoned children and old people. Let them be teachers along with you to train others how to penetrate the kingdom of darkness. Invite volunteers to learn from my servants.' From July until the end of November, four nights a week, we trained people in how to reach out in faith and love to the lost. Each night we went to war in prayer for the salvation of the neediest people in our city. Some of our students go to the prisons, others are reaching out to children addicted to glue. Drug addicts are experiencing that Jesus is greater than Satan or sin. Satan to Jesus must bow!

There are hundreds of lost young women like Janet roaming the city streets of Colombia. At 32 she was hooked on drugs, a single mother with four children. Temporary relief appeared when she took refuge in a home for addicts. On Christmas Eve, the call of drugs was stronger than her desire for help. She simply disappeared back into the darkness of the drug scene. Two weeks later, she seemed a hopeless case. At least three different Christian workers had pleaded with her in vain. What a shock it was when my friend Wilma saw poor Janet. Her face was black, caked with dirt. A cap half-covered her distorted face. She was a pitiful sight. Gone was the bright, happy Janet that Wilma had known just two weeks earlier. As Janet drew near, the Holy Spirit spoke to Wilma loud and clear: 'Don't say a word of reproach. Simply place your hand on her shoulder and my love, not yours but mine, will flow through you and melt her heart.' Janet's reaction was amazing. She reached out to Wilma and hugged her to her heart, weeping. Everyone was touched by the powerful presence of God. Right there and then four other addicts gave their lives to Christ and now Janet is safely back in the home of refuge.

Television evangelism

Evangelistic spots appeared between news items on nationwide TV. The titles of the soap operas chosen would make any grandmother blush; the seamier the better. Why? We were following the time-honoured admonition of General William Booth: 'Go for souls and go for the worst.' Right in the midst of these horrific programmes, loaded with illegitimate sex and violence, came the message of the glorious gospel of our living God, mighty to save. Light came to those in darkness and in the shadow of death.

Fifty years ago in Colombia, Willie Easton, a British WEC pioneer missionary, had been made to crawl naked through human excrement. I wonder if he ever imagined the kind of church that God would raise up. The fruit of the affliction of those early missionaries is lasting. Just a month ago a would-be assassin employed to murder my pastor, came to confess his sins and receive Christ. After he saw the pastor's programme on TV he was convicted of his sins and realized he couldn't kill a good man like that.

Diary of a prayer journeyer
Liz Hentschel

Her feet inched closer to the edge. Below lay a drop of some six metres. Was she going to jump? Was she being pushed by some unseen force? I slowly and carefully reached out and took a firm hold of the back of her T-shirt. That touch seemed to bring her back from her mesmerised state. I coaxed her away from the edge, all the time maintaining my firm grip on her T-shirt. The scene? A Buddhist monastery in Shigatse, Tibet.

Five months before, six of us (from five different countries) had started preparing for this prayer journey. We studied material related to Tibetans. We read their history. We turned ourselves inside out trying to comprehend their particular style of Buddhism. We prayed together weekly, and not just, 'God bless us and make us good little Christians' type prayers either. This was to be heavy stuff ... but did we realise how heavy?

Our plane circled, descending into one of the trickiest airfields in the world, Kathmandu, Nepal. 'Fly with the national airline,' we had been told. 'At least their pilots are experienced in take-offs and landings at this airport.' Tricky? Scary? Breath-taking? All of the above! How does one land a plane on a small airfield which is surrounded by such high, snow-capped mountains? Our pilot did. The pre-monsoon heat hit us squarely in the face as we left the plane. Exhaust fumes, smoke, and who knows what else made the air thick and oppressive. Welcome to one of the most polluted cities in the world! This was to be our base for the next week. It was here that we would prepare for our journey across the mountains to Lhasa, the capital of Tibet. It was here that we would spend time to ensure we gelled as a group. There was to be no division in our camp. We needed a well-trained army, not a bunch of individuals spending all their precious energy on any unresolved interpersonal conflicts.

Day one: I had led a prayer journey team before and vividly remembered the first night. It was the worst night of my entire life. Drunken men tried to break into my hotel room. Fear gripped me as fear had never gripped me before. I had been around, and had dealt with drunken men in my time, so this was no normal fear. Then there was the depression. It hit like a ton of bricks. And the accusations: 'Who do you think you are to lead such a prayer journey!'

That was four years ago. This time I told myself, 'Take no chances. Get your team to pray for you.' An extremely good night's sleep followed, despite the noise of traffic, the heat, and the humidity. For Ralph, however, it was different. Dogs barked. There is nothing unusual about that. But why for so long, and so loudly, and so many? Ralph sensed it was because of demonic activity in the area. The sensitive dogs were picking it up. Was that simply Ralph's vivid imagination? Suddenly he knew without a doubt that demons were trying to throw him from his bed. Yes, folks, we were off to quite a start! This was no vivid imagination.

Day two: This morning we looked at Psalm 135. We 'walked' our way through it. We praised, we sang, we ministered to the Lord. We reminded ourselves that we were chosen, a treasured possession, and we rejected and stood against intimidation and fear. One team member, Harry, led us: 'We say 'NO' to the devil!' We remembered what God had done. We spoke out the truth about him. The idols are nothing! We went on to ask God to do a Romans 10:20 again, that is, to reveal himself to those who did not ask for him. Less than an estimated 200 Tibetans knew the Lord Jesus. Oh, too few! We were fed up with the enemy keeping these people in fetters!

Day five: The stupa loomed high above us. This particular stupa represents a mixture of Buddhism, Hinduism and black magic. Our job brief? To walk up the steps alongside the pilgrims who have come to spin prayer wheels, chant their mantras, and do their prostrations. To pray quietly. To proclaim that Jesus has overcome the powers of darkness. To pray for the salvation of these pilgrims. 'Holy, holy, holy, Lord God Almighty. All Your works shall praise Your name in earth and sky and sea ...' Two of us stood in a corner and quietly sang this magnificent hymn. Suddenly blasphemy sprang into my mind and almost escaped over my lips! What was this? There I was, worshipping the Lord. Proclaiming truths about Him. Why on earth was I about to sing completely wrong words? Why on earth? Because the god of this world was making a song and dance about losing his authority back to the Lord Jesus, that's why!

During that first week our different roles in intercessory prayer emerged. There were the 'priests' who, as they prayed, identified themselves with the pain, anguish and lack of hope experienced by those we met. There were the 'prophets' who opened the Word of God and read just the right scriptures for the occasion. There were the 'warriors' who loudly and boldly prayed in the application of Christ's intercessory work. There were the 'singers' who often marched at the rear of our 'procession', their songs gently wafting over the rest of us. Each team player fully participated, but this was no game.

Day nine: The eight of us set off in a couple of four-wheel drive vehicles on our five day trip over the mountains. But for God, four of us would have had our life on earth abruptly ended that day. Our experienced driver skilfully drove the vehicle up, up, up, round, round, ever upwards . . . 3000 metres, 3500, 4000 ...

The narrow, pot-holed, dirt road took us through breath-taking scenery. The road gave way to magnificent views of the lush, vegetated valleys below. No safety rails. No road signs. This was the bush! Suddenly another vehicle all but flew around the corner and headed straight for us. It was going too fast to stop in time! How do two on-coming vehicles pass on a road which is only really wide enough for one vehicle? And what speed! Our driver pulled sharply to the right as the other vehicle whizzed past. Was it just one centimetre that separated our vehicle from the edge of that long drop deep into the valley? There is no way anyone could have survived that fall. The two drivers stopped their vehicles, opened the doors, and peered back at each other. Not a word was exchanged. But for God ...

Day ten: Up, up, up. What heights! What altitude sickness! The two men on the team were hit hard. Vomiting and near dehydration. Ralph felt as if he was punch-drunk. Harry wanted to die. We anointed them with oil and prayed. They became even worse! There was something horribly eerie about this town. The squat toilet would win the prize for the filthiest loo in the whole wide world! We fell into bed.

Day eleven: Five in the morning and I awoke with a thumping headache, part of altitude sickness, so I am told. Anne leaned over from her bed and informed me that she had seen a demon at the window. It was trying to attack her. Would I please pray? First a couple of Panadol for the headache.

Our prayer team hits the road again, and we reach Shigatse. 'Dark' and 'putrid' are the words that sum up this place ... both physically and spiritually. My grip on Mary's T-shirt does not loosen until we are a safe distance from the edge of that drop to the courtyard below. 'Did you think I would jump?' 'I don't know, but I do think something sinister was trying to push you over.' Mary and Anne are both under attack. They seem to have that knack of discerning what is happening in the heavenlies, and the enemy comes with his reprisals. That evening, back in the confines of our hotel room, we read Ephesians 2:1-10. If God could build His church in the idolatrous city of Ephesus, He can do it here.

Day fifteen: Lhasa, meaning 'place of the gods'. It is 6:30am and we join the Buddhist pilgrims as they trudge around the road which encircles the old city. They spin their prayer wheels, finger their prayer beads, and prostrate themselves. I get the impression that with each prostration, the pilgrims become more and more entwined in the demonic. Prayer flags along the route flap in the wind. All of this is in an effort to gain some merit for a better rebirth (next time around). Our purpose is entirely different. We form a procession to honour the One True Living God! Quiet songs of praise. Aching hearts for those who are walking in darkness. Verbalised prayers. Intense anger that the enemy has set himself up against the knowledge of God.

Day seventeen: The last day of Saga Dawa. The Potala Palace stands as a mighty fortress, towering above the city. We climb the ancient stone steps. Room after room of Buddhas. Burning butter lamps. Buddhist scriptures. Monks with shaven heads and clad in saffron and burgundy-coloured robes. Tourists who appear to think all of this is quaint. Friends pose and cameras click. Two by two we quietly move from one room to another, praying in our hearts. Pilgrims chant their mantras. Father ... what darkness! Abigail, my companion, and I feel suffocated after two hours. We have had enough. We have to get out. But where is the exit? We ask a monk. He sends us back through yet another room filled with Buddhas. This place is like a maze. Where is that exit? Narrow dark corridors. More pilgrims. More stench. Ah, sunlight! We slowly walk down the long stairs, our backs to the palace. 'No other name but the name of Jesus ... is worthy of honour ...' is the appropriate song for the occasion. How dare the enemy keep people in bondage!

Day eighteen: As we begin to pray in our team meeting, a snarling demonic image appears and hovers above my head. My physical eyes do not see it, but I know what it looks like. Every contour of its face. Intimidating, hating, accusing, violent. My team prays in a good dose of Colossians 1:15-23. The devil may be powerful, but he sure is stupid! Doesn't he realise that the more he attacks, the more we rise up and fight against him?

STOPTHINK&DISCUSS

- Read 2 Chronicles 20 for yourself, and ask God to speak to you about intercession, faith, promises, prophecy, and victory.
- What have you learned about the spiritual state of Thailand from 'Gates of Chiangmai'? How would you pray for the church to grow in this country?
- What can we learn about prayer and faith from 'A church in Peronne'? Do you believe that Fursy's prayers still influence life in Peronne today?
- Describe the impact of a word of knowledge (1 Corinthians 12:8) on the situation in the opening paragraphs of 'You are my battleaxe and weapons of war'. Check pages 85, 222 and 236 and compile suggestions for how to use this wonderful gift.
- What shocks you from 'You are my battleaxe and weapons of war'? What can we learn about prayer, endurance, unity, planning, and hearing from God?
- What alarming tactics of the enemy were experienced in the prayer journey to Tibet? How were the problems overcome?

12
SPIRITUAL CONFLICT IN EVANGELISM AND CHURCH PLANTING

John Bardsley

'I am sending you to them to open their eyes and turn them from darkness to light, and from the power of Satan to God, so that they may receive forgiveness of sins and a place among those who are sanctified by faith in me' (Acts 26:18).

A *kairos* for every people

Jesus prayed 'Father, the time has come' (John 17:1). There are two Greek words for 'time'. One is *chronos*, from which we get so many time-related English words like chronometer, chronicle, chronological. It is a simple word, and is not the one used in John 17:1. The other word is *kairos*. It means not only time, but opportunity, and carries implications of well-laid plans and strategies coming to fulfilment.

Imagine the use of a similar word by Mordecai when he said to Esther, 'You have come to royal position for such a time as this' (Esther 4:14), or by God himself when he promised Abraham, 'At the appointed time I will return, and Sarah will have a son' (Romans 9:9).

Imagine the Godhead planning the day for Christ to be born. They planned with meticulous accuracy, even before they created the world. This was the crucial event which would make the creation of human beings a success. It had to be just right. 'But when the time had fully come, God sent his son . . .' (Galatians 4.4).

Peter was expecting a *kairos* when God would visit, and people would give God the glory he deserves (1 Peter 2:12). Luke comments in Luke 5:17 that the power of the Lord was there to heal. The logical deduction is that on some other occasions, it was not there. Sometimes there was a *kairos* for healing, sometimes not.

Illustrations of *kairos* in the Old Testament

Can you imagine a more discouraging job to do than the one God handed to young Isaiah? No wonder he needed such a glorious vision of the Lord! 'I heard the voice of the Lord saying "Whom shall I send? And who will go for us?" And I said, "Here am I. Send me!" He said, "Go and tell this people: 'Be ever hearing, but never understanding; be ever seeing, but never perceiving.' Make the heart of this people calloused; make their ears dull and close their eyes. Otherwise they might see with their eyes, hear with their ears, understand with their hearts, and turn and be healed." Then I said, "For how long, O Lord?" [I would have asked the same!] And he answered, "Until the cities lie ruined and without inhabitant

... until the LORD has sent everyone far away and the land is utterly forsaken. And though a tenth remains in the land, it will again be laid waste. But as the terebinth and oak leave stumps when they are cut down, so the holy seed will be the stump in the land"' (Isaiah 6:8-13).

Isaiah was born at a time when Israel's history was already on the wane. The results of generations of sin and idolatry were being felt in the decadence of the nation. Judgement had already been decided in heaven. So Isaiah's call was not to bring repentance, but to plead with an unresponsive crowd, and to predict that after the exile they would receive mercy. This doesn't mean he was an unsuccessful prophet. He said what God told him to say. We need confidence in God, even if his *kairos* is not now. He sees the whole sweep of history as now.

We need to be able to see God behind the curtain of the world stage, controlling destiny, planning his *kairos* for this ethnic group and then that one.

God had a tough task for young Jeremiah too, so God created the right man for the job. "'Before I formed you in the womb I knew you, before you were born I set you apart, I appointed you as a prophet to the nations. You must go to everyone I send you to and say whatever I command you." Then the Lord reached out his hand and touched my mouth, and said to me, "Now, I have put my words in your mouth. See, today I appoint you over nations and kingdoms to uproot and tear down, to destroy and overthrow, to build and to plant"' (Jeremiah 1:5,8,9).

So Jeremiah was commissioned for the actual time of the fall of Jerusalem, when the kings were dumb and dumber, rebellious and idolatrous. Much of his task was to predict destruction. It was not a popular ministry! They called him a traitor! He needed endurance until the fullness of time.

Kairos today

God had told Israel they would have to wait four generations to return to the promised land. 'In the fourth generation your descendants will come back here, for the sin of the Amorites has not yet reached its full measure' (Genesis 15:16). God has enormous incredible 'stretch-fabric' patience! The Amorites were filling their cup of sin, slowly. Can we draw a parallel with modern religious and political anti-God regimes? Could we say 'The inadequacy of the satanic counterfeit is not yet fully demonstrated'? Some examples:

Mao's cultural revolution and the students' goddess of democracy proved that communism doesn't work, and the *kairos*, the appointed time, was created for a surge of church growth in China. Ayatollah Khomeini convinced many Iranians that Islamic fundamentalism was not the religion of choice for them. The Hindu Nationalist Party in India finally exhausted the tolerance of the outcast Dalit population, driving them to choose other religions. The Sudanese government policy of ethnic cleansing drove hundreds of people into the churches in southern Sudan and Darfur.

Discerning the kairos

Strategy is about discerning the *kairos*. We who pray for God's kingdom to come want to be like the men of Issachar, who understood the times and knew what

Israel should do (1 Chronicles 12:32). Jesus said to the Pharisees, 'You cannot interpret the signs of the times' (Matthew 16:3). Can you? Can I? Can we spot a *kairos*?

The Jola people have a lot of local kings who are really priests of the fetish. These men pour out oblations of wine and sacrifices of pigs' blood, lead the initiation rites, and make and sell charms and curses. I suggested to one of the Jola churches that they could offer Jesus as a superior King/Priest, one who poured out his own blood, in whose honour we drink a cup of wine. He could lead a superior initiation rite, in which the children learned bushcraft and met their Creator. One of the elders replied, 'It's not time yet to suggest that to the whole Jola people. But I will use it in a communion service.' The *kairos* had not yet come.

We live in the age of grace, when every individual who has not yet heard the message is promised a hearing, and every ethnic group is promised a bunch of disciples.

In the Jola heartland, Alastair and Helen Kennedy began to sow the good seed. They were followed by Mena Gilpin and a host of other co-workers. Mena retired after 33 years (1953-86) and wondered if she had wasted her life. The church was the same size when she left as when she had arrived, although she had led six little boys to Jesus, but they had not been allowed to continue coming. Sheila Kilkenny continued with sowing and reaping. Mena came back to see the work in 1994. Those six little boys were all pastors, evangelists or Christian leaders! Hallelujah! She had not wasted her life! She had planted. Now the harvest, the *kairos* had begun. Sheila sees four stages in God's *kairos* for the Jola people: sowing 1950-80, firstfruits 1980-86, growing 1986-96, full harvest 1996-_____. It's that missing last date that I'm interested in! When will there be a chain of holy multiplying churches in every Jola language?

Getting answers to prayer is not so much about screwing up my faith, as it is about persistence until the *kairos* moment, and hastening it. 'You ought to live holy and godly lives as you look forward to the day of God and speed its coming' (2 Peter 3:12).

There was a song in the old WEC song book that went like this:

'Whenever you ripe fields behold,
waving to God their sheaves of gold,
Be sure some grain of wheat has died,
some saintly soul been crucified.
Someone has suffered, wept and prayed,
and fought hell's legions undismayed.'

You may not dig the poetry, but can you catch the passion? Could you cope with a calling like Isaiah or Jeremiah, Alastair or Mena? Will you take responsibility for praying down the *kairos* for one unreached people?

Matthew 13:24-30 is a fascinating insight into God's *kairos*. We live in an age of wheat and weeds. Both will thrive together till the harvest. Evil will flourish, but not triumph. It will be harvested first and burnt. Good will thrive in the midst of evil, and triumph in the end.

What happens when we can't see the results?
John Bardsley

Meta Dunlop came to see me when I was International Prayer Coordinator and asked me one of the hardest questions of my life. 'John, I've been trying to plant the Mandinka church in Guinea Bissau for 18 years and I'm going back only one more time before I retire. There is still no Mandinka church. Have I wasted my life? Is God going to build his church?' What would you have said to her?

I thought a long moment before I answered. 'Meta, Jesus promised, "I will build my church." Matthew 24:14 says the gospel will be taught to every people. Revelation 7:9 says every people will be represented round the throne. The Mandinka culture is an essential colour and shape in the stained-glass window of God's glory. The only thing I cannot tell you is when. If I were God I would want it done by now. I don't understand God. But we just have to trust him when we don't understand. Trust, and keep on obeying.'

Meta replied, 'Then what do I do in this last term?' My suggestion was, 'Stir up as much prayer as possible for the Mandinka. The Holy Spirit convicts of sin and makes hearts responsive. He works in answer to prayer.'

Prayer makes the kairos happen faster

Tunisia seemed to be missing out on the hunger for Scripture across North Africa. A special year of prayer in 1999 seemed to bring the kairos era for Tunisia as well. Patrick Johnstone and others saw the Fula as one of the key peoples of West Africa, and special prayer was made for the Fula. Today the Fula harvest has begun.

Decades ago Len and Iris Moules worked on the Tibetan border, because they couldn't get into the forbidden kingdom. Today a team leader has written that it is harvest time in Tibet.

Should there be a year of prayer for Uzbekistan, and one for Japan? Should there be one for the Wolof and one for the Mandinka? That's why we need advocates for each of these peoples!

Breaking unresponsiveness
Antonio Alkimim

From the Bible school in Brazil we took 13 students to Uruguay for cross-cultural mission. We did three special campaigns in the three major cities. In the first two cities we evangelised we had no problem with rejection or spiritual warfare. We had 70 decisions in one and 60 in the other, and we left people there to disciple the new believers. However, we faced difficult challenges when we came to Montevideo. We tried to get permission to put up our tent, but the mayor refused our request. We tried to evangelise door to door but the response was negative. It was raining. It was difficult to testify. It was a battle. Some students were really discouraged and wanted to give up. Team members were disagreeing, almost fighting. We organised a counselling room, and I was there almost all day talking with team members. For three days I too was discouraged. I was aware that, when challenged, a person can be afraid and lose their authority. We need to be certain of our authority (Luke 10:19).

One night, as two of us were praying, for about 30 seconds I felt some strange force trying to strangle me. I almost jumped out of the window to get air. At first I did not understand what was happening, but then I claimed the protection of the Lord. Another team member saw a vision of a strange creature high up, with the head of a crocodile and a long tail which he wound round my colleague's head to shut him up. My colleague called me to help him. He felt in his spirit that the Lord was saying, 'Call on the name of Jesus.' He said in his spirit, 'Jesus, help me.' The thing that was oppressing him unwound and left him, and went right through the wall into the next room where the girls were sleeping.

The girls said, 'The same thing happened to us.' The creature said, 'All this city is mine. I control things here. Have you felt the rejection of people? That rejection is mine. I control this place. Go away.' Some felt we should leave and return to Brazil. Montevideo was the last location anyway. The other members said, 'No way. If we obey the devil this time we will never hold our heads up again. If we run with our tail between our legs, we will never have authority again.'

On Monday, our day of rest, we were browsing round the city shops. We discovered a shop selling witchcraft material, and our attention was directed to one corner of the shop. We saw the same thing that we had seen in our vision. It was red, with the crocodile's head and tail. The Lord revealed to us that that thing was prince of that town.

We decided to fast and pray three days to change this situation. The third day we praised God, and went to the streets. The rain stopped. The air was clear. We asked permission from the mayor to erect our tent, and he gave it. A neighbour allowed us to use his location at no charge. We cleansed that place, and erected our tent for evangelism. People were responsive when we visited door to door, and in streets and squares. At the first meeting 18 people gave their lives to Jesus, and more on the following days. We felt the Lord blessing. The spirit of God was really moving. Kids, mothers and fathers went home singing the songs that we taught at the meeting. Our house was near the meeting tent. Young people came flowing into our house to talk with us about the things of the Lord and to ask questions. Every day after the meeting our house was full of people, specially young people, often till one or two o'clock in the morning. Sometimes we had to ask them to go and return next day, to give us some hours to sleep. The boys taught them songs. We spent a whole week like that.

The fights between us disappeared. Some of our equipment in the tent was stolen, so we took turns sleeping in the tent to guard it. Even the gangs came to the meetings. There were 89 decisions that week. When we finished, we packed up to go home with sad hearts because we had to leave while the Lord was moving. About nine in the morning, as we were planning to leave, 70 or 80 people came from everywhere with signs and banners to say farewell: 'God bless you, brothers and sisters. Come back again.' They were singing our songs. The Catholic people thought it was a Protestant procession. They all came into the bus station, hugging and crying and kissing us farewell, a normal farewell custom for them. I had a lump in my throat, trying to hold back my tears.

A tiny church or two in France
Matt and Margaret Paton
Le Puy

We were asked to open the town of Le Puy for a regular gospel witness. A hall had been transformed into a simple church. The opposition we received seemed out of all proportion to the insignificant church and our even more insignificant family.

We had a visit from a woman who said she was a Christian but who had some strange, threatening prophecies for us. All the Catholic churches in town warned their flocks not to have anything to do with us. Our oldest boy, five years old, was walking along a wall alone, and fell off. He said he was pushed! We rushed him to hospital.

We took a day to pray, praise, and proclaim victory over the whole area. The day began with very little sense of victory, but as the hours passed we knew we were experiencing the retreat of the enemy. In some unaccountable way, we knew we were in charge. Over the next three years the name of the Lord was glorified, and people were born again. One convert was an ex-nun who had been released from the convent to care for her old mother. This nun had very poor eyesight. One day after a very simple prayer, she was healed and saw well.

Today a church worships in that town with its own French pastor, spreading God's love.

Roubaix

A nationally-known fortune teller was coming to Roubaix. He had a programme on the most popular radio station in France, and travelled from theatre to theatre, town to town. Some Christians decided to come against this evil in the name of Jesus, praying together before the show. A few of them distributed tracts to warn people of the danger as they went in. Others stayed in a car nearby to pray. What an encouragement the next day to read in the newspaper that the evening had not been a success. The fortune teller admitted he had lost his power that night.

They try but don't know how
Traugott Böker

I went to the island of Nias for four weeks of evangelism. It is an animistic area. We had numerous sessions of personal counselling. Of them all, there was only one counselling appointment in which occultism played no role, in which there was no contact with the unseen evil world.

Sometimes in Indonesia Muslims are converted and take Jesus as their Saviour, but make no progress in faith and show no keenness to evangelise. They are Christians in name only. When sick, they go to someone who speaks a spell rather than to a pastor who could pray for healing. Some fall back again into Islam, perhaps because they marry a Muslim partner. The call of the minaret has pulling power. Mr Wagiono, an ex-Muslim now serving Jesus, says, 'The call of the minaret was like music for me.'

The world of demons constantly surrounds the non-Christian people. They know it. They try to fight against it, but they don't know how. Some try to cast out one demon through another, which only makes things worse. Physical healing may produce spiritual sickness. As missionaries we must know the wiles of the devil, and how we may help free those who are still bound. One of them said, 'It is as if we were rowing in a boat but we forgot to untie the rope holding the boat to the jetty.'

Breakthrough – and yet not quite
Colin Bearup

People we were witnessing to and praying for were accepting the Lord in a place where years of labour had produced almost no fruit. A breakthrough – and yet not quite. We found again and again that while we saw evidence of the Lord touching the lives of these individuals, and while they said they believed all the right things, they did not flourish. Their appetite for teaching was modest, their prayer lives never got going and they would not witness to others. Above all, we were frustrated at their aversion to fellowship. Each one would accept contact from the person who had witnessed to him, but did not want to meet any other believers. You can't build a fellowship with people who reject the idea of meeting together. We had just one man who wanted fellowship.

One day I prayer-walked right around the perimeter of the town. At one point, out on the southern edge, I suddenly felt different. The atmosphere felt lighter. I shrugged it off and carried on. A few days later I was talking to a senior worker who said how she had been on a trip out of town and had felt the difference as she had gone past the edge of the town. When she had looked back, she had the impression of a huge dark cloud over the town. That reminded me of my experience, and we started sharing other experiences and insights. We started seeking the Lord to see how the spiritual atmosphere of the town could be changed.

We read all the books we could find that seemed remotely relevant and passed them around the team. We researched the history of the town and prepared to set aside extra time as a team to pray for a break in the spiritual darkness.

The area had been a kingdom founded and united by Islam and enriched by slaving. Despite the Islamic foundation, some pagan practises remained central. For example, at the enthronement of each king, the community would gather at a particular site on a mountain. There the new king would enter a hut to meet the ancestor spirit, which appeared as a large snake. Having been accepted by the snake, he descended the mountain. At seven points on the route two children, one boy and one girl, would be sacrificed. They were the only children of poor parents, who were compensated with wealth. The new king had to step over the blood.

The intention of those events was that the kingdom entered or renewed a covenant with the powers of darkness. They were seeking power for their king and their kingdom. Generation after generation had performed this ritual. When the area was conquered by the colonial powers the practice was modified. Goats were substituted for children. There was, however, no clean break with the past. No repentance. The covenant had never been repudiated. For generations these people had invited in the powers of darkness and had done nothing to reverse it.

Principles/method/evidences

We met as a team and spent time in praise and worship, focusing on the Lordship of Christ and who we were in Him. As we prayed for the town, we stopped frequently to consult each other as to how we felt the Spirit was leading us. We only tackled issues when we had unity on what to pray about and how to pray. There were times when some were selected to go and pray at a particular site. When the Lord told us to pray that the walls of the mosque come down we discussed whether this was figurative or literal.

One thing we could not do was repent on behalf of the people. Repentance is a change of behaviour, and we were not in any sense part of the wrong doing we were praying about. We could, however, pray for mercy, for forgiveness, and cleansing. We also prayed for bondages to be broken or loosened. It was in some ways a nerve-racking process. In our room we wrestled with unseen darkness. Outside everything looked the same, yet we needed to maintain a unity of faith in the face of this lack of evidence.

Evidence came after a while. The town's chief imam was sacked, reinstated, and sacked again in the course of a fortnight. Scandal was coming out. Blindfolds were coming off. One item that caught our attention was the high rate of miscarriages and pregnancies requiring emergency evacuation among missionary wives. There had not been a normal birth in the area for years. We prayed against this and sought the blessing of God. Within a year we had three safe births.

A number of things started to happen that undermined the unchallenged dominance of Islam. From this time a division between the locally dominant brand of Islam and a dissident group became progressively more bitter and public. The confidence of people in their religion was seriously dented. The Islamic authorities were much more fired up about their Muslim rivals than about Christian activities. Rumours circulated saying that people from the town had become Christians in a neighbouring country. Then the Lord brought a man back from abroad who had given up on Islam. Over a period of time he became a bold Christian and is now a household name. A fellowship has grown up around him.

Two observations

Personally, I am convinced that the town is a long way from being liberated. At some point a group of local believers will have to take up where we left off. As representatives of their people, they will need to repent of and repudiate the works of darkness.

The two of us who had led this extra intercession found our prayer lives falling apart during the following year. It became really hard to pray. It is difficult to describe, but far from being gung-ho about taking on another such situation, our first reaction was reluctance. It cost us something.

Slavery

One of things we prayed about was the spiritual legacy of slavery. In a culture which has slavery in its past, we can sometimes discern ongoing consequences in attitudes and relationships, both on the part of the slavers and the enslaved. I don't know how we can establish by any objective method how or why there is a spiritual heritage, but we found ourselves led to pray along those lines. Taking and trading in slaves is about establishing control over people and the manipulation of fear. It is often reinforced by beliefs, and it could be argued that there are plenty of openings for the demonic. Whatever the theory, we found ourselves led that way and prayed for God's mercy on those that did the slaving and against the way the slaving mentality shaped the people. We also prayed for the cleansing of the site of the main slave market.

A couple of years later a black missionary couple joined us. They were living, as most of us did, in rented accommodation. One night both husband and wife had nightmare experiences. The wife said it was as though she woke up but was bound and unable to move or speak. There seemed to be a man standing over her. She was in distress for some time, but called on the Lord and it passed away. Her husband awoke and found a man standing by his bed. He saw him clearly and heard him ask, 'Why are you here? Why are you still alive?' He shared the experience with us. His description of the man matched the traditional clothing and build of the people group who had been the dominant traders in the town and had made their fortune in slaving. The house belonged to one of their descendants. So we praised the Lord, affirmed who we were in him, cleansed the house and there was no recurrence. Subsequently we found out that Africans from other regions renting other houses belonging to that family were experiencing similar visitations. I don't have a detailed explanation of the spiritual mechanics of it, but my feeling that there is a spiritual legacy received confirmation.

Perseverance in Europe
Paul Finch

Most of our warfare here in Italy has not been in the overt, visible sort of deliverance situations. Our warfare here has been more in the sort of faithful perseverance towards God. Many workers seem to be in situations which are far more mundane, monotonous, ordinary – and there is the temptation not to think of it as spiritual warfare. The natural tendency is to see it as a duty, as a spiritual calling demanding faithfulness, and to slog away rather joylessly, silently telling ourselves that the only way through is that of sad sacrifice.

Much of spiritual warfare is against sin, against unbelief, against laziness, and against Satan's subtle temptations to compromise. Our own battle here in Italy is not to lose the vision, not to think God will not deliver because he has not thus far, not to settle back for less than his full victory, however he might choose to give it. Somehow I tend to think that Job was as much involved in spiritual warfare as was the apostle Paul in Philippi.

What good fortune!
Walter Mohr

Bolat, a Kazakh, celebrated his first spiritual birthday three days ago. Just a little over a year ago, he was seriously contemplating suicide. Although only 38 years of age, he assumed that the only way out of his hopeless mess was to end it all. Life's problems were so overwhelming. Then another idea arose. 'What if my fortune is about to improve? Why not find a fortune teller? Perhaps there is hope . . .' Usually these evil spiritual guides abound in the local market. That day he could not find any. 'Could you tell me where the fortune tellers are?' he asked a lady selling sunflower seeds. 'You don't need a fortune teller. You need Jesus,' she responded firmly. God had led Bolat to a fellow Kazakh who was a converted fortune teller. Soon she was eagerly sharing the good news of Jesus who saves from sin and despair. That day Bolat met Jesus. I met him as one of thirty students soaking up all we could teach at the Central Asian Leadership Training Centre. Bolat is preparing to serve the Lord. Many of his family are now followers of Jesus. His 62 year-old father audited the classes we taught. What a blessing it was to hear the testimonies of these keen believers. The majority were Kazakh, but we also had Kirghiz, Tajik, Uzbeks, Turkmen, Russians, Koreans and a Jewess. Sometimes weariness attacked us after endless hours of teaching and answering questions, yet we were refreshed daily by God's Spirit as we witnessed how he is moving in Central Asia.

'If you want to be a Christian, leave the village!'
Jim Dawson

The message from the spirit doctor and village headman was clear. 'If you want to be a Christian, then you must leave the village!' There were several Christians in the village, and a legal attempt was being made on their behalf to prove their rights to meet as Christians. The situation was potentially explosive. A group of them decided to visit Pastor Yat of the Tak church and ask for his advice.

A rickshaw driver by trade and barely able to read and write, Yat had been endowed by God with gifts of wisdom and pastoral care, especially in the villages. After listening to the Christians' side of the story he said, 'Now let me go and listen to what the non-Christians are saying.' A few days later, I went with Yat to meet the offended party at the appointed time. That day `happened' to coincide with a day of prayer that the missionaries had set aside – and pray they did.

It was a formidable thought that I was going to meet face to face with a headman, spirit doctor and his followers who were very angry at what I hold to be precious. However, as we travelled to the village, there was no fear, rather an increasing sense of peace and faith that God was in control. There were twelve of them in the 'welcome committee' sitting in a semi-circle, and looking very grim. After venting their complaints about the village being divided and the spirits being angry, they gave their simple ultimatum again. 'If people want to become

Christians in this village, then they must leave.'

Pastor Yat had carefully noted that some of those complaints actually did deserve an apology from the Christians, and he made it clear that he would ask them to give it. He gently added, though, that there needed to be respect given on both sides as they performed their religious beliefs. Then, in reply to their insistence of all paying homage to the spirits, he launched boldly into his own testimony of when he was a spirit worshipper and also a spirit doctor. They listened intently as he spoke of the fear and slavery to spirits and of his wife's illness and possession by these spirits, and of how he and his family were eventually freed from all of that by the Greatest Spirit of all, this same God who is worshipped by some of their own people.

Finally, he read Revelation 3:20 and invited them to consider inviting this God of power and peace into their own lives. One could almost have closed the meeting in prayer, such was the atmosphere. Everyone left on good terms and another date was set to meet with the Christians again.

The second visit seemed to be mixed with victory and defeat. Some of the Christians realised their error in not attending the non-Christian funerals, and not informing the headman of their desire to show Christian films. So, an apology was given and accepted by the headman. However, the spirit doctor, who had considerable influence, called a meeting that night to insist that all the Christians move their houses to one corner of the village. The majority of people decided that to be the best compromise, but in effect it would mean dividing the village and hindering future conversions. There and then, another appeal was made to the living God against such a decision. There was also an opportunity to pray for a believer who had been sick for days and to transport her to hospital. The following day she felt so much better that she caught a bus straight back to her village.

Several days passed by and no fresh news had filtered down to us as to the outcome, so prayer against the enemy's influence there was continued and victory claimed in Jesus' Name. Then Pastor Yat was visited by a believer from the village who had been very sick and was being forced by the folk there to do a spirit ceremony. Miraculously, the spirit doctor said, 'Leave him alone. He's a Christian,' and then promptly told the man to go and seek God in Tak and seek healing from him! So, he went to see Pastor Yat, who prayed for him, took him to the hospital and the next day he went home completely well.

This same believer said that there had been no shifting of houses, and that most of the folk there were interested in the gospel, and were waiting for the old spirit doctor to die so the whole village could become Christian! Yat and all those who had interceded during this spiritual battle were overjoyed at this victory that God had achieved.

Anything to stop a church from being born
Jim Dawson

In May 1989, two small groups of Thai believers were meeting about two kilometres apart. One group of four which met near the town of Wangjow, had been in existence for about 15 years, led by two keen Christians. The other group had five believers with spiritual life and depth. Some other scattered believers from around the villages used to come in occasionally.

A leader called Bluang had been involved with all sorts of cults, and over the years had split several village groups. But this year Bluang had held an evangelistic campaign in Wangjow, and 8-10 people had been healed, converted and baptized – all within a couple of weeks.

These new believers began meeting in town and there was much excitement and fervour. Bluang once again put his foot in it by mishandling church funds and was promptly cast out. One or two went with him and they began to meet in Wangjow market. However, the two halves began to meet together at each other's venues, and then began to discuss how they could merge on a permanent basis. The suggestion was to meet near the town where transport is convenient. They decided to meet at the local Wangjow school which they have free of rent. Numbers average around 10-12 people a week.

The believers and a couple of missionaries met together for spiritual warfare at the main spirit shrine in Wangjow. They prayed for the binding of this spirit's hold over people's lives, and then travelled up to a hilltop and prayed for the releasing of souls for Christ in Wangjow according to Matthew 16:19: 'I will give you the keys of the kingdom of heaven; whatever you bind on earth will be bound in heaven, and whatever you loose on earth will be loosed in heaven.' The following year was harvest time with 18 people being added to the church. A regular prayer meeting along this vein was now started, attended by most of the folk living near the town. The missionaries likewise prayed each week for the Wangjow area.

The Combined Churches' Annual Youth Camp was held at a high school only five kilometres south of Wangjow. It was a terrible site and required two full days of cleaning and rewiring the lights. However, there was a good spiritual atmosphere and a good speaker, and many young people made first time commitments and rededications to Christ. Included in these were some young people from Wangjow. A church intern began to meet with them on Saturday once a fortnight. The nucleus of a church youth group was beginning to take shape.

There had been quite a few conversions during this time amongst some older folk as well, through two church members who had developed a gift of evangelism. In one month Wangjow had six baptisms. There were many contacts to follow up and numbers began to increase on Sunday mornings. The believers began talking about buying their own land and building their own sanctuary. The total number of believers in the Wangjow area now numbered close to 30, with about 15-17 meeting each week. Some of the believers were scattered far and wide, and others were old or crippled so could not attend. Nevertheless God was at work in Wangjow and the believers were excited. So was I.

Just when the numbers were increasing and the church was becoming excited about being together, the enemy struck another tragic blow to the Wangjow church. Two young couples eloped! Some of these young people had just become Christians at the camp. Normally, this kind of eloping can be settled by the parents concerned, but when money, greed and pride take over, then it gets very messy.

The situation was eventually handled by the police.

As the number of believers slowly began to increase, so did their desire and vision to buy land for a church building. They began saving and praying. Several options were considered, but each had its own particular problem. Finally, one Christian offered to sell her land very cheaply to get out of debt. It was ideally located on the main road and only a few hundred metres from the main market in the town. The money came from varied sources, about half from the believers themselves.

The next big step of faith was a church building. The Lord answered prayer again through a local believer, an isolated farmer. He wanted to move to his wife's home area, so he offered to sell his house to the church for a bargain price. The believers hired a ten-wheeled truck and within a day had dismantled the house, loaded it on the truck and transported it to the new church site.

Work then began on extending and erecting the pillars to make it a two-storey building. The upstairs could be used for accommodation in the future, while the downstairs could be used as a meeting place. The believers made a concerted effort to pour the downstairs floor before Christmas. It was a great occasion as 60 people gathered to celebrate Christmas together, 35 of them from Wangjow and some more from the parent church.

It had been a year since the young people eloped, and ever since then one member had not come to church. The believers had especially invited her for this Christmas, but she declined and remained in her unforgiving and embittered state. The police eventually caught one couple. He was put in prison with a 15 year sentence. He has since become a Christian in prison.

It's an allegiance issue
Jonathan Hacker

Barth, my African co-worker, and I were 50km from the town of Vavoua, out in the bush in rural Côte d'Ivoire. The villagers said that no one had really explained to them about Jesus before. So we sat under a mango tree and talked about the power of the gospel to free those who are held prisoner by animistic beliefs. A group of youths stayed to listen more. Some accepted copies of one of the gospels in French.

After a meal we decided it was time to leave, but the villagers wanted us to pray for Frank, a young epileptic boy before we left. Can you imagine how we felt as we stood in the middle of the village, surrounded by people, all watching us? There was no escaping behind trite religious phrases. We had said that Jesus was more powerful than their fetishes. Now they expected us to prove it!

We gently laid our hands on the boy and prayed for his healing. Then we left. Had anything happened? Was our message still credible? We returned to the village a few weeks later. A lady had become a Christian since our previous visit, and wanted us to explain more of the good news. She told us, 'That little boy has not had an epileptic fit since you prayed for him'. I almost cried for joy.

Some months later we revisited the village to show the JESUS film. We were well received and made visits to several courtyards in the village before setting up the TV, video, sound and lighting equipment. Everything functioned perfectly. The stars shone. A large proportion of the village (200-300 people) turned out to watch the JESUS film in Gouro, their mother tongue. Afterwards we showed 'Le Combat'. Nearly everyone stayed to see the second film, and a few stayed to talk afterwards. I didn't get a great deal of sleep that night! On Sunday morning we held a service. About 15 new people came, mainly young people. We prayed for them and encouraged them to commit their lives to following Jesus.

A backslidden Christian asked us to pray for him. He wanted to destroy his fetishes and rededicate his life to Jesus. It was a privilege to take part in this service of bondage breaking.

I was saddened and somewhat confused to learn that Frank, the little boy for whom we prayed during our first visit, had begun to experience epileptic-like fits again. He had been free from these fits for several weeks after we prayed for him. What had gone wrong? Had we let God down? We found Frank and were encouraged to see his much improved demeanour – he was all smiles. He came to the service on Sunday and expressed his desire to trust in Jesus. When we spoke to his widowed mother we challenged her to choose to commit her life (and the lives of her two children) to Jesus, rather than to animistic practices. Then we discovered the problem. It would seem that she has reverted to trusting in fetishes and traditional remedies. We prayed for Frank again. But if his mother does not renounce fetishes, charms and sacrifices, he can be re-infested.

Abina refuses genital mutilation
John Bardsley

Abina was the first educated woman among the Kaan people of Burkina Faso. After her higher education in the capital, she returned to her home village as a believer. The grandmothers approached her: 'Abina, you have not submitted to the tribal custom of female circumcision. You must do this, or the spirits will be angry.' 'Sorry, I cannot submit to this. The government has forbidden it. It is against the law. It is medically dangerous because your knives are not sterile. It causes difficulties in childbirth. Spiritually, it belongs to your old tribal religion, but I am a Christian and I cannot do those things any more.'

In the tiny church she found a believing young man, and they became engaged to be married. The grandmothers approached her again: 'Abina, you must be cut before your wedding, or the spirits will be angry.' It was difficult for this young woman to show respect for her elders and at the same time refuse, but that is what she did.

The wedding day came, and Abina was the first Kaan girl ever to be married genitally intact. The grandmothers came to her: 'You must be cut before there is a baby'. She said, 'No.' When they saw she was pregnant, they became very disturbed. 'You must be cut before the baby is born, or the baby will die.' She refused. They went away with the witch doctor and cursed her and the baby.

WEC and Wycliffe both had workers in the area, so messages came back to both missions to pray with her and her husband. We all prayed. The baby died! I was shocked. If I had been God, I would not have let it happen. How can the success of a curse bring glory to God? Then the grandmothers approached Abina again. 'Now will you submit to being cut?' What would you have said? She said, 'No.' It was just like the three Hebrews threatened with being thrown in the furnace if they did not bow down to the idol. They said, 'Our God is able to deliver us. But if not, we will not bow down.' We knew, the Wycliffe workers knew, and Abina knew that God can deliver. If he chooses not to, that is his concern. Job said, 'Though he kill me, I will trust him.'

Then Abina fell pregnant again. Again the grandmothers came with persuasion and threats. 'If you are not cut, the baby will die.' She refused. The second baby died. Admittedly there was an epidemic of typhoid fever at the time, and lots of babies were dying. All the same, I was smashed, utterly smashed. 'Oh God, glorify your name! Uphold your honour! Defend your people! Awake! Awake, O arm of the Lord! Was it not you who pierced the dragon through?' The grandmothers came again. 'Now will you submit to mutilation?' 'I will not.'

Abina and her husband became pastors of that tiny church. She is not cut, and they now have two healthy children. The Lord has defended his name. Why did the Almighty allow the first two apparent defeats? Was there insufficient prayer? Did we all need a lesson in fasting? Did Abina and her husband need to have this experience in order to counsel other couples facing fearsome grandmothers with the powers of witchcraft behind them? All of the above? I don't know. Maybe I will never know this side of heaven. I used to tell this story twice a year to each new intake of candidates hoping to join WEC. It is a sobering story, but we can proclaim the glory of the conqueror.

The snake, the fear, and the name
Ken and Cecily Booth
Hayat was a teenager from the Rawat clan of the Johari Bhotiya people who live in the Mansiari valley of the Gori Ganga River in the State of Uttar Pradesh, north India, in the Himalayas. He belonged to the warrior caste, the second highest group in the local Hindu community. The Johari Bhotiyas are of mixed Tibetan and Rajput stock, and are traders between Tibet and India. Much of their lifestyle is Tibetan.

As a new believer Hayat shared with me most mornings in worship, Bible study and prayer. He was our house help and cook in the Bhotiya village of Tiksen, located at the southern end of the valley at around 2,700 metres above sea level.

All around us was living evidence of spirit worship mixed together with Hindu philosophy. Sacred stones and miniature shrines were located under certain trees in auspicious places. Food offerings and libations were regularly put in and around these objects. On special evenings folk would gather round fires and be 'entertained' by the coming of spirits on local mediums. There was fascination and terrible fear as the spirit world was approached in this way, with requests for help and answers to the many unanswered phenomena of daily life, whether personal, family, or social.

Hayat and I had been studying the written statements of Matthew and Mark concerning personal experiences in following Jesus Christ. Over and over again we read of the revelation of the power and authority of Jesus over the unclean spirits, and how the spirits recognised Jesus as the Son of God and knew of his final judgement on them. We saw how the disciples had gone into the villages under the authority of Christ's direction and power. They had come back saying even the unclean spirits were subject to them in the name of Jesus Christ of Nazareth.

One morning Hayat came from his home in the valley, his face shining, his eyes bright and sparkling. Obviously there was something special which he had experienced and I was eager for him to share it.

He had had a dream that night in which he was walking past a small shrine at a shady spot on the path near the creek just north of our village. This was a place of terror for all the people and no less for Hayat. This time too he was terrified. Suddenly a big snake came from the shrine and wrapped itself around his legs. It wound itself round his body until it started to choke him. Hayat, almost unable to speak, remembered the word of God, the authority of Jesus and the power in his name. In a shrill voice he yelled out, 'Stop in the name of Jesus Christ!' In his vivid dream, the snake stopped choking him, dropped to the ground at his feet and shrivelled to the size of a worm which Hayat was able to squash under his foot!

So this morning Hayat had actually walked past this special place without fear. He'd sung a song extolling Jesus. He'd felt free in his spirit and experienced a release he had not known before.

Killer bees attack
June Whittaker

Ronaldo and Rosanna returned to Ghana for the dedication of the Konkomba-Limonkpeln New Testament which they had translated. They were travelling from Kpassa into Koni in a four-wheel drive pickup driven by Nkrumah, with his wife Grace and their two small children. On the way, the vehicle became stuck in the mud. Ronaldo and Nkrumah got out to see what they could do when suddenly great clouds of bees descended on them. They ran into the bush with the bees chasing after them. Ronaldo said he would run a little way and then stop but the bees kept coming after him. After he had run some way, he began to worry about Rosanna and Grace with the baby and small child as he feared that maybe some of the bees could have entered the vehicle even if there was just a small gap in the window. As he ran back to the pick-up he fell down three times and each time the bees came down on him and started stinging him on his head, face and arms. In fact, there had been some bees in the pick-up but Grace, Rosanna and the small child had quickly killed them.

When Ronaldo got to the pick-up, he had no choice but to jump in and slam the door bringing more bees in with him. So they all had to set to and kill the bees again. Then Ronaldo began to feel that his finger tips had gone cold and his heartbeat had become very irregular. His hands and arms were also beginning to swell. Rosanna tried to reassure him that this was just an allergic reaction and he would be OK. All the time Grace was praying, calling on the name of Jesus.

Nkrumah returned with a message from an old fetish man from a nearby village that if Ronaldo would send the money for a bottle of schnapps, he would pour a libation to his fetish to stop the attack. But Ronaldo sent back the message that it was OK, they didn't need that, they would pray to Jesus. However, Ronaldo's reaction was becoming more severe and his heart started missing beats and stopping for long periods before it would start again. He was sure that he was going to die and the feeling was so awful that he was beginning to wish it would soon be over. He was giving his final words to convey his love to his children. Then his eyes started rolling back and he started to salivate and go into convulsions.

Rosanna, a nurse, realised that they needed to get Ronaldo into some water to stop any further reaction. Nkrumah saw this, took over helping Ronaldo and called to Rosanna, 'Mama, run to save your life!' They were able to get Ronaldo to a pool of water and use it to bathe his head and arms and remove some of the stings. By this time he had passed out completely.

Thankfully, the staff at the clinic were expecting them to come at a certain time and when they did not arrive came to look for them. One of the clinic workers came on a motorbike and was able to carry Ronaldo on the bike back to the clinic to treat him. They had to cut off his ring because his fingers had swollen so much. When Ronaldo came round he was in a room in the clinic surrounded by women looking down at him. He was not sure whether he had died and gone to heaven! Treatment with antihistamines brought down the reaction. When he showered later, he said that many stings came out of his hair. Altogether, they counted over a hundred stings that came out. It was a real miracle that he survived and that two days later he was even able to stand up in church to preach on the Sunday morning!

They discovered that the old man who had offered to pour a libation had called on the fetish to summon the bees. But it seems that he could not control the swarm, so the bees had actually been attacking his village before homing in on the car and Ronaldo. They recalled that the car was black with the bees crawling all over it, and there were black clouds of bees in the sky above. Nobody had ever seen anything like it! It was especially unusual as they say that bees don't like diesel fumes and would normally stay away from a diesel-fuelled vehicle. As the old fetish man was trying to see what was going on, the bees came and attacked him and stung him all over his body.

The old man said that it had not been his intention for the bees to attack Ronaldo. He knew that Ronaldo was a good man who had helped the community by building the clinic. He had summoned the bees to go and attack three of his enemies. Clearly, it had gone wrong, which just shows the folly of thinking that a person has power to manipulate the spirit world. Clearly Satan had other intentions! The old man was swollen from the stings all over his body and face. Then Ronaldo realised how good God had been to him because Ronaldo's face did not swell at all. The old man was in a very bad way, but he did pull through.

Ronaldo has had several flashbacks and bad dreams and for a while felt dizzy if he stood too long. Remarkably, Rosanna sustained only three stings.

The dedication of the Konkomba-Limonkpeln New Testament went very well, in spite of the drama en route. The programme was well organised and well attended. There was great jubilation when the Bibles were unveiled and both the men and the women had to do their traditional circle dances around them before the proceedings could continue. The first five copies were auctioned and then there was a great rush as everyone was very eager to get their hands on the books. All 200 copies were sold out in a very short space of time and people were still asking for them. Another batch came up from Accra later, and then the main bulk was distributed to all of the 48 main places, including 16 in neighbouring Togo, where Limonkpeln is spoken.

Put to sleep
Bruce Rattray
A man who used to be the leader of the meeting had backslidden. He must have become demonised. Although he still came to the meeting I could tell he was very dark. Every night he would clap his hands and sing the songs, but the moment I started preaching he would go sound asleep. As soon as I said Amen he would wake up again. I put up with this for a couple of nights, but the night came when I thought it had gone on long enough. I started to preach, and sure enough he went off to sleep. I stopped and said, 'Let's pray.' Everyone bowed their heads. 'In the Name of the Lord Jesus Christ I command the spirit of sleep to leave this place immediately!' The man jumped up as though he'd had a pin stuck in him! He hung on to every word and when I gave an invitation he responded. I don't know how he went on spiritually, but the proof of the demonic power being broken was dramatic.

Spiritual scud missile
John Bardsley
The president of the WEC churches in Côte d'Ivoire was sitting in his office one day when a witch walked in. He knew who she was as she led a coven that had caused him a lot of trouble. 'What do you want here?' he asked. She said, 'I want to become a Christian'. He was a trifle suspicious. 'Why?' In reply she asked him some questions. 'Do you have indigestion?' 'Yes, I do. I have serious, long-term indigestion, troublesome enough to ask my brothers in the West to pray for me.' 'I thought so. We cursed you with that.' Then she listed other symptoms they had cursed him with as well. 'But last week,' she went on, 'we decided to kill you outright. We prepared our most powerful curse. We watched as it visibly left our building, rose into the sky, and came down onto your roof. Then fire came out of your roof and destroyed it!' ('Spiritual scud missiles!' I thought to myself.)

'That was our most powerful weapon of all! Your power is stronger! I don't want to belong to the second greatest power. I want to belong to the greatest.' She had no idea at that time how differently the two kingdoms are structured, and how differently power is distributed and used. Satan seems to give actual power in increasing amounts to create a hierarchy of evil, in which minor demons fear and serve major ones. In the kingdom of God, God is the only one with power. We are given authority to use it to the extent that we are submitted to him, and tuned in to hear his will.

We pull down what opposes God
Jean Forbes

My local pastor in Kent UK was contacted by the minister of a church in a place called Beltinge, near Herne Bay. The numbers attending the church were falling and there was a feeling of deadness about. We went together for a spiritual warfare evening for this church.

Near this church was a hill with a water tower. In the Spirit we saw a huge enemy warrior guarding the water tower. We felt that water represented the Holy Spirit, or the water of life. As we pulled down that warrior in the Spirit he crumpled, and it seemed he was only made of silver baking foil – just a ploy to deceive. We prayed the Holy Spirit over the area and new life to all the local churches. Within weeks the church which had requested our warfare was seeing new people attending.

In the Thanet area that our fellowship covered in prayer, there was a country road with a bad camber which, together with speed, caused many accidents and deaths. As we prayed, we felt there was a spirit of death and destruction over this area. We walked this road rebuking the spirit and bringing in a spirit of life and attentiveness and all that was the opposite of destruction. The road accidents on this road dropped dramatically over the next year.

In this part of south-east England, there are high cliffs overlooking the sea. At one particular spot seventeen suicides had occurred during one year. We went there to pray against such death and destruction and to pray the opposite – life and hope – into that place. During the following year the Samaritans started up and there were only three suicides that year. The Samaritans claimed credit for the lower suicide rate, and so did we, as the Lord uses all methods to accomplish answers to our prayers.

Psalm warfare in the Buddhist world
John Oswald

John Oswald has conducted a survey across the Tibetan Plateau, interviewing many people, including Tibetan Christians. He examined the animistic underlay of Tibetan Buddhism and sought advice from the Psalms about what Christians can do about this enigma. This is his experience.

A few years ago, in the cold, early weeks of February, I was heading for Repkong on a dusty road in north-west China. Several questions had brought me here with my notebook. Every summer, the Tibetans of Repkong assemble for a festival. I met a believer who had attended it recently and I had read some research notes about it. A central focus of the festival is a trance-medium ritual in which a chosen man becomes demonized. This trance is induced by incantations and the beating of a drum and climaxes when the man's eyes roll back, his voice becomes high-pitched and the spirit speaks auspicious words through him. My believer friend had witnessed this bizarre spectacle and as he watched, he prayed to Jesus that this demon would not take possession of this man. After much effort, the man was still not able to induce the trance but succeeded on a second attempt. I wanted to find out more.

We were introduced to four monks of the Yellow Hat Gelukpa sect who sat reciting Buddhist scriptures for the merit of the householder. Crispy, fried dough sticks called khapsey and butter-tea were offered round, while we enquired of the maroon-robed monks about Repkong's oracle festival. They made it plain that while this ritual did not represent orthodox Buddhism, it was 'beneficial' for the community. It was the regional god Nyenchen who was invoked, they said, and we could visit his shrine a few minutes' walk away. This was a striking sight – two simple shrines side by side: on the right the 'god-house' for statues of Nyenchen, his wife and son, and on the left a more orthodox Buddhist shrine with a statue of Padma Sambhava, the Indian tantric master credited with successfully introducing Buddhism into Tibet by 'converting' Tibet's pre-Buddhist gods to Buddhism. Thanks to him, this regional god Nyenchen still seems to exert a fearful power over the inhabitants of that area.

My quest
Faced with such occult practices, I began to research more about the Tibetan spirit-world and dig into the Bible for the answer to two questions, 'Are there territorial spirits?' and 'If there are, what can we do about them?' How can we cut through the power of regional gods like Nyenchen?

Talk about 'territorial spirits' can rely more on exciting anecdotes than satisfying biblical interpretation. Nonetheless, it points to a reality which is almost tangible among the Tibetans, namely, that there is an anti-God spirit-world keeping Tibetan communities in their grip. The battle for their salvation and spiritual freedom in Christ is real.

Dirty tricks
It is clear there is a battle raging around all those who minister to Tibetans. Some find that weaknesses, old and new, suddenly flare up – depression, anger, sickness, accidents and relationship problems. Not a few report increased sexual temptations in Tibetan areas. (There is widespread promiscuity among Tibetans and Tibetan Buddhism is blatant in its sexual imagery.) Some relate how video or tape equipment mysteriously fails to work just before a key presentation, such as the JESUS film. Some find the responsiveness of non-Tibetans more satisfying and turn from Tibetan ministry to more receptive audiences. Who can blame them? The work is tough. True, these 'battle scars' can be symptoms of culture shock, stress or ministry burn-out, but sometimes circumstances point to more sinister forces at work.

The repellent attraction of Buddhism
Tibetan Buddhism is a strange phenomenon. On the one hand is its friendly, philosophical side, its talk of compassion, peace and harmony. Buddhism seems to offer the post-modern age an adaptable, 'politically correct' spirituality. Tibetans speak in hushed homage of the Dalai Lama and the West adores him.

On the other hand, visitors to Tibetan monasteries often experience a shocking bombardment of their senses. They encounter hideous images of copulating or skull-crushing deities, the stench of butter lamps, the raucous and intrusive soundscape of the monastic band, and all of this shrouded in a claustrophobic darkness, for lack of sufficient daylight. As part of tantric practice, human skulls are used in the construction of some damaru ritual drums, and human thigh bones for some kangling trumpets.

In this spiritual atmosphere, some workers become fearful of Buddhism. They shy away from exposure to its rituals, shrines and teachings. This can hinder them from acquiring an adequate first-hand understanding of the worldview of the people they have come to reach. Fear should preferably be dealt with before embarking on Tibetan Buddhist ministry.

Others are so keen to 'bond' with Tibetans that they are in danger of adopting Buddhist thinking or practice. One lady hired a room adjacent to Tibetan monks who chanted a lot. To her horror, one night she awoke to find herself also chanting Buddhist mantras. Another worker asked his Tibetan friends about Buddhist teaching on 'non-attachment' so that he could free himself from distracting thoughts. This would necessitate a complete imbibing of Buddhist teachings and meditation. I heard of one young woman who set out to reach Tibetans for Christ – and six months later converted to Buddhism. These are some of the spiritual realities of the Tibetan world.

There is a middle way
Is there a way to minister effectively to Tibetans, without being drawn either into the marsh of fear or the tentacles of compromise? Resoundingly, YES! The Bible leads the way as ever. 'Your word is a lamp to my feet and a light for my path' (Psalm 119:105).

Worship is the way
'Love the Lord your God with all your heart and with all your soul and with all your mind and with all your strength' (Mark 12:30). This is the way of Christ – worship – a pouring out of our whole being for God. Jesus lived for the glory and worship of God the Father. The Spirit lives to glorify Jesus. The Father loves to glorify His Son Jesus. Worship abounds in the Godhead. It is beautiful to behold, and the task of the Church is to bring the nations in worship before the King of kings and Lord of lords. Not only is worship the single most important thing to do. Worship is also the best way through the testing times of ministry to Buddhists. Firstly, worship keeps our focus on Christ. Then, as we truly worship, we rediscover an energy that overcomes fear, the enabling of the Holy Spirit (2 Timothy 1.7).

Psalms 95-97
The psalms may appear to be a strange source of instruction about spiritual warfare, but the writers of Psalms 95-97 knew what it was to worship when they were surrounded on every side by the unfettered worship of false gods. They give us vital insights into the type of praise warfare that the Holy Spirit led them into. Their essential message is 'The Lord Reigns!'

Intercessors could do no better than pray that workers among Buddhists and the new Christians will be able to maintain a high worship life. Is this not why the apostle Paul prays for the Ephesian Christians' inner life with God (Ephesians 1:17, 3:16) when they were surrounded by worship of the false goddess, Diana, the most prominent deity of the whole Ephesus region?

No other rival
The type of false worship depicted in Psalm 95:3-5 is remarkably like the animistic underlay of Tibetan Buddhism. Like the Canaanite primal religionists, ordinary Tibetans fear the spirits of the land, the waters, and the mountain peaks. For the Psalmists, by contrast, Yahweh is not limited to localities. He is the Creator of all these features!

1) The earth and waters
Tibetans call the spirits of the earth 'land owners' (sapdak), who jealously guard the earth. Before the 1950s, Tibetans did not mine the earth or lay surfaced roads to avoid upsetting such spirits. Another class of spirits rule the rivers and springs, one reason Tibetans regard catching fish as sinful. These water spirits hate their 'property' to be plundered. Other spirits are viewed as guarding certain 'territories' – a region, a city, a household, the hearth. Some of these spirit-protectors have very prominent names, such as Palden Lhamo, the protector goddess of Lhasa, Tibet's capital.

For Tibetan Christians to find true freedom in Jesus, it is vital that such spiritual ties are severed in Jesus' name. One fierce and greedy spirit, Shukden, is revered and feared by various groupings of Tibetans. He is noted for his insatiable appetite for money. A young Tibetan, Geoff, was released by his father from filial obligations to worship Shukden, their household deity. He was told it was better not to start worshipping him because the misfortunes Shukden imposes on his devotees for incorrect rituals are not worth the cost and effort (e.g. sickness, death, economic hardship). Some time later, Geoff came into contact with a group of Christians, who found him unusually free from the spiritual baggage which many Tibetan enquirers seem to carry.

2) The mountains
Fighting for their lives against the cruel elements, the idea of mountain gods come easily to Tibetans. Every craggy pass of the Tibetan plateau is marked by a lhabtse, a cairn of stones said to represent the spirit's dwelling. Tibet's mountain gods (tsen) go back to pre-Buddhist days and were connected to the local chiefs. Spiritual domination and human rulership were inextricably linked. A common title for kings was tsenpo (from tsen). Some kings took the name tsen, such as the famous Songtsen Gampo. There are many mountain gods, such as Repkong's Nyenchen, Golok's Machen Pomra, and Mt. Everest's twelve goddesses. Most revered of all is Mount Kailash in Western Tibet, the 'centre of the universe' in Buddhist cosmology.

What Does The Bible Say About These Tibetan Gods?
1) The gods of the nations are 'idols'
Psalm 96:5 states that all such gods are 'idols'. The Hebrew word (elilim) implies that these gods are 'as nothing'. Paul says, 'We know that an idol is nothing at all in the world and that there is no God but one' (1 Corinthians 8:4). The statue is indeed 'nothing', just a physical object made by men (Psalm 115:2-8). But is that all?

2) The gods of the nations are 'demons'
The Greek translation of Psalm 96:5 gives a different angle. It says bluntly that the gods are 'demons' (*diamonia*). In the Bible, this is the hidden reality behind idols; 'the sacrifices of pagans are offered to demons' (1 Corinthians 10:20), not simply to statues. Idolatry is not just harmless superstition.

3) Demons attach themselves to places
Jesus told his disciples that demons are restless to find an earthly abode and some clearly have territorial interests. The Bible, however, does NOT give a systematic analysis of these things. What Jesus does indicate is that His disciples have authority to overcome ALL the power of the evil one (Luke 10:19). This is sufficient, surely?

Psalm warfare
John Oswald
Psalms 95-96 show us four simple things that we can do when surrounded by false worship, using a type of 'praise warfare' which focuses on God, not the enemy. This 'Fourfold Path' of praise gives us a clear example to follow. We could perhaps call it psalm warfare!

Step One: Praise God among the nations
The process of unashamedly worshipping God from our hearts not only pleases God and gives us great delight, it can also initiate spiritual and physical victories. This is the first thing we should do.

Expelling demons from places?
What about commanding demons to leave places? This practice has raised suspicions in the minds of many Bible-believers. Driving out demons from people is a part of the normal apostolic mandate (Luke 9:1-2) and Jesus led the way in this. On the other hand, expelling demons from places is nowhere described or commanded. Jesus' approach was always to individuals afflicted by demons rather than casting demons out of geographical areas (Mark 1:21-28, 5:1-20). Demons' 'rule' over territory is dependent on their human following. Conversion radically affects the spiritual status quo!

In Ephesus, a significant number of people exchanged their occult practices for Christ (Acts 19:17-20). There was a backlash from the Diana cult, but the hold of the Ephesian gods was beginning to loosen. It was God's Holy Spirit in his people that set about this change in the spiritual climate (vv. 1-7). Writing to these Ephesian believers some time later, Paul tells them to engage in spiritual warfare by standing firm in Christ and by persistent Spirit-led prayer (Ephesians 6:10-18). It is our focus on God (rather than on the demons) that is Paul's emphasis.

Praise in the context of the nations
The Psalms also direct us to fix our gaze on God. The refrain of Psalms 94-99 is 'The Lord Reigns'. Psalm 96:10 tells us to declare this openly and explicitly 'among the nations'. The setting for these psalms is not a quiet chapel in cosy Christendom. The nations steeped in their primal religions are the backdrop against which God's ringing exaltation is repeatedly and joyfully commanded.

Abraham in Canaan
In Genesis 12 and 13, Abram worshipped God in full view of the Canaanites around him. In villages like this, building an altar could hardly be done in private. The whole neighbourhood of Shechem came along to watch! Abram was surely saying among the nations, 'The LORD reigns!' as he raised his voice to his God.

Step two: Declare that God reigns over all
In a climate dominated by Buddhism, Christian praise can also become an implicit proclamation to the 'powers and principalities' that their so-called 'territory' belongs to God alone; their rule is an illusion and their time is short. Psalm 95:3-5 says there is no crag or stream, no patch of grass or snowy peak that Yahweh did not make. He owns every bit of their supposed turf! Scriptures like Psalm 24:1 sum it up, 'The earth is the LORD's, and everything in it.' Singing or reading aloud verses like these can help intercessors to pray for workers in countries where false worship is dominant.

Abraham at Moreh
The 'great tree at Moreh' seems to have been a centre for Canaanite worship. Right on the site where animistic rituals were usually practised, Abram 'called on the Name of the LORD' (Genesis 13:4), publicly extolling Yahweh, perhaps as 'God Most High, Creator of heaven and earth' (Genesis 14:22).
There is a power in worship. Tibetans have been known to visibly soften in their interest in Christ when songs of praise to Christ are sung. Music and praise can have a transforming effect on spiritual resistance.

Step three: Command all creation to worship God
The Peoples
Gospel preaching is a primary weapon of spiritual warfare. There is a call to worship bedded into the Gospel message; those who find salvation in Christ become his worshippers. They realize that 'all the gods of the nations are idols, but the Lord made the heavens'. Their eyes are opened to the one true God (Psalm 96:4-6). The psalms invite the multi-ethnic 'families of nations' to 'ascribe to the Lord the glory due to his name' (Psalm 96:7-9). The end-objective of all

Christian mission is worship - billions of worshippers for Jesus from every tribal group on earth!

Nature
Biblical worship includes the command to all natural creation to praise God (Psalm 148). In Psalm 96:11-13, nature is directed to 'rejoice', 'be glad', 'be jubilant' and 'sing for joy' before the Lord. Psalm 98:7-9 bids the sea, the world, the rivers and the mountains to celebrate the Lord. This may just be poetic expression; who has ever seen a mountain singing? The literalist may not have seen it, but in a deeper sense the whole cosmos speaks of God's glory and praises his name.

Spirit-beings
It is no surprise when the psalms encourage the angels to make their praises heard (103:20-22, 148:1-2). Angels are the worship experts (Isaiah 6:1-4, Revelation 5:11-12). But what about demons? The summons is no different, for the proper posture of all created beings before God, rebellious fallen angels included, is prostrated in worship before the 'Great King above all gods'. Psalm 97:7 voices this thought explicitly, addressing all idol-gods to 'WORSHIP HIM', for the Lord is the Most High over all the earth and exalted far above all gods (v.9). In other words, the entire created order is to worship God and God's people may command all of it, including the gods of the nations to acknowledge Christ as Lord. This means not the statues, but the spirits (demons) behind them (1 Corinthians 10:20). In the end, Christ will bring everything under his control (Philippians 3:21) and every knee will bow to his supreme authority (Philippians 2:10-11). These are biblical 'command prayers'. In the Buddhist world this type of spiritual authority is one of our key weapons. It has 'divine power to demolish strongholds' (2 Corinthians 10:4).

Dagon before the presence of God!
We may wonder what effect worship and using such command-prayers can have on rebellious demons. The humorous story of the Philistine god Dagon falling prostrate before Israel's Ark of the Covenant illustrates some of the spiritual dynamics involved when demons are brought face to face with God's presence (1 Samuel 5:1-5). It is a power-encounter between idols and the living God. The ark of the Lord symbolized God's worship, his presence and his word. This ark was captured by the Philistines and placed in Dagon's temple. Right in the territory given to Dagon by his worshippers, the idol-god could do nothing other than bow before the Lord! There was no way that he could stay upright (vv. 3-4), unless the symbol of God's presence is taken away. The first commandment, inscribed on one of the two stone tablets inside the ark says, 'You shall have no other gods before me.' This seems to have had particular force in the pagan shrine of Dagon!

The story demonstrates two fundamental facts. Like Dagon, demonic spirits posturing behind non-Christian religions have to fall before the presence of God. Like the Philistines, people reinstate their fallen idols and remould their beliefs.

The Church is like the Ark of God

When God's people enter a Buddhist area, they bring the presence of God, rather like the ark. When they live and preach the Bible or worship the Lord, the same thing happens. Not surprisingly, demonic forces get uncomfortable. Though it may take many years, their power is gradually weakened as their devotees start to question the power and integrity of their gods. Like the Ephesians (Acts 19), the people see the power of the Holy Spirit at work and turn away from occult practices. When Christ's church is birthed in that place, the ark has truly come to take up residence! 'Dagon' must fall, for God is among them.

Step four: Worship God on location

Do Christians have to physically pray in places to effectively pray over them? The simple answer to this must be 'No'. God is able to hear us wherever we pray! We must advise against rich Christians being little more than 'tourists for Jesus'. However, prayer trips can have many positive spin-off effects.

Abraham engaged in his worship in the land God had called him to inherit and he walked the length and breadth of it (Genesis 13:17). Jesus also walked the same land proclaiming, living and demonstrating the reign (kingdom) of God. The apostles travelled to many nations to do the same. All of these announced among the nations, 'The Lord reigns.'

Many Christians have prayed around the key sites of the Tibetan world. They have sensed in their spirit a direction from God how to pray. Many have been led to sing out their praises, to stake out the land for Jesus. The ark of the Lord has been brought near! As Tibetans hear and respond to the love of God, the Dagons of Tibet will gradually crumble and fall.

Conclusion

Tibetans seem bound by forces greater than human powers can overcome. Their gods and Buddhas hold the Tibetan communities in their grip, and some of these spirits are feared by regions, clans, households, monastic orders and cities. To this degree, they are territorial. Human societies have allowed this to be so. However, from the Bible's point of view, these gods and spirits are all demons and, as such, their territorial 'rule' is both illusory and temporary. It is illusory because God is the one who created the whole universe and all of it belongs to him, not to them. It is temporary, because their only authority is derived from human sin and idolatry. When unbelievers turn in faith to Christ, the power of these spirits is diminished and at the second coming of Jesus Christ, they will be subject to judgement.

The psalms show us a four-fold way we can deal with these spirits, through worship. We might call this approach 'psalm warfare'. First, worshipping God glorifies God, releases us and can precipitate spiritual victories. We are encouraged to worship God 'among the nations'. Secondly, worship is an implicit declaration to the false gods that their 'territory' is God's. He alone is King. Thirdly, in worship we command all the created order, including angels and demons, to join with us in giving God his rightful glory. These demons should also worship HIM. Fourthly, God's people sometimes travel to the very sites of false gods in order to declare God's kingship and judgement in that place, and as the gospel advances among its people there is an inevitable shift in the spiritual balance of power.

This type of 'psalm warfare' emphasizes that spiritual warfare is not a set of techniques and formulas, but is a by-product of our love of God. It delights in the exaltation of God over all other rivals and determines not to get drawn into side-alleys but to keep the main thing as the main thing!

STOPTHINK&DISCUSS
- Discuss the concept of *kairos* in your situation.
- Write down a useful practical point from each of the stories.

13
EXPECT A POWER CLASH AND A TRUTH IMPACT

John Bardsley

I chose Romans 7, victory over sin, when I preached in a Dayak longhouse in Kalimantan. Bruce Rattray, senior missionary, told me, 'That would have been a good message back in Australia, but that is not what the Dayaks need to hear. They are not worried about sin. They are fighting unfriendly spirits. Their huge question is "Is your God stronger than the spirits I fear? If I believe in your God, could he protect me when my old gods get angry?"'

If the spirit bird called, or a snake crossed the path while a Dayak was walking to his field, he was supposed to return home. It was taboo to go to the field, for fear of bad luck. But Dayak farmers needed to go to their fields to protect them from monkeys and birds, and to weed and harvest them. One Dayak farmer confided in me, 'My neighbour is a Christian, and is not afraid of those taboos any more, so when he goes to his field, I go with him.' I suspect that man became a Christian before too long.

'Does a wooden face have the power to kill?'
Graham Chalker

Graham and Janet Chalker worked among the Baoulé people of Côte d'Ivoire. In their area were three small village churches, each with a congregation of twenty or so, but not one of these churches was growing.

One day Graham and Janet were driving into a village when they noticed an unusual number of men out on the road. People started yelling out, 'Janet, close your eyes!' She didn't see why she should, but as they turned the corner into the main street Janet saw something she shouldn't have seen.

If the villagers want to curry favour with their god, they take a sacred mask and place it on a dancer who is completely covered in an outfit of straw. As he dances through the village with supernatural strength, the village men sing and dance in adoration of their god. This is a man's show. The women all have to stay indoors. It is absolutely forbidden for any woman ever to see this mask, but if a woman does happen to see it, she will die – and this does happen.

Janet had seen the mask, and everyone knew it. One of the village elders came over to the car and said to Janet in a solemn but dispassionate way, 'Janet, you have seen the fetish of the men, which is taboo for a woman to see. The spirits will be angry, and you will die.' The man was not angry, but felt he had to tell her what he believed would happen. Graham recalls: 'Nothing could strip us of the bravado associated with being a super-spiritual missionary in the service of God

161

quite like those words did. This was no idle glib superstition. His statement was based on a reality that these people live out daily. It quite unnerved both of us.

Graham continues: 'Do you believe a wooden face has the power to kill? We do, because we believe that behind these things is the power of one who by nature is a destroyer and murderer. By prayer we took refuge in the One who disarmed all the principalities and powers (Colossians 2:13,15).

'Several weeks later we had an unexpected visit from one of the elders of that small village church. Janet was hanging washing out in the garden. When he saw Janet, he looked at her in awe. "Janet . . . you're not dead! You're not even sick!" He couldn't contain his amazement.

'We knew immediately why that church was not growing. Even the elders of the church still lived in fear of the fetish. They did not realise that Jesus has defeated the devil. We knew that we had a brilliant opportunity here to demonstrate the power of Jesus to those fearful Baoulé people. Straight away we began planning an evangelism campaign targeting this village and the two neighbouring ones, with a showing of the Jesus film, and another film called 'Le Combat' about the fight between Christ and Satan, and Christ's victory on the cross. In between films, Janet herself was to be 'Exhibit A'.

'The Christian ladies in these three villages were so excited when they saw Janet with me. It was very moving. When Janet stood up in the village that night, it was the turn of all the villagers to go goggle-eyed. "Your God is stronger than our fetish! Even the fetish of the men!" That night the sixty believers in those three small churches had another eighty people wanting to know more about this power that conquered their mask.

Praise God, it's gone!
Bruce Rattray
Yepta, an intelligent, hard-working young man, had been training to follow his father as a witch doctor. He became a Christian, and Bruce was discipling him to become a pastor. Yepta wanted everything God had for him, and one day he was learning about the filling of the Holy Spirit. As he opened himself wide for the Holy Spirit to come in and take control, suddenly he became agitated, and grabbed Bruce by the arm.

'Bruce, pray with me. Pray with me!' Then he relaxed again, saying, 'Praise God, it's gone.' It seems that a demon which had infested Yepta when he was a sorcerer's apprentice had managed to remain concealed in Yepta until that day when the glory of God was being revealed in him. The control of God was pushing into every corner of his life, and the foul spirit could not stand the glare.

Truth and power and allegiance
There is a lot of discussion as to whether this was a power encounter or a truth encounter, but I claim it is both. There was also an allegiance issue. It does not really matter which comes first. In the case of Yepta, truth came first, and as Yepta responded to the truth, that demon was revealed. For Graham and Janet, it was the power encounter that became the catalyst for the truth encounter. Expect the

power encounter to prepare people for a truth encounter, when you can explain to them who Jesus is, why he is stronger, why he died, and how they must repent and acknowledge Jesus as Lord over their lives. Teach the truth at this teachable moment. God has gained their attention.

Breaking a 200-year Buddhist chain
Patrick McElligott

Although his wife had been a Christian for eighteen years, Mr O showed no interest in his wife's faith. A gifted musician on the saxophone and clarinet, he had formed his own modern dance band and was its leader. He was very popular in the music world. He considered himself a 'self-made man'.

However, he began a battle he could not win. He had cancer. Even after major surgery it was not completely eliminated. He became so ill he was close to death, but survived one more operation.

During one of my visits to see him in hospital he confided that he was very frightened about dying. After hearing the gospel he opened his heart to Christ, confessed his sinfulness and professed faith in Christ as Saviour. His wife, daughter and brother-in-law, all Christians, wept for joy when they heard him pray. The prayers of years had been answered.

For the next seven months he was confined to hospital. Often we visited him to sing and pray. We held tiny worship services for him there in his hospital room. He grew a little stronger, and was discharged for a while, then had a relapse and died. It was not a sudden death. All the relatives had time together. I was there seeking to comfort them with the Word of God.

Before he died he made it plain that he wanted a Christian funeral. This was a big problem to his aged mother and the relatives on her side of the family. That family had been connected with the local Buddhist temple for over 200 years. To them a Christian funeral was almost unthinkable. However, his wishes were respected. So began one of the busiest weeks in our missionary lives, with the responsibility for all the Christian aspects of the funeral.

I met with the undertakers to arrange a funeral which would have no Buddhist priests, no Buddhist altar, no incense and no candles, no praying or speaking to the dead, and no idol worship. The day the body was placed in the coffin, a short ceremony of prayer and Bible reading was performed. The next day a wake was held in which testimony was given and hymns sung. On the day of the funeral itself over 300 people gathered. Each was given a printed explanation of the meaning of a Christian funeral. It taught about the grace of God, the cross, the resurrection and eternal life. Instead of burning incense and praying to the dead, each participant placed a flower in front of the coffin and spoke words of solace to the relatives. A message from the scriptures concerning the Christian hope was broadcast over loudspeakers to all those who were unable to find seats in the marquees provided. It was probably the biggest Christian funeral ever held in that part of Kyoto.

After the funeral, close friends and relatives gathered at the crematorium. Just before the coffin was committed to the flames we sang 'What a friend we have in

Jesus'. The members of his band insisting on joining in with all the Christians. It was a moving time as we said 'Goodbye' to our friend and brother in Christ, and tried to comfort his grieving wife.

The whole funeral was a triumph for the gospel. A spiritual battle against the powers of darkness had been won. A chain of 200 years of temple connection had been broken. It left us exhausted, but what a delight and privilege it was, as foreigners, to be so deeply involved on such an occasion. Will there be any fruit from among those who attended? We shall see.

'I want Christ': Ferreiro, Preta, Natalie
Hazel Wallis
Ferreiro

Ferreiro was a very important man on his island of Uno. He was old, he had completed all the ceremonies, and sat on his throne. He owned large numbers of cattle. He had also been the number one witch doctor on Uno, the one who had supervised the initiation rites for both men and women.

Ferreiro heard testimonies of Christians. He stopped speaking to the spirits for people, explaining, 'I am going to become a Christian.' One day Gene McBride, the missionary, and Pedro da Silva, the pastor, were passing the village. Pedro said to Gene, 'Let me go and greet my uncle Ferreiro.' Ferreiro was really pleased to see them. He called the whole village together. 'I am going to become a Christian.' He collected all his idols, some from the village idol house, some from the bush. 'These belong to me. I bought them and I am going to burn them. These others belong to the village. Take them. They can no longer stay in my idol house.' He burnt the lot. Everybody opposed him. They were really angry. Some people acted as if it was his funeral. His colleagues from the initiation rites asked, 'What have you done! Why have you become involved in this white man's business? You have lost all respect, you have lost your name. Aren't you going to enjoy sitting on your throne, now that you are old?'

He replied, 'What is that to me? I have enough rice in my store. What do I need with tribute paid to elders? I want Christ.' Some time later one of his friends from the initiation rites came to visit, and was surprised to see him alive and well. He said, 'Now I know your God is powerful! We did a ceremony with a white cock so that you would die. Your God has power!'

Ferreiro had a new idol house that he had not even used. He dedicated it as the very first church building. It was not long before his sons and other family members had also become Christians.

Preta

Preta said to her friend Joaquina, 'One day I will become a Christian too.' That very night Preta could not sleep. She could wait no longer. She had to accept Christ immediately. She went and woke Ferreiro. He took her to the church where Gene McBride and Michael Tarrant were sleeping. At midnight she confessed her sin and accepted Christ. They changed her name from Preta (Black) to Joia (Jewel).

It was only in the morning, when she burnt her idols, that her friend Joaquina realised what she had done. People were angry. Her husband threw her out of the house. Her family refused to give her food. All the women of the village got together and cursed her. Each age group brought a chicken and together they performed a ceremony so that she would either die or once again take her place in the forefront of the dance of the spirits. She had been a renowned dancer. Joia knew nothing of the ceremony or the curse, but Joaquina knew, and it made her afraid to become a Christian.

The ladies would look at Joia carefully and ask how she was. They were amazed that she was so well, that nothing had happened to her. A whole year passed. Joaquina saw how the Lord had protected Joia. She then had the courage to accept Christ for herself. That was when she told Joia all about the curse. Joia even worked for the women who had been responsible for the curse against her. Later they too were converted. They could see the power of God.

Natalie

Another renowned dancer was Natalie. She told us, 'My mother was already a Christian, but I was not. I used to dance with the spirits of the dead. When my mother refused to let my little sister be initiated, I took her myself, against her wishes. She was ill the whole time until the ceremony was over. I was scared and sad and guilty for my disobedience. That time, I could not dance.

'When we returned home, my sister recovered, but my leg grew inflamed. I took medicine, but it made no difference. The doctor sent me to the city so I could go to hospital for an injection every day. I stayed with Christians. Every day they explained the word of God to me. I knew God was speaking to me. One day I accepted Christ. Straight away I was healed! The swelling on my leg burst, and black stuff spilled out. I have not had any pain in that leg since.'

STOPTHINK&DISCUSS
- Can you find a biblical principle in each of these stories?
- How might a power encounter be expressed in a modern urban environment?

14
DEMONIZATION AND DELIVERANCE

Dietrich Kuhl, Traugott Böker, Stewart Dinnen, Trevor Kallmier,
Hans Rothenberger, John Bardsley

The Greek New Testament does not use the word 'possessed'. It is disappointing that such an excellent translation as the *New International Version* has used it. We would like to take seven examples where 'possessed' is clearly a mistranslation and provide a better alternative.

In Matthew 8:28 *duo daimonizomenoi* would be more accurately translated 'two demonized men', and Matthew 12:22 *daimonizomenos* would be better translated 'a demonized man'. Matthew 15:22 'suffering terribly from demon possession' is *kakos daimonizetai* meaning 'badly demonized'. In Mark 1:23 'possessed by an evil spirit' is *en pneumati akatharto* meaning simply 'with an unclean spirit'. Mark 7:25 'possessed by an evil spirit' is *autes pneuma akathartoi* which could be rendered 'with an unclean spirit'. Mark 9:17 'my son who is possessed' would be better 'my son who has' to translate *huion mou echonta*. Luke 8:27 *aner echon daimonia* is literally 'a man having demons'. If the word 'possessed' does not occur, why put it in? Use instead 'to have a demon', 'to be demonized' or 'to be under the influence of a demon'.

In our view 'possessed' is an unsuitable term because it makes no differentiation between various levels of demonization. 'To be with a demon' creates a less frightening mental picture. 'Demonised' covers the whole range of demonic influence, from oppression and obsession to possession.

Symptoms of demonization
Not all symptoms might be present or obvious. At times symptoms might be dormant. Mark 5:1-20 gives a good account of a case of heavy demonization: unusual physical strength, continuous self-injuries, schizophrenic tendencies and split personality, clairvoyant powers (the demonized man knew immediately who Jesus was), malevolent or ferocious behaviour, restlessness, demons answering when asked, the fact of transference of the demons from the person to the pigs, complete deliverance after the demons had been commanded to come out from the person.

Dr Paul Lechler, a Christian medical doctor and psychiatrist in Germany, found the first seven symptoms of the following list in all his cases of heavy demonization, a diagnosis which he established only after eliminating every other possible medical explanation.

● Double voice, i.e. the demon speaking with a different voice from that of the person concerned. It is a rare condition.

- Clairvoyance, i.e. extra-sensory perception of unknown facts without the use of the known senses. Quite common are premonitions or pre-visions of funerals or fatal accidents. This is fairly common.
- Sudden seizures, convulsions or sudden cries, sudden fits and compulsions, becoming violent, fits of rage and madness. They can easily be confused with a psychiatric condition. Paroxysms during the process of casting out demons (examples have been given by PM John in Ghana, and Rev P Takaliuang in Indonesia). In some cases demonized people fall asleep or become unconscious.
- Great bodily strength not normally available to that person. (See for example Acts 19:16.)
- Strong, at times angry, resistance to spiritual truth. There may be hatred of Jesus. The person may be completely unable to say or read the sentence, 'You are Jesus Christ, the Son of the living God.' They may feel uneasy or disturbed when you pray. They may dislike God's word, go to sleep during preaching, be unable to understand the Bible. These are all indications.
- Spells of unconsciousness, especially when people start praying or preaching. On the other hand, this may be totally innocuous and without any demonic connection if someone is overtired.
- Tormented by emotional factors: Restlessness; inexplicable and non-reactive mood swings with euphoric highs and depressive lows; inexplicable and almost panicky fear, e.g. in dark rooms, alleys or woods, inexplicable worry or anxiety. In 1 Samuel 16:14-16; 18:10 we read that King Saul was tormented in this way.
- Compulsion and compulsive actions, (see chapter 5) e.g. compulsive lying, thoughts, sexual drive, cursing, blaspheming, kleptomania, uncontrolled violent temper and frequent bursts of anger, obsessive suicidal thoughts. Obsessive or compulsive disorders can also occur in Multiple Personality Disorders (MPD) without any link to demonic influence. Repeated self-injuries can also occur, probably on the basis of compulsion and impulses rather than being stimulated by oppressive circumstances.
- Voices in the mind, murderous thoughts, continual fear of death, repeated nightmares, compulsive suicidal thoughts that are not related to a particular situation.
- Moral depravity, constant uncontrolled unclean thoughts, total lack of moral restraint (Romans 1:24-32). There is a common aspect which may be caused by a variety of circumstantial reasons. Habits that will not respond to counselling may find a complete cure after the expulsion of demons.
- Sounds, knocks and apparitions near a demonized person, hearing voices. According to Kurt Koch, this occurs only in a location where occultism has been practised actively and with a person who has mediumistic gifts present in the location.
- Constant illnesses that defy medical explanation. Constant pain unrelated to illnesses or injuries.

The first seven symptoms are normally seen only in cases of heavy demonization. The last eight symptoms are ambiguous. Don't jump to a conclusion. Discernment is necessary.

How can we differentiate between demonized and psychiatric cases?

It can be extremely difficult to differentiate between these two conditions. At times a clear and firm differentiation may be possible only with the gift of discernment of spirits (1 Corinthians 12:10). Sometimes a person might suffer both conditions. At times a diagnosis might be established only after all other options have been excluded, after other treatments have failed, or after a successful deliverance.

Look for any of the first seven symptoms.

Is there any change of personality without reason? Is it possible to link that personality change chronologically with an involvement in the occult?

Are there suicidal thoughts and actions without adequate reason, i.e. internal impulses or compulsive actions that are not reactive? Is there evidence of compulsive self-mutilation without any adequate reason?

Are there perceptions, voices or visions that don't seem to be symptoms of a mental or psychotic disorder (e.g. schizophrenia) or a result of drugs? Schizophrenia normally goes hand in hand with disorientation about reality and destruction of the personality. This is not necessarily the case in demonization, although in cases of heavy demonization the person may seem to be completely mad and disorientated about himself. In case of schizophrenia these symptoms can be influenced by medicines (Neuroleptica) whereas in case of demonization these symptoms are normally resistant to medication. It is also striking that the content of voices and visions caused by the occult are highly charged with demonic, sexual and/or self-destructive aspects.

None of the symptoms is conclusive in itself. A diagnosis can be made only after all aspects have been investigated. These criteria do not replace the gift of discernment. They are meant as additional help to avoid errors.

Unresolved conflicts such as guilt, and traumatic conflicts after child abuse and incest, may lead to a splitting of the personality, disintegration of mental life, a loss of inner freedom.

Jesus Christ has come to destroy the works of the devil (1 John 3:8). The battle has been decided. The victory is won. Liberation from subjection to the dominion of Satan requires only a return to the finished work of Christ. The Greek term *euangelion* in its secular meaning originated in the language of war, as the technical term for the announcement of victory. God wants to set the captives free. He has done everything to achieve this. It is not automatic, but it is available. It must be appropriated by faith. After deliverance, wrong behavioural patterns and habits need time for healing and a transformation process.

Possible causes of demonic influence or control

1. Deliberate disobedience

A deliberate continuation in unconfessed sin amounts to deliberate disobedience, for example an unwillingness to forgive and a persistence in bitterness (Ephesians 4:26-27; 1 Samuel 15:23). A married person who persists in an adulterous relationship, even without sexual intercourse, may open himself or herself up to deceiving spirits.

2. Unconfessed involvement in the occult

This could have been before or after conversion. It could be through Western sects and movements such as New Age, Freemasonry, Scientology or Christian Science. It could be through Eastern religions such as Hare Krishna and Yoga. It could be through any of the activities prohibited in Deuteronomy 18:10-13. It could be as a participant or as an onlooker. Transfer of demons can occur by health procedures or protective treatments that are linked to the occult, such as using a pendulum for diagnosis, or washing with water that has washed Koranic verses off a slate. What specifically is being transferred? A dependence; a foothold from where spirits have a legal right to influence a person.

Harassment may come through objects with magic power or locations infested with evil spirits. We need to make a clear distinction between the object itself and the demon behind the object that is associated with that particular object. This association may also be with a house or a certain location. Souvenirs from mission fields or tourist trips are an example. I was in Gambia browsing the market for gifts to bring home. One stall-holder offered me a juju (charm). I shocked him by the vehemence of my automatic refusal.

Divination refers to various ways of tapping secret knowledge, so would include tarot card laying, palmistry, rod and pendulum, ouija board, table lifting, automatic writing, glass movements, teacup reading, interpreting omens, astrology and consulting mediums.

Jola funerals
Sheila Kilkenny

The Jola of Senegal have the pall-bearers at a funeral stand still while the medium asks the spirits a question: 'Did someone kill you? Was it a curse?' They believe that movement backwards or forwards by the body will indicate yes or no. If they believe the person was cursed, they will ask who did it, and they have ways to interpret alleged movements by the corpse to indicate who it might be.

Magic includes various forms of tapping secret power, for healing or protection or simply because of a lust for power. It includes telekinesis and levitation, lifting the human body by demonic power, spells and curses, hypnotism, charms and amulets, witchcraft and spiritism.

3. Ethnic and cultural bondages

Culture is that unique blend of a people's beliefs, value system, language and lifestyle which identifies its members wherever they are. The Lausanne Covenant includes this warning: 'Culture must always be tested and judged by scripture. Because mankind is God's creature, some of his culture is rich in beauty and goodness. Because mankind is fallen, all of it is tainted by sin and some of it is demonic. The gospel does not presuppose the superiority of any culture over any other, but evaluates all cultures according to biblical criteria of truth and righteousness. It insists on moral absolutes in every culture. Churches have sometimes been in bondage to culture instead of to scripture. Missions have sometimes exported an alien culture.'

4. Heredity

Unresolved and unbroken ancestral involvement in the occult leads to a disposition open to the occult. A mother may dedicate her child to Satan. It may lead to a passive disposition in the form of mediumistic gifts which can be activated, reinforced or aggravated by any involvement in the occult. In Scotland they say someone is 'fey' if they are more likely to be conscious of the spirit world. Field studies show that compulsions and mediumistic gifts persist into the third and fourth generation of active shamans and occultists. Members in these family lines seem significantly more susceptible to demonic influences and involvement in the occult.

a. Evidence in Scripture for the influence of ancestors on the living

The prayers of Ezra, Nehemiah and Daniel in Ezra 9, Nehemiah 9 and Daniel 9 seem to indicate a solidarity of guilt in families. In a positive sense, see expressions like 'for David's sake' in 1 Kings 15:3-4. Other texts seem to indicate a solidarity of guilt that goes beyond the individual and covers the family and even the clan: Joshua 7 (Achan); 1 Chronicles 21:7-15; Isaiah 50:1; 65:6-7; Hosea 4:6; Amos 7:9 (against the house of Jeroboam; when God punished a king, often all male descendants were wiped out, including children); Zechariah 5:1-4.

b. Counselling experience

How can we explain cases of demonic attacks based on ancestral involvement in the occult, and mediumistic gifts in family members of the second to the fourth generation of shamans and magicians? It seems that the spiritual law of sowing and reaping plays itself out through the principle of solidarity with ancestors. In other words, my true identity is not merely 'Dieter Kuhl' but 'Dieter Kuhl son of Wilhelm Kuhl, son of Heinrich Kuhl'. There is also the possibility of the continued activity of 'familial spirits' that operate in connection with family lineage. Spirits live forever. These spirits claim a legal right to remain in the family based on the unresolved sin. They claim the right to harass the offspring of that person. This does not make the child guilty of the sins of the parents but it does give the demons a foothold from which to influence the life of the children.

5. Curses

Demonic attacks may be based on curses and magic by shamans and occult practitioners. In the case of Christians this is possible only if, for one reason or another, they have left themselves open to attack. Curses cannot afflict a person unless they deserve them (Proverbs 26:2). Curses may be deliberate (Numbers 22:6, Ecclesiastes 10:20) or may be simply hasty words (Matthew 5:22). When realised, footholds can be renounced and attacks can immediately be resisted in the name of Jesus.

6. Trauma

A terrifying experience as a child; uncontrolled mourning after loss of a loved one; fearful, stressful or abusive relationships; being the object of violence; unnatural death such as abortion or murder may all open the way to demonic influence, or to a harmful 'soul tie' which will need to be broken.

Deliverance

Self deliverance

If a Christian is conscious of some demonic influence hobbling his life, he is to cut it off under the authority of Jesus and retake all ground ceded to the enemy. To do this, he needs to discern how the enemy gained a foothold. Recognise the lie! If the entry point was wilful sin, he has to repent and confess it. If it was occult involvement, as well as confessing he needs to destroy any compromising artefacts and renounce their use, and renounce any ceremonies. If the entry point was from his ancestors or some other curse, he can renounce that. Then he can accept the pardon of Jesus, confessing his faith in Jesus as Redeemer. He can assume the authority given by Jesus to break all the chains of the enemy, repudiate him and all his works, and re-consecrate his life to Christ, asking to be filled and controlled by the Holy Spirit in exactly those areas where the devil had stolen some control.

The ministry of the church today

We have been given a mandate to proclaim and demonstrate the kingdom of God on earth: Matthew 28:18-20, Mark 16:15-18, Luke 24:46-49, John 20:21-23, Acts 1:4-8, 2 Corinthians 5:14-21. The church today has generally been good at proclamation but weak in the area of demonstrating the dynamic nature of the kingdom of light. The two need to go hand in hand. One of the main reasons many non-Christians reject the message of Christ is that the church is perceived by them to be irrelevant, ineffective and powerless. Have complete assurance in the efficacy of Christ to set people free. Trust the Lord for the empowering of the Spirit of God as you prepare to minister in Christ's name.

Individually and collectively we need to ask ourselves if our lives and our service for Christ clearly proclaim and authenticate the gospel of the kingdom of God. How can we more effectively demonstrate the authority of Christ in our world?

Preparation for ministry

We should not underestimate our spiritual foe and our own frailty. Spiritual authority and holiness cannot be separated. Guard carefully your relationship with the Lord. Ensure there is no unconfessed sin or other unresolved problem in your life. We should be accountable to someone else and give that person the right to ask us questions.

If necessary set aside special time to wait on the Lord in prayer and in the word, possibly fasting. Having said that, Jesus did not have to go and fast before he cast out the demon that goes out 'only by prayer and fasting'. Why not? He must have had a lifestyle that included fasting. We guard our relationship with the Lord every day, don't we? We ensure there is no unconfessed sin or unresolved problem every day, I hope. So we can be prayed up, ready prepared, at any time the challenge comes. Holiness is not meant to be exhausting, but resting in Jesus.

It can be mentally, spiritually and physically draining, so we need prayer support. Prepare a team to minister with you. At least one other person should go with you. The team members can pray specifically while you are involved in deliverance. Never minister alone to a person of the opposite sex. Antonio Alkimim said, 'Some women came to our church to trap the church leaders, including me. But I discerned the spirit. No one should do deliverance alone, unless clearly hearing the Lord about it.' Demons always explore the weakness of people. They have a desire to have a body; they express themselves through a body, e.g. drunkenness, witchcraft, greed, prostitution; they need a body because they are looking for a place to stay. If a person gives way to one demon they may get many, because the first demon invites more. There are many ways demons explore the weakness of Christian leaders, for example through greed, pride or sexual appeal. They will make temptation easy for a Christian leader.

Before going to minister, specifically ask the Lord to protect your immediate family, for often the enemy endeavours to counter-attack by causing trouble for members of the family. When an evil spirit manifests, the sensation is not fear, but the kind of feeling you have before you meet a very powerful, important man. You may have goose bumps, or imagine something is crawling on you. We have a more powerful authority, and the spirits have to be subject to us in the name of Jesus.

Suggested Guidelines
Minister to people privately, not publicly. Don't lay hands on people in this ministry. When a person comes for counselling, don't pray with your eyes closed, because you need to see the signs God will give you.

1. Observe and analyse the symptoms
Symptoms of occult bondage must be differentiated from symptoms of physical and psychological disturbances, yet if any of the physical and psychological disturbance originates in occultism, this must be discerned. Be sensitive to the Holy Spirit. He is the divine radar. Pray in your heart, asking the Lord for understanding of their real problem. If they have simply a physical or psychological problem, advise them to pray and consult a doctor or psychiatrist. If the Holy Spirit assures you that there is a spiritual problem, then proceed.

Look for occult involvement: playing with a ouija board or tarot cards even as a game; reading a horoscope even as a hobby; consulting a witchdoctor, or taking a friend to a witchdoctor, even as a curiosity; bowing to a shrine or holy place even if you don't believe in Satan; keeping antique relics of ancestors, especially ancestors who may have practised occultism; trying hypnotism or yoga even as an experiment; keeping a book about occultism.

Look for satanic attack or disturbance by demons, perhaps at a certain hour of the day, or on a special day. Ask if they experience nightmares, depression, aches without medical reason; hatred of the name of Jesus, the Bible, prayer, or Christian meetings; compulsive anger or suicidal thoughts; unexpected filthy thoughts; compulsive desire to commit adultery or to go gambling.

Look for people who sometimes lose their personality through demons, speaking with a different voice, demonstrating supernatural strength, but still capable of clear reasoning, and not a crazy person. Is there a hardness in their face? Can you tell a demonic laugh from a holy laugh? Are they living in confusion? Is there sorrow, distress, weariness, anxiety, despair without any reason? Are they afraid of death? Are they controlled by bitterness and a desire for revenge?

Take time. We have to make a proper diagnosis. Check whether the individual is under medication or has a history of mental illness. Check whether they are receiving counselling or ministry from others. Ask lots of questions. Get the whole story. Listen and make notes.

If the family has brought the patient, have the family confess their sins such as pride or unbelief. Counsel the family too. If the family members earnestly repent, sometimes the demon spontaneously leaves.

2. Expose and bring to light all occult practices (Psalm 90:8)

We can do this in two ways, first by asking questions about a long list of occult activities. Ask about amulets and fetishes, clairvoyance, crystal balls, white magic, whether special days or dates are important to them, charms, spells, incantations, spiritism, mediums, séances, fortune telling, teacup reading, sorcery, hypnotism, levitation, writing in blood, letters of spiritual protection, superstitions, divination, names of a witchdoctor or wizard, the meaning of their own name, bad dreams and nightmares, trances, meditation, astrology, horoscopes, card laying, palmistry, invulnerable magic, psychometry, black magic, telepathy, yoga, numerology, fire walking, omens, voodoo, black mass, books on occultism, holy water, holy places, and taboos (which can be about food, days, hours, dates, people, places, animals or trees).

Secondly, ask about their parents and grandparents with respect to occult practices. Ask what was done to them in their mother's womb, and when they were born. Ask the meaning of their name, and why they were given that name. Were there occult practices when they were children, or students, or to do with a love affair, marriage, illness, or a problem? Are they members of any cult, secret society or anti-Christian religion?

The purpose of these questions is to know the hiding places of the devil. Never pass over one single occult practice in a patient. While you are asking these questions, write the significant practices on a sheet of paper, so that you can deal with every sin exposed. Those who practice occultism live in darkness. It is important to bring all such practices into the light so they can be delivered. Ask in the power of the Holy Spirit, because without the light of God, Satan can darken their mind and make them forget something he wants to conceal. We can do nothing without the Lord and his Spirit.

Ask for their willing cooperation and participation in everything. Demand absolute honesty and sincerity, hiding nothing. The patient needs an open heart.

Any duplicity or covering of issues in his or her life will inhibit deliverance. The patient needs a humble spirit. There must be recognition that they have a problem they can't resolve by their own ability. They need to be aware of their need, and reach out to the Lord to help them.

We are not suggesting strict rules or a formula that has to be followed slavishly. Wordings are not important. Deliverance is not in saying the right phrases. When counselling in a cross-cultural situation it is important to keep in mind that 'form' and 'meaning' in different cultures might be quite different. It is not sufficient to act on certain 'forms' but we have to get to the real meaning behind the forms.

It is more peaceful if you bind in Christ's name the demonic powers that are active in the person so that they do not become disruptive or violent.

Be aware that you could be wrong. If you have a word of knowledge about a problem, offer it sensitively as a suggestion.

Businessmen in Java may offer the sacrifice of a goat to the spirit who lives in the active volcano Mount Kawi. They make a pact with the spirit in order to become wealthy. The spirit of the volcano tells them that he wants one of their children in return. If the businessman agrees, he does grow wealthy, but one of his children goes insane or dies a violent death. Satan is taking his wages. That person gives Satan and evil spirits a legal right to a foothold in his life or the life of his family members. This pact must be broken, annulled and dissolved by a conscious repudiation on the part of the person subjected.

3. Renunciation

Involvement in the occult means a legal pact with the kingdom of darkness. Renunciation nullifies that legal pact with Satan. Renunciation is an official declaration before witnesses, and you and your team are the witnesses. The meaning of renunciation is made most clear when we analyse the meaning of the corresponding Greek word *apotassesthai*, which means 'to step out of line in battle'. He who renounces Satan steps out of the devil's battle line and becomes a follower and soldier of another lord, Jesus Christ. Renunciation should be spoken aloud. You may have to assist them phrase by phrase. It can often be a time of great spiritual struggle, sometimes producing demonic manifestations. Be prepared for that. The early church included in its public declaration of faith the following sentence: 'I renounce you, Satan, and all your works and ways.'

STOPTHINK&DISCUSS
● Discuss the difference in meaning between 'demon possessed' and 'with an unclean spirit'.
● Discuss the causes and symptoms of demonisation.
● Look up 'renunciation' in the index and discuss when confession is sufficient, and when renunciation is necessary.

15
DELIVERANCE

Traugott Böker, Dietrich Kuhl, Pondsius Takaliuang,
Antonio Alkimim, Hans Rothenberger

A possible deliverance session

1. Explain the process to the afflicted person

Explain the conditions for deliverance given in James 4:6-11. Be humble, because 'God opposes the proud, but gives grace to the humble'; 'Humble yourselves before the Lord, and he will lift you up.' Genuinely repent and confess sin: 'Wash your hands, you sinners. Grieve, mourn and wail. Change your laughter to mourning and your joy to gloom.' Submit to God wholeheartedly: 'Submit yourselves to God'; 'Purify your hearts, you double-minded.' Purity has two aspects. 100% pure means not only that there is no dirt, but also that there is no alloy or mixture, no other loyalty. Come near to God: 'Come near to God and he will come near to you.' Resist Satan. 'Resist the devil and he will flee from you.'

2. Proclaim the authority of Jesus in word, prayer and song

Some possible texts would be Philippians 2:5-11, Hebrews 4:13, Revelation 5:9, Isaiah 53, Psalm 18:30-39, Psalm 97, Isaiah 33:1-2.

3. Pray for direction and revelation

4. Lead them to confess sin by name in prayer

Confessing sin related to occult practices must be done clearly and by name. If God lists our sins in the Bible with specific names, we must confess those named sins. If it is done clearly, the bondage of it is broken definitely. Let them confess their sins in their own language. If it is difficult for them to remember them all while they are praying, let them look at your list. Sins such as anger and hatred commonly occur with occult sins. When a patient is open and honest in confessing, let them confess these at the same time. If sexual sins are confessed at this time, let it be done privately or under four eyes only.

'Those who oppose him he must gently instruct, in the hope that God will grant them repentance leading them to a knowledge of the truth, and that they will come to their senses and escape from the trap of the devil, who has taken them captive to do his will' (2 Timothy 2:25-26).

There are some cases where people cannot pray, or find it difficult to pray. You can lead them in prayer, sentence by sentence. If they are fearful to confess aloud the name of certain spirits, encourage them with the assurance that the blood of Jesus protects those who confess their sins. They may ask if they can confess their sins alone. Yes, they can, but it is better if they have a trustworthy Christian present, both as a witness and to help them. Remember, we who hear must be trustworthy in keeping these confidences.

Explain that the devil hides behind unconfessed sin, and that these unconfessed sins give him rights in our lives. One condition of deliverance is confession and purification by the blood of Jesus. Unconfessed sins may include:

a. Sins of the spirit, against God: Occult sins, rebellion, hypocrisy, lying, pride, idolatry and anything that takes the place of God in their life (Exodus 34:12; 1 John 5:21).

b. Sins of the soul, against other people and against ourselves: Animosity, bitterness, refusal to forgive, anger, jealousy, avarice, misunderstandings.

c. Sins of the body: adultery, incest, perversions, habitual masturbation, gluttony, drugs, drunkenness.

After confession, teach the enquirer to accept the pardon and the cleansing of the Lord.

5. Lead them to renounce any rights the devil has had

You may often have to have the patient repeat a prayer after you, if it is difficult for them to speak because there is resistance from the demons. They must continue to pray even if they feel this resistance, even if physical manifestations occur.

In the first century, candidates for baptism were asked, 'Do you renounce the devil and all his works?' In the Anglican catechism, the third answer is, 'I should renounce the devil and all his works.' These are in agreement with 2 Corinthians 4:2: 'We have renounced secret and shameful ways.' In Greek there are two words for 'renounce': *apeipon*, used in 2 Corinthians 4:2, means to disown; *apotasso*, used in Luke 14:33, means to forsake. In this act, patients disown all relationship and contact with the devil, and say farewell to all the old 'visitors', 'friends' and 'spirit guides', and they forsake all occult practices.

There are six elements needed in the prayer:

● I approach you, God, in the name and by the blood of Jesus.
● I affirm that in Jesus I have received forgiveness and cleansing from my sins.
● I submit all my life to you.
● I ask you to bring out into the light all the enemies of Jesus that are in me, and deliver me from them.
● I want to close all the demonic entry points in my life, whether opened by myself or by my ancestors, and retake in the name of Jesus the following ground which I had left open for the demons: _____
● In the authority of Jesus I separate myself from all demonic influence. Father, I ask you in the name of Jesus to deliver me from all the wicked spirits, by the power of the blood of Jesus poured out for me at the cross. Thank you for your mercy.

All occult objects must be destroyed: books, knives, cups, clothing, idols, charms, pendulum, ouija boards, music, anything used for any occult purpose (Acts 19:19-20). Failure to do this sometimes enables the demon to resist eviction, so if there is resistance, ask, 'Do you have anything that belongs to the enemy that must be destroyed?' (Deuteronomy 7:25-26).

Those who practise occult activities usually keep occult articles such as amulets, fetishes, a book of charms, a book about the horoscope, a cassette on occultism, a lecture on spiritism, antique articles, magic rings or bracelets, the bones of animals or wood from a sacred tree. These must be burnt or thrown away into the river or the sea.

What about expensive articles of gold or silver, perhaps a cross or a sacred dagger? According to the word of God, they must be burnt. Sometimes a patient will argue that those articles will be better sold and the money used for church or orphanage. Don't allow such argumentation. We must obey the word of God more than any reasoned argumentation. If people don't allow their expensive items to be burnt they are not serious in their repentance, and they are not delivered. Anyone who truly meets Jesus will destroy their expensive articles. When a patient finds the Best, he is happy to abandon the rest.

Sometimes a patient will not want to burn an article from their parents because of honouring their parents, and will even cite the fifth commandment. Explain that the fifth commandment is preceded by the second commandment, which prohibits putting anything in the place of God or regarding it as more important than God. We must obey God rather than parents or ancestors (Acts 5:29).

There are occult articles made from the Bible. Must they be burnt? We don't destroy the word of God, and it is not wise to burn a Bible in front of the congregation. But we must destroy everything used for the devil, the special paper it may have been wrapped in, any paper used for the devil.

There are occult articles using money. Must it be destroyed? Yes, it must. The basic principle still holds, that we never allow any of Satan's articles in their life. Everything must go completely.

There are occult articles such as gold or silver needles or a jewel placed in the body under the skin. These can be removed surgically. Or you can pray, and sometimes in the name of Jesus they just come out, sometimes painlessly, sometimes preceded by a loud groan or shout, then they fall down. Sometimes you can watch them coming out, sometimes they just seem to disappear. When they are gone, the patient experiences a wonderful deliverance.

How can we discern the difference between neutral carvings, statues or pictures and occult ones? If you enter a home, and see certain articles hanging on the wall, don't directly command them to destroy such articles. Ask questions first. Can those articles be taken into the toilet? If they say 'No', then those are occult articles. If the answer is 'Yes', then those articles are not dangerous. Have those articles been 'purified' in a special ceremony on a special day? If 'Yes', they are occult articles. If 'No', they are neutral. Would you be fearful without those articles? 'Yes, I am fearful without them' means that they are occult things. If they are unsure, they can pray. If God gives them peace in their hearts, those things are neutral. If they are unhappy, it is better to destroy them.

People often keep indecent books along with occult materials. They can be destroyed along with the occult material. They belong to the devil too. How about memorised spells? Pray to the Lord that the blood of Jesus cleanses their brain and their mind so that they can memorise the Word of God instead. If sinners don't burn their occult practices, they will all be burnt together in hell. Destroy the occult paraphernalia, so that the patient will experience a glorious deliverance. Articles can be destroyed before or after receiving Christ.

I bought some souvenirs for our daughter who was three years old. She had nightmares. One night her eyes were so round I thought she was demonised. She froze. I picked her up and my flesh crawled. I told the demons to get out and that they had no right in our family. Then I put her in bed again. 'How did these things happen in my house, Father?' God told me: 'Go to the wardrobe.' There I found the souvenirs. Even in the soap I was looking at the shape of an evil spirit. I destroyed it. It never happened again.

6. Expose the enemy

a. Explain to the patient the purpose of this next phase. Demons which may be hiding in the enquirer must be revealed in the light of God. We are not asking the enquirer himself to respond, but to be aware of every internal impression (a name, a word, a feeling such as sorrow, hate, etc.) and every physical reaction (vertigo, tension, nausea, etc.) and to tell us what is happening inside all the time.

b. Bind the spirits. In the name and authority of Jesus, order all spirits not assigned to the enquirer to leave the place. Forbid the spirits to call any other spirits, or to do any harm to the enquirer or the team.

c. Expose the spirits. Order all the spirits hiding in the enquirer to show themselves, either aloud or by an impression in the enquirer's own spirit. Ask the enquirer to tell you the spirits detected. It is not necessary to engage in conversation with the demons, except to obtain information which may help in deliverance: the names of the spirits, their number, their plans and purposes, their entry point, and their leader. It is necessary to place the demons before the throne of God and in his light to ensure the truth of what they say. (This information may not be indispensable for a deliverance. In Luke 8:30 Jesus merely asked the Gerasene demon its name). There is always a chief spirit. Demons usually have companions, competing with themselves to dominate the person. They seldom come on their own.

7. Expel the demons

Order the spirits in the name of Jesus to leave the enquirer. You have no need to shout to be heard. A resolute tone will suffice. For example: 'Enemy of Jesus called _____ , I bind you with all those who are with you and under you, and I command in the name of Jesus that you leave now the life of this person, and go to the place assigned by Jesus for you, and never return.' Demons are often clustered together, and it is useful to group them together when casting them out. The departure of the spirits does not have to be accompanied by dramatic signs, but can be demonstrated by a feeling of relief and liberation, a sudden chill, a foul smell, coughing or vomiting.

If the spirits resist and do not leave, search to see if there still remains a sin unconfessed or an artefact undestroyed which still gives rights of occupation to the demon. If necessary, another session can be set. Don't put yourself under pressure. It is Jesus who delivers! In Luke 8 Jesus asked the demon its name after he had commanded it to come out. Obviously, then, this demon did not come out the first time Jesus commanded. So he asked its name to find the reason why, and discovered there were hundreds of them.

8. Lead them to faith

If they have not already done so, lead them to receive Christ into their heart as Lord (John 1:12). Our Saviour and Deliverer tells us that if the house has been cleansed, Satan will invite seven other more wicked spirits to live there (Matthew 12:43-45). The expelled spirit will return if the heart is empty. They must receive Christ definitely and fully (Isaiah 57:15, Ephesians 3:17, Revelation 3:20). When sinners act according to these verses and receive Christ, the Spirit of God works at the same time, and the miracle happens. Sinners are delivered from the dominion of darkness and enter the kingdom of God. Children of Satan are born again to become children of God.

Ask them to yield their whole life to the Lord (Romans 12:1-2). After receiving Christ, after destroying Satan's junk, they must pray a prayer of total surrender to the Lord. Jesus is not only Saviour and Deliverer, but he is Master, Owner and Lord. Formerly, sinners belonged to the devil; now they belong to their new and gentle Master. To him they wholeheartedly commit their entire life. Their body, soul and spirit, their possessions, their wealth, their family, their jobs, their talents, their all belongs to Jesus, and must not be used for demons or evil spirits. They cannot have two masters (James 4:7, Psalm 31:5, 37:5, Ephesians 4:24).

Ask for the filling of the Holy Spirit. The person delivered needs to offer himself to God to be filled and controlled by the Holy Spirit, specifically in the areas that have recently been under demonic control. He must consecrate his newly purified life to Jesus (Matthew 12:43).

9. Verify the deliverance

'Are there still any spirits hiding in you?' 'Do you confess that Jesus Christ actually became a human being, and is the only Redeemer?' (1 John 4:2). 'Do you declare that you are in complete harmony with Jesus Christ and the Almighty God?' 'Do you abandon Satan as a false god, a liar and a defeated enemy, and do you totally refuse him any authority over you?'

Let them thank the Lord for salvation and deliverance (Psalm 103; Exodus 15:1-21). The outstanding sign of real deliverance is praise and thanksgiving. This is an important point in deliverance. Those who are set free from jail and come home will be full of joy. In the same way, when sinners experience real deliverance, they will spontaneously praise God and thank him in wonder. Hell and the dominion of darkness are full of insults, railings, scorn and complaints, while heaven and the kingdom of God are full of praise, songs, joy, thanksgiving and peace. Psalm 103 and Exodus 15 are examples of praise uttered by delivered people. They praise the Lord in their own language, and sometimes in tongues. Sometimes they weep for joy. Sometimes their faces become very serious as they praise, and sometimes they laugh, breathe a deep breath, and pray a long prayer.

Be patient with them. This is worship and gratitude.

If people cannot utter a single word of praise and thanksgiving, it is an important sign that this sinner is not delivered. If the patient is continuing in complaint, in asking forgiveness or still asking for deliverance, they are not yet free. They are still in darkness. There may be hidden sins, or they may be heavily demonized. We must pray that the Lord gives more light, and wait for the Spirit to lead us in examining him or her. They may even speak out some formal praise, but be stumbling or seeking for a word. They are not free. From a free heart flows spontaneous praise like fresh water from a spring.

10. Care of the delivered person

Deliverance must be followed by discipling and teaching. Delivered people need to grow in the knowledge and the fellowship of Christ through Bible study and prayer. They need to testify publicly about Jesus and his deliverance. They must know their status, position, rights and riches in the Lord! Now they are God's children (John 1:12); God has become their heavenly Father (Romans 8:15) and they have the right to pray the Lord's prayer (Matthew 6:9-13). Now they are not alone, because God's Spirit lives in them and he is greater than any other spirit in the world (1 John 4:4). Their sins have been forgiven and forgotten (Isaiah 43:25). They have received eternal life (1 John 5:13). God preserves their life (Jude 24; 1 Thessalonians 5:23-24). The angels of God watch over them (Psalm 34:7). They have power to overcome evil spirits and temptations (1 John 5:4). God is faithful to provide and meet their spiritual and other needs (Philippians 4:19). In the Lord they have unlimited possibilities to live an abundant life (Ephesians 3:17-20).

They must know their duties and tasks in the Lord! They must keep reading the Bible and meditating on it (Colossians 3:16, Psalm 1:1-3, 1 Peter 2:2). The Lord will give enabling and understanding to grasp the word (2 Timothy 2:7, John 14:26). Teach them about a daily Quiet Time. They should keep praying (Colossians 4:2). The Holy Spirit will help them to pray (Romans 8:26-27). They need to keep meeting in a good fellowship where the Word of God is clearly taught (Hebrews 10:25). No Christian can live a normal Christian life on his own (Galatians 6:2). Tell them there is no perfect church in this world, and they must be patient with other Christians who fall and do wrong. We all do, but we keep looking to the Lord (Hebrews 12:1-2).

They must keep testifying about God's goodness to other people (1 Peter 2:9-10). They must begin some family fellowship (Joshua 24:15). They must use their all for the Lord, including their body (Romans 12:1-2), their time (Ephesians 5:16, 1 Peter 4:2), their strength (Mark 12:30), their money (Philippians 4:17-18), their talents (Matthew 25:16-17, 22-23). It is good if they ask the church leaders for a job in the church.

They must do their duty in society, working as well as possible for the glory of God (Daniel 6:1-4). God will enable them to do their duty with a strength and wisdom not their own (2 Timothy 2:1, 1 Corinthians 15:10). They must do everything for the glory of God (1 Corinthians 10:31) and in the name of Jesus (Colossians 3:17).

They must know their enemies in the Christian life! Never tell them that everything will run well after they believe. A Christian is a soldier. There are enemies. Tell them honestly that this is a war, with three kinds of enemies, starting with the devil and evil spirits, which attack a Christian from outside. The powers of hell will do their worst to oppose, deceive, or allure every Christian without exception. Satan will organize schemes or methods to trick every true child of God, especially those who have been delivered out of occult bondage. The word of God gives complete spiritual armour for combating the devil and his hordes. They are defeated enemies, because Jesus has overcome them on the cross. Attacks of Satan against believers are allowed by God so that we can practise to be a soldier and be prepared to help others who are under Satan's control. Jesus was full of the Holy Spirit but he was still tempted. At the first sign of a demon trying to manifest again, they have the authority to tell the demon to go away. Demons will try any chance to get back the possession they lost. Soon after deliverance a spirit may whisper things into one's mind. It is easy to slip back again into old habits which invite demons in.

The second kind of enemy is the world around us, driven by forces that do not acknowledge Christ, constantly trying to allure us and to separate us from our Lord (Ephesians 2:2, Mark 4:19, 2 Timothy 4:10). The world can be in us (1 John 2:15-16). We can overcome the world by saying 'No' as Joseph, Daniel and his three friends, Moses and Jesus all did (Genesis 39:7-8, Daniel 1:8, 3:16-17; Luke 4:3-12; Hebrews 11:24-27). 'No' is a key word for overcoming the world.

The third enemy is my old self, my physical appetites. This is a subtle enemy because it is in me. It is a source of filthy feelings, disobedient mind and will, worldly thoughts and all kinds of sins (Galatians 5:19-21). How can we overcome it? There are some principles in Galatians 5:16-25. The new nature and the old nature are in conflict, but the old nature has been crucified with Christ, so has no power over us. When we are tempted to do what the old nature desires, we are to crucify it again, and be ready to be led by the Spirit.

Christians must know their reward in the Lord! As Christians, God blesses us because our past life is forgiven, he blesses us every day in the present, and he blesses us in our future. Every Christian has a bright future. Every faithful believer will be rewarded. We will be glorified with Christ (Romans 8:17), and will reign with him (Revelation 22:5). We will live with him forever (1 Thessalonians 4:13-18). We will judge the evil spirits (1 Corinthians 6:3). We will win a crown (2 Timothy 4:8, James 1:12, 1 Peter 5:4), and live in the new Jerusalem (Revelation 21). Hallelujah!

Some ancient prayers of exorcism

Deliverance is not a new thing, but has been practised by the church in every generation, as these prayers demonstrate. We don't reprint them here for you to use, but simply to see that this is not some new fad! We don't print any formula for you to use, because deliverance is not based on a formula, but on Christ's authority.

Rituale Romanum (1614, revised 1952)
Depart from him, unclean spirit, and give place to the Holy Spirit, the Paraclete. I exorcise thee, every unclean spirit in the name of God the Father Almighty, in the name of Jesus Christ our Lord and Judge, and by the power of the Holy Ghost, to be gone from this person _____ made in the image of God, whom our Lord in his goodness has called to his holy temple that he himself may become a temple of the Living God, and so the Holy Ghost may dwell in him. Through the same Christ our Lord who will come to judge the living and the dead, and the world by fire.

From the first Prayer Book of Edward VI (1549)
I command the unclean spirit, in the name of the Father and of the Son and of the Holy Ghost, that thou come out and depart from these infants whom our Lord Jesus Christ has vouchsafed to call to his holy baptism, and be made members of his body and his congregation. Therefore thou cursed spirit, remember the sentence, remember thy judgement, remember the day to be at hand when thou shall burn in fire everlasting prepared for thee and thine angels. And presume not, hereafter, to exercise any tyranny towards these infants whom Christ has bought with his precious blood and by this his holy baptism called to his flock.

From the East Syrian rite (7th century)
I adjure you, O evil spirit, through God the Father Almighty, and through Jesus Christ his Son, and through the Holy Spirit the Paraclete, that you depart through His power from the vessel which you hold captive.

Old Mozarabic rite for exorcism of places (7th century)
O God the author of blessing and fount of salvation, we earnestly pray and beseech you that you may pour out the manifold dew of your grace together with the abundance of your blessing upon this dwelling of your faithful. Amen. May you grant it prosperity and drive away adversity. Amen. May you destroy the devil and author of evil. Amen. May you place herein the angel of light, the guard and defender of good, and by the multitude of your mercy may peace abound for those who dwell in this place. Amen. May there always be present here, O Lord, those of your gifts which are profitable to all. Amen. Send O Lord to this dwelling place your good and holy angel as watchman and sentinel and guard, to resist evil things and provide good things, so that all disquiet and disaster be banished from this house. Amen. May your presence keep far from here need, pestilence, sickness, and attacks of evil ones, so that where your name is invoked, abundant good may follow, and evil attempts of devils be put to flight, and your protection and the help of the saints take their place. May the Lord bless and sanctify the tabernacle of his servants, and grant them the riches of the kingdom of heaven. Amen.

STOPTHINK&DISCUSS
● Is this a pattern you would feel comfortable to use yourself, if the situation arose?

16
EXAMPLES OF SPIRITUAL ENCOUNTERS

In Brazil spirits have a surprise
Antonio Alkimim

There were 80 people at our house church meeting when a witch arrived. She said, 'After my son became a Christian and his friends started praying in my house, the spirits don't come any more. Even when I try to invoke them, they don't come.' Although she herself has demons they don't manifest, but she is not yet ready to ask for deliverance. People like her are accustomed to powers and can see spiritual things, both angels and demons. If your religion is just words, they do not respect it. If they see signs and wonders, they will choose God, because they are accustomed to power. We already have five converted witches, and although this witch was defiant, she was noticing that God was hearing the prayers of his people and healing people,. People testified to what God did. This kind of person always feels uneasy in the presence of Christians. The woman had planned to stay in the house we meet in, but she was disturbed and uneasy, so she left. She couldn't stand the presence of God in that house.

One day I went into the mechanic's shop. One of the mechanics observed every move I made. He took his courage and asked me a question: 'Are you a priest?' 'Why?' 'Because my spirits are making me see a huge light around you.' 'No, I am a pastor.' I took the opportunity to testify of Jesus. I was not feeling especially 'spiritual' that day, but God in his mercy made him see.

An evangelist was witnessing to one of the strongest demon practitioners in Montes Claros. The man didn't want to be free. The evangelist asked, 'May I pray for you?' He said, 'Pray,' but it had no effect, because this man was willingly serving the devil. Spirits cannot be cast out of people without their consent and presence. The person must have the desire to be freed. Those deeply involved in witchcraft know what they are doing, so it is more difficult. They know they are serving Satan.

In Brazil the spirits always have a surprise to give. Sometimes they behave like snakes; they may assume the identity of their African deities; they may appear as sexual deities or behave like a sensual person and do striptease. You never know what kind of demon will appear. It may identify with the religion of the country. Because of syncretism between Catholicism and African religions, the spirit may have a saint's name but will also have a name from some African religion. Depending on the spirit, it may ask for gifts, or threaten to hit you, or tell you, 'I'm here to kill.' Their main objective is to make life miserable, to destroy a person. When I see what demons do to people, I hate them.

Prostitutes often have demons. Homosexuals can have a demon that causes people to act with sensuality, or a demon to act like a woman. Some do not come to church because they know they will lose the demon!

One day I was in the church when a beautiful young lady came for prayer. I called the female assistant to be present. The young lady said that she had had a vision the previous night that her grandmother had died, so I knew that something demonic was happening. When I began to pray she became disturbed and started biting herself. As I was binding the powers of darkness, she cried out, 'Stop doing this!' The whites of her eyes were bloodshot and full of hatred. She was gnashing her teeth and trying to punch me. She said, 'I hate you. I am a legion.' A thousand thoughts went through my mind at that kind of aggression. I grabbed her wrists and said, 'I don't care how many you are. I come in the name of Jesus. Come out of her.' They came out, disarmed. I sensed that she was free. We counselled her for a few minutes and she went home. The spirit never manifested again.

Another time when I had tried to expel a demon it had seemed easy. Later, however, the patient had again showed signs of demonization. I had not found them all! You have to tell the chief spirit to manifest. Here we call the chief spirit a falange, a cluster. Tell the chief spirit to come out, and then the others to come too. Normally the chief spirit is powerful. Tell it to come out without violence, in the name of Jesus.

Resistance to deliverance

I don't have patience to talk with the spirits again, asking them to come out repeatedly. I have heard people say 'I spent x hours in a deliverance session.' I am sure of my authority, and say to them, 'I will give you just one order. Come out.' The demon must go out, because it is defeated by the Conqueror. The prayer of the righteous has great power against the powers of hell. Afterwards I sing and praise God for deliverance. When I feel that the person is calm, I ask for the name of the person. If the person is free, they will tell you their real name. If the demon is still there, they will not answer.

There are some cases in which a complete and immediate deliverance seems almost impossible. I believe there are always reasons for this. People might not be delivered because certain conditions are not fulfilled, e.g. confession of sin and full surrender to Christ. At times the counsellor needs to probe for deeper issues and causes. We should ask the demonised person to pause and pray and ask God to show them what the problem is. We can ask God ourselves for a word of knowledge or insight. Perhaps in making his confession the person has consciously omitted those sins which were more serious. Perhaps the seeker was only concerned to get rid of his mental vexations without wanting to follow Christ. Perhaps there are secret commitments with which he is unwilling to break or of which he is not aware. Maybe there has been child abuse, incest or satanic rituals in childhood. It could also be that our diagnosis might have been wrong or simplistic. Our weapons are spiritual. We should then form prayer groups of believers who will be prepared to pray regularly and often for the demonized person.

In counselling one difficult client, we often came up against a roadblock, a demon who refused to budge. Then we knew it still had rights in her. After she had forgiven her father she said, 'I need to forgive my stepfather too.' Once one of the team had a picture of a flick knife, and asked her what it meant. Then she confessed that she had used a flick knife, initially to defend herself against abuse, then later to terrorise people. When all that was renounced and confessed, we made progress.

A bitter root
'See to it that no one misses the grace of God and that no bitter root grows up to cause trouble and defile many' (Hebrews 12:15). The bitter root operates through the law which says we reap what we sow. When we are forgiven all our sins at the cross, but continue to harbour resentments against others, we bring all our debts back on ourselves, like those of the unforgiving servant (Matthew 18:23-35). A bitter root in us actually affects the way people treat us. If we are feeling rejected, super-sensitive and interpret any negative experience as rejection, we tend to send out rejection signals which others pick up and act on. It is a stronghold that must be renounced before deliverance can proceed.

An inner vow
As a result of an embarrassing or traumatic situation, we may promise ourselves, 'I'll never again get myself into that.' It may be small, like being embarrassed in a first attempt at public speaking. It may be huge, such as 'I have always been mistreated by men, so I will never trust a man again.' If the promise was made in childhood it may even have been forgotten, yet it remains in the background of the personality, influencing decisions, resisting change, creating bondage, resisting release. Deliverance may be obstructed until forgiveness and the authority of Jesus shatters the vow.

'Ask Jesus what he wants to say to you about that'
Someone may have so dominated the patient in the past that he finds himself continually relating back to that person. It may, for example, be in despair ('He ruined my life'), in hate ('I'm planning my revenge') or in a sense of rejection ('You will never be any good'). Some call it a 'soul tie'. Discuss the issues with the patient. It is beautiful to have him or her ask Jesus what he wants to say about that relationship, and to watch his healing flow in. Break the soul tie, and deliverance can proceed.

Unwilling to lose the 'gift'
Jean Goodenough
Peter and Sandra lived in the same block of maisonettes as I did. Peter was deeply into science fiction, UFO sightings, and anything weird. Tony, who lived nearby, was the opposite of Peter, down-to-earth and rational. (Names have been changed.)

I was visiting Tony when Peter and Sandra dropped in with a problem. Peter had bought an antique clock that took his fancy. They began to experience classic poltergeist activity, when objects moved or disappeared, lights and gas were being turned on and off, and there was an increasing feeling of cold.

Tony had experienced this cold when he visited Peter and Sandra. One night they had been so spooked by what was going on that they asked Tony if they could spend the night at his place. He went round to give them a hand with their bags, and a picture flew off the wall and hit him. He also experienced something very cold coming up to his neck. He made a rapid exit and waited for the others outside. He wanted to find a rational explanation for what happened, including the feeling he had, which seemed to go far beyond a reasonable fear reaction. He did not use the word 'evil' but he did say privately that he never ever wanted to experience anything like that again.

As I talked to Peter, I discovered that he had experienced strange things in the past, including a degree of clairvoyance. His mother had had similar experiences. As delicately as I could, I said I felt that he had a familiar spirit, and he could only be free if he was prepared to move out of the dominion of darkness into the kingdom of light. I asked if he would like a visit from my pastor.

The visit took place, and my pastor chatted with all three for about two hours. He told me afterwards of Peter's reluctance to lose his 'gift', so the process could go no further. However, they did dispose of the clock. The phenomena stopped when it was banished to the meter cupboard.

Having heard the account of all the strange goings-on, I returned home and remembered noticing some recent unexplained draughts when no doors or windows were open. Again I experienced a fear reaction as I wondered if there was a connection with the poltergeist – not that I had any sense of evil with the draught! I affirmed that my home belonged to the Lord. Before settling down to sleep, I read Daily Light. It spoke of God giving generously to those who ask, so I asked the Lord for a generous portion of his peace. He gave it to me – I slept like a log.

Tied by a demon
Dramé Mamadou Esaï

I am Ivoirian, born in 1973 to a Muslim family in Abidjan. From early childhood I was captivated by traditional music and folk dancing to such a point that it dominated my life. I was effeminate, and used to dance in traditional ceremonies. In reality, it was a satanic gift inherited from my father, who used to dance the goumbe in his youth. Little by little I was secretly drawn towards homosexuality and debauchery, though outwardly I was reserved and polite.

The problem accelerated when I began to imitate a Congolese singing artiste who had a particular dancing style. Unconsciously I was bound more and more to adore her, and to dance like her. I thought like her, and spoke like her. I bought her records, cassettes, magazines with her photos and interviews. It was really idolatry. I made such a spectacle in my high school that all my classmates called me by her name. It was pitiful for a young man to do such a thing. Some insulted me, some mocked, but others encouraged me. For myself, I believed that this was youth, this was life, and that all young people modelled themselves on their own favourite artists. But the Bible says, 'There is a way that seems right to a man, but in the end it leads to death' (Proverbs 14:12).

So it was that in spite of my fame, I was actually worried and sad, and longed for peace of heart. Alone in my room I wept over my effeminacy. I was miserable, until 17 March 1992 when some Christian young people, who shared the high school accommodation with me, invited me to the weekly meeting of Scripture Union. A Christian student had been invited to share the living word of God with other students. His message was 'Without holiness, no-one will see the Lord' (Hebrews 12:14). I accepted the Lord Jesus Christ as my Lord and personal Saviour. The Son of Man came to save the lost (Luke 19:10), and in my life, where sin had flourished, now grace super-flourished! (Romans 5:20).

I was instantly delivered. The same day, helped by the pastor, I decided to destroy all my CDs, cassettes, photos, posters and magazines relating to that singer. My heart was filled with joy, love, and friendliness. I looked at the sky as if all nature was new to my eyes. The Bible is right when it says that 'if anyone is in Christ, he is a new creation; the old has gone, the new has come!' (2 Corinthians 5:17).

Two weeks later it was the Ramadan and Easter holidays, and I returned home. I announced the good news of my conversion to my father. He reacted violently, beat me, inflicting wounds all over my body. He threatened to put an end to my education. All my older relatives were astonished, because it is like blasphemy for a Muslim to change religion. They treated me as someone mad, or lost, because I had abandoned the dance and had accepted Jesus who said, 'I am the light of the world. Whoever follows me will not walk in darkness, but will have the light of life' (John 8:12 CEV).

In spite of the persecution to make me change (whispering, mocking, rejection by parents and by Muslim religious leaders), I remained firm by the grace of God. I knew that Jesus had succeeded in transforming my life. No other is able to do that, because Jesus said, 'I am the way and the truth and the life. No-one comes to the Father except through me' (John 14:6).

It's true. God is good. He pardons, transforms lives, undergirds the oppressed and gives eternal life free to those who are looking for it with a genuine heart. I was baptised by immersion in 1994. The Bible says, 'Do you not know that the unrighteous will not inherit the kingdom of God? Do not be deceived: neither the sexually immoral, nor idolaters, nor adulterers, nor men who practice homosexuality, nor thieves, nor the greedy, nor drunkards, nor revilers, nor swindlers will inherit the kingdom of God' (1 Corinthians 6:9-10 CEV). 'He who conceals his sins does not prosper, but whoever confesses and renounces them finds mercy' (Proverbs 28:13).

Instant deliverance, partial deliverance, or none
Mike Boling

During my time in Equatorial Guinea in 1991-92, I saw many cases of demonized people. Some were instantly delivered, others received partial deliverance, and still others showed no sign of deliverance after repeated prayer. I think the most important thing I learned is that there is no set formula. Each situation needs discernment from the Holy Spirit on how to work deliverance in that situation. We saw many people who seemed to possess an animal spirit. During deliverance, they would begin to walk or crawl or act like a particular animal, depending on which spirit was inhabiting them. Demonization was also frequently linked with previous visits to the local healer. The local healer would invite a spirit (to him, it was a spirit of the ancestors; to us, obviously a demonic spirit) to inhabit the body of the sick person in order to reveal the reason for his sickness. Demonization also came through curses put on a person. The following incidents might be helpful.

'My dead husband appeared'
An elderly woman asked for prayer since she had been having scary dreams in which her dead husband appeared to her. The pastor first asked the woman if she was willing for Christ to take total charge of her life. At first she was resistant but then agreed. This initial part was quite important in aiding the subsequent deliverance. When the pastor began to pray for the woman a voice in the local dialect cried out repeatedly, 'I won't go, I won't go.' Finally, the woman tumbled off the bench where she was sitting and became silent. When she arose, all was calm, and she confessed that the demon had left.

Spirit healer dance
We prayed for a young woman who was having dreams of a demonic nature. Before we began the deliverance, we sat in the room with the woman and prayed for the Holy Spirit to come and take control. As we were praying, the woman began to dance in a similar fashion to the local healer. After rebuking the demon and commanding it to leave, the woman became calm.

She hit the floor
We were praying for one young woman and commanding the demons to leave her. Suddenly it was as if an unseen hand had picked the woman up by the collar of her dress and thrown her backwards! She hit the floor and appeared to be unconscious, breathing heavily. We left her for the moment and began to pray for another woman nearby. As we began to command the demons to come out of this other woman, the woman on the floor began to move one arm up in the air. Obviously, the demon was trying to fool us. We went back and continued to pray for her. We saw further body twisting as evidence of demonic activity. Finally, she became calm and stated that the demons had left her.

Distractions
A young man was brought for prayer by a family from another village. He was a tall, husky youth, and I prayed that God would protect us from any violent demonic manifestation. When we began to pray he began to argue with one missionary that there was nothing wrong with him, and tried to distract him from praying for him. Every time he responded he would sneer as if he were mocking everyone in

the room. As we continued to pray for him, he would get up and wander aimlessly about the room as if he wanted to leave. We saw no sign of deliverance after a lengthy time of prayer.

Unwilling to renounce
This last episode was related to me by Rob Brynjolfson, my colleague. A young man came into the church walking with a stiff, unnatural gait, similar to someone who has had a spinal cord injury. He wanted prayer for deliverance and said this ailment was caused by a curse put on him by his grandfather. As it turned out, the grandfather was in the congregation. The young man was having sex with one of his father's wives and the grandfather said he had only cursed him because he refused to stop after being warned. In this particular situation, a decision was made not to pray for this young man since he was not willing to renounce his immoral activity.

Breaking satanic bondages
Bruce and Annette Rattray
Late in 1990 Obed had been ministering in Sungai Mariam (Mary River), a village half an hour by river from Nanga Lebang. The Spirit was at work amongst the people. When Obed had to leave for ministry elsewhere he asked Bruce to visit this place.

Obed had told us about a little old man, Anca, who had been demonised. He was quite mad and had become so violent that he would run out of his house with his machete when people came by. The villagers had put him into a cage the size of a large coffin. It was only a little wider than the width of his own body and a bit longer than his own length. It was made of strong timber tied with rattan. It could be opened at the end, but that was tied up too. The only way to move him in and out of the cage was by untying the end. Food was put for him just outside his cage. He could barely sit up. Pak Obed had already prayed for him and he was no longer violent, but his relatives were afraid so they kept him in the cage. When we arrived he was just like a corpse, stiff and cold. The folk said, 'We won't let him out of the cage. He'll just have to stay there.'

His wife had left him and returned to her own village. His brother was worried about him and told us that all they did was put food out for him, but he never ate it. The villagers said they would just leave him there until he died. Bruce and I felt very badly about this. They told us that every time he heard the sound of a white deer (it wouldn't have been a deer at all, it would have been made by a spirit) he would go mad and become violent. Even after Obed prayed for him, he would tremble violently when he heard this sound.

We prayed for him and Bruce then asked for him to be taken out of the cage. They were willing for that while we were there, but said he would have to go back in the cage when we left. We brought him out and tried to talk to him but he couldn't respond at all. It was as if he was deaf and dumb. He hadn't spoken for several weeks. A couple of days later I took him some food. He was just as we had left him. We managed to get him to sit up and drink something. Every time I wanted him to take a mouthful of food Bruce would have to pray and insist in the Name of the Lord Jesus that he would eat. On this second visit we brought him out of the cage and Bruce prayed against the deafness and dumbness; he began to respond and spoke a few words to us. He was very dirty, so I bathed him. The people thought I was quite mad. We went back three times. Each time I took soft foods for him, but we realised he was soon going to die because he only ate when we were there.

After prayer we made the decision to bring him down to our home. Before we left we heard the deer noise. We commanded the spirit making the noise to go and never come back again. It has never returned. We took Anca down to Nanga Lebang and put him in a room in the main headquarters house. I fed him. Gertrude helped too. At first we made him stay in his room, and then we would take him out for a walk. He was really very weak from being so long without food and exercise, but he kept improving. When Pak Obed came back he took him very slowly (in the local dialect) right through the way of salvation. Anca said he wanted to believe and he received Christ. He stayed in our home for the last week before he went back to his village. He was so happy, and followed Bruce around all the time. He worked for us, ate with us, and talked and talked. After we took him home Obed visited him regularly. His brother and seven other people came to Christ. Sadly, his wife did not return, but Anca was now quite capable of looking after himself.

He wanted to be free
Norma Hunt

I had been told about a very powerful witch doctor and some of his healings. For example, he was called to someone who was sick. He wiped his fingers around the person's throat and under his chin and removed a handful of deer fur which he put onto a plate in front of him. The person recovered. A witch doctor costs money, so he would not be called unless someone was quite ill. In remarkable ways he healed many people.

One day a delightful and charming man came to my medical clinic. I talked to him about the gospel and showed him a chart called 'The Two Ways'. It had scripture verses on it, and if people could read I asked them to read a verse. Mostly though, I just explained the meaning of the verse I wanted them to know about.

This particular day I felt the Lord was telling me to read out Colossians 1:13-14: 'He has rescued us from the dominion of darkness and brought us into the kingdom of the Son he loves, in whom we have redemption, the forgiveness of sins.' At first I refused, saying that the man would not have a clue what I was talking about. Eventually I gave in! As soon as he heard the verses, the man said, 'That's what I need. I need to be delivered from the dominion of darkness'.

He told me he was a witch doctor, not by choice, and not one who did evil things. He only helped the sick. He related to me a number of things that he had done, and suddenly I knew that I was sitting beside the powerful witch doctor that I had heard so much about. A lovely man!

He explained how he had become a witch doctor. One day out in the rice field he saw a snake as big as one of the big trees that had been felled, about a metre in diameter! He fainted. The next thing he knew was that he was back at the long house, and that he had power he had never had before. If someone was sick, the spirits would come to him and tell him even before he was called by the sick person's relatives. These spirits would tell him what to do. Sometimes they brought him things that belonged to other people!

He told me he was afraid of the spirits and showed me a little piece of wood that he carried in his hat to protect him from them. He wanted to be free from them. I explained to him that if he accepted Christ as his Saviour and Lord he could be free. However hard it may be for those of us in the Western world to understand, it is not a simple thing for such a process to take place. This man lived a long way from me or from any other Christian help, and though he went some way in believing in the Lord, I don't know to what extent he progressed.

Detailed diagnosis
Joan Eley
Painful memories
Fanny cried as she described how her parents separated when she was only two years old, and she never found her mother till she was sixteen. She stayed with her father, a hard man who would hang her up by her feet naked and belt her. He died when she was eight but she held a lot of resentment against him. Wherever else she stayed she was also cruelly treated. On several occasions men tried to violate her. As she was telling her sad story her husband sat weeping. He knew she had suffered but didn't know the details.

She was forever seeking her mother. Seeing a woman in the market, she would ask herself, 'Could this be my mother?' When she was sixteen, someone told her where her mother was, so she went to visit. It was not far away. She had a lot of resentment for her mother for deserting her, and for living so close all those years and never looking her up.

Her mother was ill, so Fanny bought a house and brought her there to care for her until she died five years later. Even during those five years her mother never responded to her as a mother to a daughter, but treated her like a stranger, and was not interested in her. Fanny still did not want her mother to die. One of her sisters beat her, accusing her of killing her mother.

Her tears as she told me this made it obvious she needed healing of these memories. I asked Jesus to go back through her life and heal that little girl within her who was still uncomforted. She cried as if her heart would break, but it was not now the crying of an adult, but of a little child. I felt a demon had taken advantage of her extreme sadness. It was cast out in Jesus' name, along with all the rest of the sadness, loneliness, rejection and fear which had entered during her childhood.

After this the change in her was tremendous. She could now talk about her childhood without crying her heart out, and was at rest in her emotions and rejoicing in the Lord. All those childhood memories had been healed and those tormenting demons had been sent to the pit in Jesus' name. Glory to our Lord!

Dragging his feet

Francisco had problems with his devotions. He said he felt tired and something hindered him when he did have them, so they were disorganised and lacked harmony. He worked like a slave, not that he loved money but he was concerned for his parents. His father worked hard but never made enough. Francisco made promises he could not keep, became distracted and entangled by other things, and was irresponsible. He had always been like that. He liked sports, and had sometimes put them before the Lord. He loved music, and spoiled his testimony by singing in dubious places. Carnal thoughts disturbed him, and only his love for the Lord had prevented him from falling into immorality.

Some of the demons in him gave their names and their work. Vanity worked to make him put sport and music before the Lord, and hindered him from asking for help from others. Lies made him speak quickly without thinking. Lasciviousness made him struggle with morality. Sleepiness hindered him from praying and reading. Greed caused him to work so hard he missed church. Fear produced nightmares and illusions. Unbelief tried to make him believe he was not saved. Infirmity was working in his kidneys, his eyesight, muscles, tendons and hands. Entanglement worked with Sluggishness and Irresponsibility to spoil his efficiency at work.

Francisco knelt before the Lord, and the demon spirits lost ground as he tearfully dedicated himself 100% to the Lord and his will. Then we worked on curses, and cast out the related spirits in Jesus' name. The demons left, some with big yawns. Now he has perfect liberty to pray without hindrances. There is a beautiful confidence and harmony between him and the Lord. He feels so light, the joy of his salvation shines brightly. Christ is real, his liberty is real. Since then he has gone on with the Lord, serving him with a beautiful Christian wife.

Unsuspected pride

Ruth felt self pity because of her poverty, and developed an inferiority complex. Her life consisted of going to school, coming home and weaving hammocks, but her mind was free to roam while weaving. She stole, smoked cigarette butts, and took the ends of the witches' candles to mix with kerosene for polishing the floor. Apart from playing sex with two friends when she was little, and some minor petting when engaged, she had kept herself pure, and was a virgin at her wedding.

Her husband Elias has lived a pure life since his conversion five years ago, but Ruth admits to jealousy and a grudge towards a bad-living girl he was with before that. Elias had begun to reject her when she tried to draw close. Other times she bossed him, making him feel he knew nothing.

Ruth was proud of her mind, very proud of her figure, face, singing, and her ability to lead worship. She was proud of her mud house, the best in the village, and of her growing flock of goats. The enemy had gained terrible power in that area. Some minor spirits were leaving, but Pride was staying put. It was very offensive, arrogant, racist. When Ruth kneeled down, I said to Pride, 'That is where you should be!' Pride sprang her to her feet, saying, 'That wasn't me, it was her!' We had fun.

Pride claimed the revealing blouses and tight skirts she wore to show off her figure. She made a bonfire and burned them. One blouse with gorgeous buttons was going on the fire and Pride exclaimed, 'That is mine! At least take off the buttons! You are going to leave me naked!' She threw a cassette on the fire because Pride said it was his to dance to. One thing after another had to be dealt with to pull down the stronghold of pride. Ancient serpent was there and he left like a snake unwinding itself. A demon called JJ was causing her gastritis, and was going round and round in her intestines. It left with sourness and acidity. I had never before worked on a case where demons so controlled the mind. No sooner had one been revealed than another one took over. They made so much noise in her head that she couldn't hear the teaching in the seminar, and they kept her awake at night.

She herself worked hard with self-deliverance on sadness demons, and had good results. There was already a tremendous change between her and her husband. Jealousy and envy had gone. Concerning Pride, the Lord led me to Isaiah 14:11-15 and Ezekiel 28:12-17. 'You found me out,' it said, and left with vomiting. It was followed by the devil and King of the World the same way. What a victory after five and a half days' work! Ruth and Elias are now strong leaders in the church.

Abandoned and cursed

Matilda had been very active in the church, so when I heard that she had resigned from her responsibilities, was under discipline, and had cleared out from home for a couple of weeks, I visited her and spoke to her about the possibility of curses over her life. It was too hard for her to speak of the sad, dark events of her past, so she decided to write them down.

At the age of two she was abandoned by her mother, because she resembled her father whom her mother hated. Her father took her to her grandparents to bring up, and she spent seven happy years with them. Then her mother stole her from her grandparents' home, not because she loved Matilda, but to take revenge on Matilda's father. For a year she lived with her mother, who cursed her and treated her more cruelly than ever. Then she was in foster homes where those responsible had been told to beat her, as she was good for nothing. Her mother's lover twice tried to violate her, but she fought back with her feet and teeth. She ran away to Caracas, the capital, where she stayed for three years with a kind family. Her father had spent a fortune trying to find her, and they met in Caracas when she was 17. Her grandfather had longed to see her again before he died, and this made her hate her mother more than ever. When she was 18 she met and married Antonio to escape another relationship. Antonio had had five women, and one of his lovers insulted and taunted Matilda in the street, making her life unbearable. She felt she didn't love Antonio, and had no desire to continue to be his woman. He insisted that since she was a Christian she must accept him and his women!

It cost her terribly to forgive her mother who had made her suffer so much. She cried as if her heart would break as she said, 'I forgive.' After this, curses were broken and demons left. Hatred was the boss. He, Rejection, Coward and Lies left and made their way to the pit in Jesus' name. She went to her mother's home and said, 'Mother, I forgive you for all you have done to me'. Three months later the mother came to Matilda's home, crying uncontrollably and asking for pardon.

Matilda confessed that although she had truly forgiven her mother from her heart, she was still battling to forgive her mother's lover who had tried to violate her, and to forgive another who had made life so miserable for her. She confessed fear, desperation, anger, loneliness, unrest, hatred, desire to die, confusion and resentment, for which she asked forgiveness. Only then could they take back all the ground given to the enemy through those sins.

In order to forgive her mother's lover (now dead) and the ex-lover of her husband, she again cried her heart out, but in the end she found strength and grace in the Lord to forgive them. She had asked the Lord on numerous occasions to forgive her, but was never sure if she was forgiven, or even if she was saved, because of not having forgiven these two people. After this all her doubts about her salvation were gone for good. What a relief!

Then hosts of other demons left, leaving her saturated in baths of perspiration. They left through the eyes and nose, with tremblings and goose pricks.

Since then she has felt wonderful. God gave her such a deep love for Antonio, and he came to the Lord. A few months later her mother was gloriously saved, and threw away her many idols. Her father came to the Lord, repented of all his spiritist practices, and when both her father and her mother came to a wedding anniversary for Antonio and Matilda, the two were able to speak to each other without hatred. What victories!

Matilda asked her mother, 'Why did you hate me so much? Why did you hate my father so much?' Her mother related her own tragic story. Her parents had been desperately poor and starving. When she was fourteen, a 25 year old man fell desperately in love with her. Her father sold her to that man for a few sacks of corn! He took her to his home, but she ran away and hid. Her family knew where she was and persuaded her to return to him, otherwise they would have had to give the corn back! Matilda had been the first child of this forced union.

His house was contaminated
Sister Ezbel had been caring for her ex-husband in his last years. He had been such a blasphemer and hater of God, but came to the Lord only minutes before going into a coma and dying. The house was contaminated with his demons. As we did house cleaning, some terrible fear demons manifested. They left in Jesus' name, and the whole atmosphere of the home changed.

Esther had cooled
Victor and Ezbel asked me to come quickly. Their eighteen-year-old daughter Esther had cooled in her Christian life, and had come under attack. She became engaged to an unbeliever in clear disobedience to 2 Corinthians 6:14-16. This had caused some grief at home. One night demons began to speak in Esther in various different voices. Some of the things they said were so funny it was difficult not to

laugh, while others, threatening destruction and death, were so terrible they had her parents in tears.

They were led by a demon named Strength, who boasted he was so strong Victor would not be able to cast him out in Jesus name; and though Victor tried, and evicted several weaker ones, Strength defied him. Every night Esther was tormented and could not be left alone until she settled down in the early hours of the morning. Esther's sixteen-year-old brother was so afraid of what was going on that he went to stay with his aunt in Barquisimeto. After a month of this, Victor told the church that if it continued, he would not be able to carry on as pastor, because he and the family were exhausted.

I ordered Strength in Jesus' name to come forward and answer some questions – the names of the other demons and on what ground they had entered. Strength admitted they were connected with demons in her fiancé Jabier. Strength said he would leave her body with demonstrations of strength. 'Oh no, you won't!' I said. I counselled Esther not to cooperate with him if he tried to use her hands to attack us. I then forbade them from speaking any more, as we were not there to be entertained by them, but to cast them out in Jesus' name. Esther asked if we would postpone the deliverance till Jabier arrived, because the spirits always manifested more strongly when he was there. I told them the only manifesting they would do would be to leave. When Jabier arrived, so powerfully was the Holy Spirit working that demons were leaving without being told, with thick white froth, Esther and Jabier burping away. Jabier was not a Christian, and this was a problem. I asked who would fill the vacancy when these all left? Jabier answered, 'The Lord Jesus.' Yes, he was ready to receive Christ, so I handed him over to Victor who led him to the feet of Jesus.

Rosalie
Author unknown
Among the Gouro people of Côte d'Ivoire, West Africa, demonization is all too common. When a person becomes violent through insanity or demonization, threatening damage to themselves, to others, or to property, restraining them presents real problems. The traditional Gouro home is a round hut with thick walls of dried mud, a thatched roof and a bamboo or wooden door. Confining a violent person in such a building is not practical, especially if they have the superhuman strength so often in evidence.

There is an institution on the coast for psychiatric treatment, but it is not often that a Gouro living 250 miles inland could use this facility. The Gouros have developed their own solution. A heavy tree trunk is prepared to restrain the patient. A hole is cut or burnt through the centre and the patient's leg is pushed right through until the foot appears the other side. A strong metal pin is then inserted near the ground to prevent the withdrawal of the foot. Often the patient, in spasms of violence, bruises or cuts his leg on the log. This form of restraint means suffering.

Rosalie, a beautiful young Gouro woman in the village of Beziaka, became violent. She was the second wife of Ben, a fine, intelligent and literate Gouro man who had spent ten years in the army. Ben and Rosalie, like most of the inhabitants of this big village, were heathen. Although the gospel had been preached there for twenty years, there had been little enduring response. The Beziaka Gouros remained firmly attached to their old witchcraft.

Rosalie's family did all the witchcraft they could to secure her deliverance. They spent a great deal of money on healers and diviners. She only grew worse. No one could predict her next violent action. She wantonly smashed eggs, tore a man's shirt, beat a child, threw out the food she was given, and stubbornly refused to wear any clothes. Filthy, with saliva running out of her mouth and stark naked, this formerly beautiful and gracious young woman presented a shocking spectacle. The only thing to do was to put her foot in the log.

Among the tiny group of Christians in Beziaka was a woman named Naomi. She went boldly to the distressed family and told them that the 'Jesuses' (Christians) could heal Rosalie. Rosalie's father declared that if they took her to the Christians he would disown her. Lifelong ties to your parents are strong, and to be disowned is one of the worst things that could happen to a Gouro woman. Nevertheless, Rosalie's mother, her three brothers and her husband decided to take her to the mission. Pierre, Ben's Christian friend, offered to accompany them.

It took six of them to get Rosalie on board a passing vehicle, her foot still in the log. They arrived at the church to find the local Christians gathered for a weekly day of prayer and fasting, led by Samuel, the evangelist. Samuel preached to all who had come, urging them to turn from sin and devilry to the Lord Jesus as Saviour. Rosalie's mother and husband produced their fetishes and burned them as they believed in Jesus. Then they joined with all the Christians to pray for Rosalie.

By the end of the first day, several demons were cast out. Rosalie gave up fighting and struggling and became quiet. The second day, to test her progress, Samuel gave her a hoe and asked her to cut weeds. When she began to use the hoe back to front, Samuel realised she was not fully delivered. 'How many demons remain in you?' 'Two,' came the reply. The company returned to fasting and prayer. Samuel went into his house alone, crying to God with all the intensity of his being for full deliverance. His shirt was drenched with perspiration.

Complete deliverance came the third day. Rosalie's first words were, 'Jesus has saved me. Thank you, Jesus.' She passed the hoeing test, working normally. She bathed and dressed. What rejoicing there was among the Christians! Ben was so pleased that he brought a gift of a guinea fowl and yams. 'Why have you brought them to me?' asked Samuel. 'It is Jesus who heals and delivers.' They praised the Lord together. Rosalie and her mother went and bought food, and Rosalie cooked it. At once she began to testify what the Lord had done for her. Two days later she told the whole Sunday morning congregation.

After a time, through pressure from her husband, Rosalie's mother turned back from following the Lord. Ben too found the price of discipleship too high, and forsook the way. But Rosalie never looked back. Her two year old took ill, and backslidden Ben insisted on doing witchcraft. The child died. Even this deep sorrow did not shake Rosalie's faith, and she now has another son.

Several years after her conversion, she was one of twelve candidates baptised in the Bandama River near Zuenoula. Hundreds of Christians marched that day with banners and songs and testimony. Surely there was no greater trophy than Rosalie. Her demonization had been no secret, and her deliverance was not done in a corner. All the villages between Beziaka and Zuenoula had seen her driven past as a raving lunatic in the log, and a few days later return normal, completely transformed in character. 'What happened?' asked one burdened mother. 'Jesus has healed her! I'm going to take my son to the 'Jesuses' too!'

This family had a demonised and violent teenage son with his leg in the log. For a long time a famous demon of the Gouros called Zaza had pestered this boy saying, 'Give me your father!' Repeatedly the boy refused, knowing that if he agreed, his father would not live long. Finally weakening, he had it in his heart to agree. At that point the demon had invaded him. The family spent all their money on the fetish priest, then wanted to hire the Muslim priest, but had no money left. They offered him their young teenage daughter to be one of his wives if he could cure their son. The Muslim failed, and the girl was spared that tragedy. They brought the lad to the church, heard the gospel, destroyed their witchcraft and believed in Jesus. Again the Christians fasted and prayed, and the lad was completely delivered. The whole family, parents and seven children, turned to God. Praise the Lord! He heals today! He delivers today! (Names have been changed).

STOPTHINK&DISCUSS
● How closely do these stories follow the pattern given in the previous chapter? Are some steps sometimes omitted? If so, is there a satisfactory reason why they were omitted?

17
HEALING FALSE AND TRUE

Pondsius Takaliuang

Learn to distinguish between phenomena which come from God or from the devil. Demonic miracles often hinder a person hearing Jesus' claim on them to give their lives completely to him. Ask about the life of the person doing the healing. Is he converted? Does he live as a disciple of Jesus? Where did he get these abilities, and since when?

Magic healing

Witch doctors are bound by their method, time, and way of healing. If anything is changed, there is no healing. In divine healing God can heal at any time and in many ways. The Lord healed the sick through dipping (2 Kings 5:14), touching (Luke 22:51), laying on hands (Mark 8:23,25), the shadow of a believer (Acts 5:15), a handkerchief (Acts 19:11), anointing with oil (James 5:14).

Magic healing may clear up a physical ailment, but the patient suffers from a mental or spiritual problem. Although they may have been physically healed, they still suffer from anger and hatred. They have no peace. They refuse spiritual things. After divine healing, the patient is not only cured, but is interested in spiritual things. They have a holy desire for God.

Witch doctor
Pondsius Takaliuang
As a boy I suffered from a severe stomach ache. I almost died at that time. My family called a witch doctor. He said a healing spell and directly cured me without my going to hospital. But after that I could not pray or read the Bible, and I was not interested anyway. When I repented, I was healed in body, soul and mind. I love to pray and read the Bible.

Forty fits a day
Matt and Margaret Paton
Michel was 27 when we met him. He was in a state of terrible distress, suffering up to 40 epileptic fits a day. His mother had taken him to specialists in various parts of France, but the epilepsy was never brought under control. They finally decided to end their days together by turning on the gas taps.

A neighbour had invited them to the Evangelical Church, and Michel suggested that they try that last possibility. They went to the gospel meeting, and after prayer there was a slight change in his condition. Then our co-worker received the revelation that Michel's mother was a spirit healer! She admitted that she helped the sick with amazing results, even being asked by leading doctors in the main hospital to treat some hopeless cases with her prayer.

Our co-worker warned her that all the evil she was taking from people was falling on her son. She saw this immediately and renounced her 'gift'. Both she and her son were wonderfully converted and Michel was immediately delivered from his illness. Today he drives a car, has a good job and a lovely wife, and is active in church.

Breathing exercises
Terry and Diana Freeman

A young university teacher with a vibrant personality, Leah's marriage had surprisingly collapsed. Leah and her four-year-old daughter Gua Gua lived with her parents. After a few months of Bible study and friendship, Leah unreservedly gave her heart to the Lord in 1995.

Opposition came quickly. While her father was indifferent, her mother vehemently forbade her involvement in this 'Western religion'. She should give her time to her career instead of wasting it at those meetings. Her mother regularly created a fuss and used emotional blackmail to keep her at home. As time went by it became uncomfortably apparent that a more sinister force lay behind this opposition.

Leah would tactfully find ways to expose her mother to the truth. One day she was writing a new set of worship songs for a new cell, and asked her mum to help. Mum happily did so, until she came to the words, 'It's your blood that cleanses me.' She immediately became angry and again attacked Leah's involvement in the group. Those lyrics had a profound effect on her.

For four years Leah's mum had practised Qi Gong, a popular system of breathing exercises morning and evening. Adherents claim it is healthy, or even that physical healing or supernatural experiences can result. Early morning and late evening she would exercise and meditate, sometimes alone, sometimes with a group. At least once she had visited a cemetery and inhaled deeply to breathe in the energy ('Qi') of the departed. In this way she unknowingly gave open invitation to the powers of darkness to set up strongholds in her life. While claiming improvements in long-standing health problems, at the same time she became progressively more fearful and anxious. Often while sleeping she would dream of people now dead. As they came to her, she would 'shoot' them with her fingers, and they would turn into grotesque beasts. She agreed with Leah that it was the work of evil spirits, but said, 'I'll use the power of Qi Gong to defeat them!'

A year came and went. Leah learned a lot about spiritual warfare and perseverance. Each night she and Gua Gua would pray together for grandma. Tension at home was easing, but Leah began to lose hope that her mum would be saved. Another six months, and Leah had stopped praying for her. But Gua Gua had not. As was their custom, Gua Gua slept in grandma's room. In the morning, the first thing she would often say was, 'Grandma, do you believe in Jesus?'

Leah bought a book, the testimony of a Chinese believer from an earlier generation. Her mum read it and was moved. In September she surprisingly agreed to go with Leah to a secret meeting of believers. There she heard an old Chinese believer teaching about healing from the Bible. How intrigued she was. This was why she had begun Qi Gong. Over the days that followed, she responded in faith to that message, asking God to heal her headaches, leg pains and eye complaints. That brought her closer to God, and one night she came in to Leah's bedroom with these words, 'I want to pray with you.' Without prompting from Leah, she confessed her sins and admitted that for so long she had rejected the One who truly is God. The next time Gua Gua asked, 'Grandma, do you believe in Jesus?' she replied, 'Yes!' but this time she meant it!

What anger in the dominion of darkness! Counterattack came quickly. She was stricken with guilt and fear. She had betrayed her old master. What would he do? How would he punish her? She slept badly, and old health problems, supposedly cured by Qi Gong, began to reappear. Leah explained, 'Qi Gong doesn't heal disease. It just covers it up.'

In her dreams people came to beat her. She said, 'In Jesus' name, go!' To her surprise they apparently replied, 'In Jesus' name we beat you!' Next morning she asked Leah, 'How can this be?' They searched the room for objects related to Qi Gong and found a photograph of her 'Master', the particular priest she had aligned herself with. She threw it in the rubbish, along with books, tapes and all other objects connected with Qi Gong, renouncing all links with it.

While praying, Leah's mother felt God say, 'I will bless your family. I will heal you and give you the Holy Spirit. First, I will heal your eyes so you can read my Word.' She began an uncontrollable puffing action, exhaling air out of her lungs. This may have been connected with the active inhaling action of Qi Gong in the cemetery. Three nights later she asked Leah to pray with her again. Leah prayed, 'God, help her to believe and not doubt. Come, Holy Spirit . . .' and suddenly she found herself speaking in a language she did not understand. The thought in her mind was still, 'Come, Holy Spirit.' This went on for about an hour. She would stop for a break, begin again in Chinese, but find it would switch to the other language. While she spoke in the other language, her mother would exhale in a puffing fashion. After this she became very quiet, very tired, and went off to sleep again. Leah went back to her own room where she continued to pray.

As the months passed, her mother's bondage of those dark years weakened. Early the next year, visits in her dreams stopped. She is still young as a new creation in Christ, but God is close, strengthening her and teaching her the victory there is in him. The gospel is bringing the freedom it was designed to do.

Christian healing

'I would rather she die than call the witch doctor'
Norma Hunt
Until Western medicine came to the area, the people depended on occult powers for healing. Some continued to do so, and others used a mixture of both. Generally

the Christians depended on the Lord and medicine, but in difficult cases they were seriously tempted to return to the old ways.

Ana, the daughter of Christians Tangang and Lingur, became very ill. At the time I wasn't doing medical work because the government had a nurse in the next village. The nurse treated Ana but she didn't improve. Village folk said to Tangang, 'She will not get better unless you call the witch doctor. Call him.' Tangang replied, 'I would rather Ana die in the Lord than live under the power of the devil.' It was a sore test of his faith, and Lingur's, but she stood by his decision. Ana did recover.

Tangang and Lingur's faith was purified in the furnace of trouble. One of their little boys fell or was pushed into a flooded river and drowned. This was great opportunity for people to say, 'What is the good of believing in Jesus? He didn't protect your boy.'

Then one day tragedy struck again. I was called to come immediately to their home. When I entered, there was Lingur cradling her next little boy, aged 18 months, in her arms. He was white and lifeless. I was stunned by the sight. She said, 'Norma, I don't know what is wrong with him. He was playing outside and all of a sudden he called for me and said he wasn't well. I thought he was just tired, but then he went all limp like this. I thought he might have a snake bite, but there are no marks on him, and no one saw a snake.'

He had the appearance of one who has collapsed from an internal haemorrhage. He was unconscious and his pupils were large and fixed. I felt distraught. Would God let this little one die so soon after his brother's drowning? What would it do to their faith? What would others say? Tangang was called in from the rice field and rushed in perplexed. We prayed. With instructions from me, Tangang rushed off to get the government nurse. I really didn't think that he would be able to do anything; the child should have been rushed to an emergency department, the nearest one a long way away.

Again we prayed, pleading with the Lord for his life. I felt by then that this was a spiritual war, and that I needed to stand against the powers of darkness in the name of Jesus and in the power of his blood. One of the Christian girls and I went to my house to pray. We waged war specifically against the powers of darkness in the name of Jesus. The battle was in the heavenlies. I was feeling desperate.

We returned to the house and the little fellow was still white and limp. As I sat beside his mother Tangang returned with the news that the nurse could not help him. The child must be taken down river to the hospital.

Suddenly the little boy's eye gave a little flicker. I said, 'Lingur, his eyelid moved a bit.' 'I don't think so,' she replied. 'It was because I brushed a fly off.' I checked his pupils; they were responding slightly to torch light. I felt like bursting with joy. Gradually he came back to life and recovered completely.

I can't stop the bleeding!
Norma Hunt

Usually on Sunday mornings I went to minister in the surrounding villages. One morning I stayed home, because we were having a number of baptisms in the river at my village. I was still at the river after the baptisms when a man from a nearby village came running. 'Norma, come! Duba has cut himself! We put him on your veranda!' I felt a bit annoyed. 'Always, always being called by someone!' I thought, 'I'm not going to hurry!'

When I arrived at my house my annoyance was jolted out of me. The poor man was sitting on the split bamboo veranda with the blood dripping through on to the ground. Towels used to wrap his leg were soaked in blood, and he looked very pale. I felt ashamed that I had dawdled home; ashamed of my annoyance. Still, I was not worried. I had dealt with many wounds and the Lord had enabled me to repair them.

Having gathered up the necessary equipment, I carefully removed the towels from around the leg, fully expecting to see a large wound, but no, it was a tiny cut about one centimetre long, on his shin. 'What a cinch,' I thought. I cleaned the wound and washed away the blood on Duba's leg while the blood slowly trickled out of the wound. 'Not to worry,' I thought, 'a bit of pressure will fix it.' But no amount of pressure had any effect!

I began to worry. 'I can't stop this bleeding even though I am pressing hard on the bone!' I said to myself. After a few minutes I said to the men who were with him, 'I can't stop this bleeding. You will have to take him to SP1.' There was a clinic there, but it was a good two hours walk away. One of the men said, 'Is there anyone here who can do an incantation?' Horror struck me. I didn't mind having to hand him over to the medical authorities, but to hand him over to someone who would do an incantation was to admit spiritual defeat.

In a split second all that I had been teaching flashed before me. 'Jesus is all in all. Jesus' power is greater than the power of darkness. Trust him.' My mind reeled. My heart felt crushed. I was in turmoil. Hand him over, and I might as well go home. In the eyes of the people, the Lord would be defeated by the occult. I cried out to the Lord in my heart to stop the bleeding, but it went on. Praying in my heart was not enough.

The men were not believers, but I had treated a lot of people from their village. There was only one thing to do. I must trust the Lord to stop the bleeding. I said, 'May I pray for him?' They said, 'Yes.' As I closed my eyes I heard one of them say to the others, 'If Norma prays, he will be all right.' With my fingers still pressed on the wound I prayed aloud, claiming the power of Jesus to stop the bleeding. For a few seconds I kept pressure on the wound, then I removed my fingers and the bleeding had stopped. I was probably whiter than Duba who had lost so much blood! God's power was vindicated. Duba recovered well.

Ex-Pastor in pain
Joan Eley

Joseito had been a pastor for five years when he and two of his brothers backslid through a young woman. It was a disaster. Three years later he caught a terrible fever and came home. He felt as if he was dying and going to hell. In fear he came back to God, asked forgiveness from his wife, and called for the elders of the church to pray for him. It didn't work. Two years later I found him sitting under a shady tree, a wreck. I hardly recognised him. He suffered from giddiness, terrible pain in the temples, and other symptoms with colourful descriptions: 'It seems like I have something rotten inside my head. It feels like my brains are burning. My eyes are burning and stinging. My back is aching, and the pain goes down one leg in the bones and joints. For two months I have not been able to pray or read or go to church. I have not worked my farm, either – my wife and some church members are keeping it running for me. Every night I groan with the pain. The doctors say I could die at any moment, and there is nothing they can do. My relatives tell me the only solution is a witch doctor, but my wife has pleaded with me not to go. She said that God can send someone who has his power to cast out this spirit.' So I offered to pray with him. The pastor was in agreement, and we counselled and prayed with him the following day.

During the night he suffered nothing but a few shooting pains in the temples, and in the morning he went to work on the farm! So we worked on him again that night, and he is gloriously healed.

His ten year-old son had had epilepsy since he was five, which meant he had become epileptic the same year Joseito caught his fever. Joseito wondered if it was a punishment for his adultery and backsliding, and had even wondered if he had committed the unpardonable sin. Praise God, the lad was also delivered, and has never had another attack.

Final stages of tuberculosis
Bruce and Annette Rattray

At Lidung village many people were showing a positive response to the gospel. The one exception was Mr Serani, one of the most powerful witch doctors in the whole area. While the gospel meeting was being held in one of the larger rooms of the longhouse, he would walk up and down on the veranda outside beating a gong. He was a likeable little old fellow, but he avoided me like the plague!

One evening after the meeting Tugi, one of the believers from a nearby village, asked me to pray for his older sister, who was very ill. That was the understatement of the year! Leading me into a dingy little room coated with soot from the fireplace, he pointed to his sister. This emaciated wreck of humanity, clothed in rags, was little more than a walking skeleton, with every bone visible under her yellow, sagging skin. Her slightest movement brought on a spasm of violent coughing that left her gasping desperately for breath. Unable to lie down, she would try to sleep by kneeling near a 25-litre kerosene tin and resting her head on a pillow placed on the tin. It was the filthiest pillow I had ever seen!

I explained that I would pray for her only if she and her family were prepared to cut all ties to the occult and destroy all fetishes and objects associated with demonic power. I would pray for her in the name of the Lord Jesus Christ. Satan and all his demonic powers were in conflict with Jesus, therefore they had to choose to which power they would submit. The family was divided, with the larger group preferring a healing ceremony with Mr Serani, and the smaller group wanting me to pray. It gradually dawned on me that I was in a God-ordained power encounter.

After several hours of discussion, the family spokesman called Tugi. 'Tell the pastor we will have the ceremony with the witch doctor, and if she is no better, then he can pray for her.' 'No way,' I replied. 'You must choose between the two powers. It's over to you.' So they asked the sick woman what she wanted. 'Let the pastor pray for me,' she wearily replied.

So I stood in front of this pathetic wheezing, gasping wreck of a woman, my faith less than a grain of mustard seed. I was desperately trying to believe Mark 16:18: 'They shall lay hands on the sick, and they shall recover.' I laid hands on her and prayed: 'Lord, if it be for your glory and for the building of your kingdom here at Lidung, please touch and heal this poor woman.'

Next morning, the family carried her to my canoe, and we took her to my wife's medical clinic. Anne came down to the canoe to check her, and somewhat reproachfully chided me: 'Bruce, I cannot help anyone in that condition. She is in the last stages of tuberculosis!'

I explained about the power encounter of the previous night. Anne gave the folk who had accompanied her a few aspirin and something to ease her breathing, and instructed them to bring her back after a couple of days. She did not expect the old lady to live that long.

A few days later, as folk began to gather for the daily clinic, I went out to chat with them while Anne prepared her equipment. A very thin lady with a big smile was sitting on the veranda rail.

'Which village do you come from?' I enquired. Her smile widened. 'I'm from Lidung. You don't recognise me, do you? I'm the lady you prayed for a few days ago!' 'Anne,' I called. 'Do you recognise this lady? She's the one I prayed for at Lidung!' 'It's a miracle,' Anne whispered. 'Oh, praise the Lord!' The old lady quickly regained full health, and went back to work in the rice fields!

But that was not all. When Mr Serani, the witch doctor, saw what had happened, he said, 'God's power is greater than that of the spirits. I want to believe. I want you to come down on Sunday. I want to burn up all my fetishes and my occult objects.' This was a tremendous step for a witch doctor.

So we went down on Sunday morning. He brought out all his paraphernalia. He had piles of it! The folk stood around, laughing a little bit nervously, and making jocular comments. We made a big fire. We tried to burn these things, and even though they'd been in his room, and tinder-dry, some of them were almost impossible to burn. The Dayaks had told me that if you try to burn something that has occult power the fire won't burn it. I didn't believe them then, but I do now. I had to get a machete and split some of those wooden idols into small pieces before they would burn. Then we counselled Serani. This old fellow made a clear-cut stand for Christ and started coming to the meetings at Merakai. He was so appreciative. Once, he brought a present for Annette – a huge fish from the river – and kissed her hand as he presented it. He became a faithful follower of our Lord, and a much-loved brother, with a tender heart and a great sense of humour.

Fifteen years later, as old Mr Serani lay in a coma dying in hospital, I held his dear old hands, speaking gently to him of the Saviour's love, of assurance of salvation and eternal life with him. I felt somehow that he heard me. After committing him to the Lord, I walked quietly down the corridor. The young doctor, a Muslim, called out and asked me to step into his office. He came immediately to the point. 'I saw you with that patient. You love that old man, don't you? I am amazed that you, as a foreigner, could have such a close relationship with an old villager like him. What is the background to that?' So I told him the whole story. Deeply moved, he was silent long after I finished, snapping out of his reverie only when I stood up to leave. And so the chain of blessing flows on!

Dr Emile
Traugott Böker

Dr Emile was a Chinese veterinary surgeon, and the organist of his church. My wife Hanni and I spent a night with him and his wife in 1989 when I was taking a meeting in their church. A month before they had prepared a small room in their apartment which is specially to be for the use of preachers. We asked Dr Emile how he came to the Lord. He told us that his father was a follower of Javanese mysticism (kebatinan). Emile had been seeking – he 'tried out' mysticism, Hinduism, Buddhism, Islam. Nowhere did he find 'intellectual' satisfaction. He was converted through the ministry of the pastor of a Pentecostal church. However, as he had so many questions which they could not answer, he turned to a pastor of the Reformed church where he found a more solid theological basis. Soon he was voted into the church committee. He is a keen man who is concerned that his church is so little active in evangelism.

Before we left we wanted to pray for the family and asked for special subjects for prayer. They mentioned that their second son, Francisco, had a constant stabbing pain in his stomach, though not always in the same place. He had been examined by several specialists but without success.

I was reminded that Dr Emile's father was a mystic. Was there some connection? When I remarked that there were connections between mysticism and being tormented by evil spirits, Dr Emile began to tell us more of his family background.

Francisco slept in the room where his father's keris (Javanese ceremonial dagger) had been kept. Whoever holds this dagger in his hands becomes invisible. Dr Emile's great-grandfather experienced this when he seduced a girl in a village and the men of her village were after him. He had this keris with him and none of their blows struck him. When Dr Emile had been a young man this keris used to be honoured every week with an incense sacrifice. The worth of such a keris is about the price of a luxury car.

When Dr Emile became a Christian he gave the keris to his younger brother. But very strangely, once a week on the offering day he experienced a noticeable smell of incense in the air. He gave the ebony cupboard in which the keris had been kept to his medical-technical assistant. From that time on, this man had dreams at night of being chased by snakes. In that room and in the bathroom Dr Emile had often seen a mysterious figure who looked very like his grandfather.

As a student Francisco had worn a necklace with a death's head charm with which he could make himself invisible. Once, during an examination, he had an open book before him from which he was copying the answers, but the examiner went up and down the rows, passed by him, and saw nothing.

Emile himself had clairvoyant abilities. Some time before he had warned a colleague that on a certain day he should not leave the house, because he had the odd feeling that danger would lie in wait for him. In fact the colleague had a strange traffic accident that day in which he died. Another time Dr Emile had a strong impression that a dog which was a patient of his was seriously losing blood. He packed his bag into the car and drove to the house, and it was really so; he arrived at just the right moment. He was told that a dog which a colleague had treated had died of an ulcer in the womb. Spontaneously Dr Emile said, 'The dog died of an enlarged liver.' An autopsy was made and Dr Emile's clairvoyant diagnosis was correct. He was driving in his car and suddenly had a clear sense that his wife was in trouble. He raced home and found it was true.

Dr Emile did not like having these abilities and they worried him a good deal. He went to a Christian doctor to ask him to pray over him. This man held him by both hands and prayed and sang over him in tongues. From then on most clairvoyance left him. However, he began to have other supernatural abilities – he could heal, sometimes combined with clairvoyance.

Dr Emile's body has a strange radiation. Once, when he was ill, his wife would not go near him because she felt a hot radiation from him, although he had no fever. Another time, as he lay on his bed stretched out for a siesta, he suddenly felt that in some unexplainable way his body was full of electricity. His wife lay beside him and, as she turned over and touched him, she felt a shock and cried out, 'Why on earth are you electrifying me?' She did not believe that this was a supernatural experience.

When he laid a hand on the bodies of his patients, the animals, he felt that warmth, an electrical current, went out of him. After a time this came to an end, and then he often had a completely spontaneous inspiration, like a flash of lightning, about what was wrong with the animal. He never had this ability in the mornings, only in the afternoon increasing until evening. Afterwards he felt very weak, almost ill.

A dog was brought to him with a dangerous tumour. It had been operated on before, but now another operation was necessary. Dr Emile laid his hand 'in Jesus' name' on the old, still visible scar. Before the next operation took place, they examined the dog again – there was no trace of a tumour. If his wife or children fell ill, he laid his hands on them 'in Jesus' name'. Often the illness went rapidly away. He used hypnosis – if a dog was restless or dangerous he looked it in the eyes, then the dog laid down and went to sleep so that he could treat it.

Dr Emile had quite unusual strength and stamina – two veterinary practices, active in the church (sometimes playing the organ at church four times in one day) and, with all this, he slept only a minimal amount. He sometimes had a strong twitching in his face – could that have something to do with occultism? He did not have real peace in his spirit; he was a driven man. He knew no really deep sleep at night, sleeping only for an hour or so. Then he would wake up, walk about, and lie down again. His wife was used to the bedroom door being opened and shut the whole night long.

Despite all his abilities, Dr Emile was not happy. He always had such a strange feeling, as if he were not really quite on earth. He was often plagued by fears: 'If I should suddenly die, what would become of my wife and children?'

His wife Fanny, who had already thought that he and his brother were mentally ill since they had seen ghosts, asked how one could tell whether supernatural gifts were from God or from below. We named some characteristics. Dr Emile declared that he really did not want anything to do with such things, but he had to realise that there was an inherited condition. Whole families were in debt to demons because they had called upon them for help and protection.

I asked Dr Emile whether he was prepared to renounce all evil powers, all spiritual bonds to his ancestors, and to trust in Jesus Christ alone. He said he was. Then we prayed together. I asked Jesus to give him power to trust God alone. And then Dr Emile prayed. He admitted his guilt, that he had turned to other powers instead of Christ as his Saviour and Lord. Hanni and Fanny prayed too. Nothing particular happened, but Dr Emile witnessed to a new peace in his heart.

That was a start, but the two of them needed further help. Until that time they never had prayed together. Even at table each prayed silently for themselves. Fanny had depressions. There would be a good deal of personal counselling necessary. Next time we had a meeting in that city, we took the opportunity to visit the family again and stay the night with them. Hanni had a personal talk with Fanny. She said a prayer of renunciation of worship of the dead which she had practised until then. Now that she had opened her heart, we encouraged them both to pray together from that time on. One Sunday, the whole family suddenly turned up in Batu. We did not have much time together, but they told us that the previous four days they had prayed together - every morning at 5 a.m. before the children woke up.

The following year Dr. Emile visited us unexpectedly. He had some questions about Judas Iscariot about whom he had to hold a Bible study in his church. He told us that since he lost his magical powers he was reading and understanding the Bible in a way he had never known before. It was noticeable: since that time he was often asked for Bible studies. It was a joy to see how thoroughly he prepared for these sessions. He read books and heard cassettes on all sorts of themes, as much as he could. And in all this he had a good sense of discrimination - what was biblically grounded and what was just a human idea.

The final victory
Brenda Couche

'I'm sorry, Media, but there is no way I can cure your eyes.' Media had been blinded in an explosion thirty years earlier. He had spent a fortune on animal sacrifices, witch doctors and mediums, and was now trying the Evangelicals. He sat wearily under a tree, resigned to another disappointment, only half listening to the strange story of God having a son called Jesus.

After that he visited us quite often, his son leading him along the narrow rough paths by a pole they carried between them. He had four wives and several undernourished children whom he brought to our clinic for treatment. Christ's

House treatment was always supplementary to the divination and sacrifices to the spirits, and payment for the healing was always made to the witch doctor, not to us. He still listened to the gospel but made little response.

One morning we were awakened in the early hours to the sound of desperate laboured breathing outside the window. Media was having a severe asthmatic attack, and was convinced he was dying. 'I want to enter Christ's way,' he gasped. 'I'm dying and I don't want to go to hell.' We brought him in, prayed with him, gave him the necessary injection, and watched with relief as his heaving chest relaxed and the terror on his face turned to smiles. 'Thank you Jesus, thank you, thank you,' he sang.

'Now you have entered Christ's way,' we explained, 'you must leave Satan's way, burn all your fetishes and break your spirit pots.' 'Yes, yes,' he said. So we arranged to go to his home that afternoon, where he would publicly confess his faith in Christ by destroying all his fetishes. This we knew was no easy thing. Media was an important man in the tribe, and played a leading role in teaching the boys during the initiation rites. He was deeply involved in the animistic ceremonies of the tribe and knew the secrets of the witch doctors.

That afternoon, my co-worker and I went with a group of Christians to Media's house. We were met with an ominous silence. Media sat with his head down in abject misery. 'No, I can't do it,' he said. 'My wife and sons have all threatened to disown me, leave me to die, or even kill me, if I persist in entering the Christ way. What can a blind man do?'

We came home feeling more aware than ever that we were trying to invade Satan's territory and that we had lost a strategic battle. We spent several hours that night in prayer. 'Why, Lord, why?' Suddenly the Lord spoke to us very clearly, and we both knew it was from him. 'Mine is the final victory.' The clouds lifted and we felt a surge of faith. 'Yours is the final victory,' we declared with joy.

A week later, again in the early hours, we were awakened with the familiar desperate breathing. This time it was much worse. Media was barely able to speak, but managed to ask us to pray for forgiveness for him. This time he really meant it and was prepared to enter Christ, cost what it may. Miraculously, the Lord healed him again, and he went home rejoicing.

Later that day we gathered round a fire outside his mud house, where he burnt all his idols and smashed his spirit pots, shouting for all the family to hear, 'Jesus has defeated Satan, Jesus is stronger than Satan!'

He never looked back. Though the family gave him a hard time, they didn't reject him, nor did his sons refuse to work his land as they had threatened. One by one his wives and some of his children were converted, and the whole village marvelled at his testimony. He never recovered his physical sight, but God truly opened his spiritual eyes.

STOPTHINK&DISCUSS
- There is a spiritual gift of healing (1 Corinthians 12:9) but does God sometimes also heal when people without that gift pray in the name of Jesus?
- What reasons can you list for the fact that there seem to be more healings in the Third World than in the West?
- How can a believer guard against demonic healing?

18
QUESTIONS AND DISCUSSION

Levels of demonization: Can a Christian be demonized?
Dietrich Kuhl

Scriptural evidence

The New Testament uses a variety of words, phrases and pictures to describe demonic influences in people and demonic control of people. It's important to notice the difference of terminology that is used to describe such influences in the lives of believers and unbelievers. I have deliberately chosen an inductive approach to help you draw your own conclusions. Keep in mind that 'demon possession' and 'demonic oppression' are not New Testament terms.

Terms used in connection with unbelievers or likely unbelievers
1. Demonized; to act under control of a demon; under the power of a demon, expressing the mind of the demon. This is the most commonly used term in the New Testament (13 times). All occurrences are in the Gospels (Matthew 4:24; 8:16, 28, 33; 9:32; 12:22; 15:22; Mark 1:32; 5:15, 16, 18; Luke 8:27, 36; John 10:21). The term is not used in Acts or the Epistles. It is never used for people who are born-again believers. Often the terms 'demonized' and 'casting out of demons' occur in the same text.
2. 'God anointed Jesus of Nazareth with the Holy Spirit and power, and . . . he went around doing good and healing all who were under the power of the devil' (Acts 10:38): It means 'being ruled by the devil'. The same verb is used in James 2:6 where the rich oppressed (or exploited) the poor.
3. To have an unclean spirit (Mark 3:30; 7:25). Luke 4:33 speaks of 'having a spirit of an unclean demon'; Luke 13:11 speaks of 'having a spirit of infirmity'; Acts 16:16 mentions 'a spirit of divination' and Acts 19:13 speaks of 'having evil spirits'.
4. A man in or with an unclean spirit (Mark 1:23). In other words, a man under the influence or authority of an unclean spirit. It could also be translated 'in union with an unclean spirit'. The expression signifies an intimate and somewhat fixed relationship.
5. 'A man in whom was the evil spirit' (Acts 19:16). We could also translate it, 'a man with whom was the evil spirit', or 'a man in union with the evil spirit'. Both constructions in numbers 4 and 5 are used in a similar form of Jesus and the believer: The believer is in Jesus and Jesus is in the believer. This expresses an intimate relationship and union. This same basic fact is here stated for the unbeliever and the unclean spirit.
6. 'The ones being tormented by unclean spirits' (Luke 6:18; Acts 5:16).

7. Luke 22:3 and John 13:27 state that Satan entered Judas Iscariot, 'the son of perdition'.
8. In Matthew 12:45 the Greek verb *katoikein* emphasises that the spirits make that person their home (oikos), that is, the fixed settlement. The same verb is used for God and the Holy Spirit who live, remain in the believer (Ephesians 3:17; James 4:5).
9. The evil spirit had seized the demonized Gadarene many times (Luke 8:29). The Greek verb means 'to snatch or catch away'. It conveys the idea of force suddenly exercised. The description seems to imply that the spirits were dormant and at times became violently active.
10. The evil spirits often drove the demonized Gadarene into the desert (Luke 8:29). This implies control over the demonized man.
11. Satan had bound this woman for 18 years (Luke 13:16). She needed to be loosed. She may have been a believer, because she is called a daughter of Abraham, and because she immediately praised God.

Basic conclusions: A fixed, close relationship with demons; heavy disturbances by demons; control by demons at a time when the church was not yet established.

Terms used in connection with believers or likely believers
Paul was concerned with the church and for the church. His prayer life focused on the church. He does not address the problem of demonization of unbelievers — probably because it was obvious to him (Elymas, the slave girl, Ephesians 2:2).
1. Paul warns believers not 'to become sharers/companions/partners with demons' (1 Corinthians 10:20). Paul argues against participating in idolatrous feasts. He implies that someone who is born again can get entangled in a close fellowship with demons.
2. Paul warns believers not 'to give place to the devil' (Ephesians 4:27), i.e. not to give him an opportunity to do what he wants to do. How do we give room to the devil? By continuing in our sin, by harbouring resentment and having an unforgiving spirit. The solution is repentance and forgiveness.
3. Paul emphasises that the devil should not be given an advantage (2 Corinthians 2:11), i.e. he should not be allowed to obtain what is not his. (NIV translation is a dynamic equivalent: '. . . in order that Satan might not outwit us'.) How could that happen? By an unwillingness to forgive and put things right. The solution therefore is repentance and forgiveness.
4. Paul speaks of the possibility that Christians can be shaken in mind or disturbed (2 Thessalonians 2:2) by a spirit or a teaching that is inspired by demons.
5. Paul mentions a believer who turned aside (1 Timothy 5:15), i.e. away from Jesus, in order to follow Satan. It happened through persisting in sin.
6. Satan filled (aorist) the heart of Ananias (Acts 5:3). It happened through deliberate deception. Compare this with Ephesians 5:18: 'Be filled with the Spirit.' It's the same word. The issue is not space but surrender to the Lordship of Jesus or Satan.
7. In 1 Timothy 3:7 and 2 Timothy 2:25-26 Paul warns believers to be alert lest

they fall into the trap or snare of the devil, who then takes them captive to do his will. The context makes it clear that it is probably through pride. Repentance and humbling oneself opens the escape from the trap.

8. 2 Corinthians 12:7 records that Paul was given a thorn in the flesh, a messenger or angel of Satan to 'buffet' him (punch him with the fist). It means something that hit Paul from the outside.

9. In 1 Corinthians 5:5 and 1 Timothy 1:20, an unrepentant sinner was 'handed over to Satan'. The man in 1 Corinthians 5:5 had lived in incest. Hymenaeus and Alexander had continued in blasphemy. The purpose of this metaphor is to exclude the person from the congregation. This places the unrepentant offender back in the world which is Satan's domain. Such removal from the church is corrective in its intent, a last resort. If these people were truly saved, the buffeting by Satan would cause them to realise their error and forsake their sin.

10. Satan walks around like a roaring lion, i.e. a hungry lion, seeking to attack and 'to devour', i.e. to destroy (1 Peter 5:8).

11. Revelation 2:24 records that one can 'know the deep things of Satan', for example by digging into the occult. It is not just an intellectual knowing. The word implies influence and a degree of control by Satan. The way of deliverance is through repentance (Revelation 2:21).

12. Paul expresses his amazement that believers have been bewitched (Galatians 3:1). The Greek verb means 'to mislead by a charm'. Paul links this with demonic influence, although it may be indirectly through false teachers (see #15).

13. In 2 Corinthians 11:4 Paul speaks about the possibility of believers 'receiving a different spirit', listening to and accepting the lies or the influence of an evil spirit. Galatians 3:2 uses the same word for receiving the Holy Spirit. Deliverance is through repentance and renunciation. It is noteworthy that nowhere in the New Testament is exorcism as such clearly mentioned or taught with regard to believers. The emphasis is on repentance, turning away from sin and Satan, renouncing all claims, resisting the devil or fleeing from the devil.

14. Paul had to admit, in 1 Thessalonians 2:18, 'Satan hindered us'. The Greek verb *enkopto* means literally 'to cut into', i.e. hindering someone by breaking up his path or by placing an obstacle in his path (e.g. by sickness, problems with children, riots). In Paul's case it was certainly not caused by prayerlessness (1 Thessalonians 3:10). It is interesting to compare 1 Thessalonians 2:18 with Acts 16:6-10 and Romans 1:10 & 13.

15. Several times in scripture (1 John 4:1-6; 2 Peter 2:1; 1 Timothy 4:1) we are warned 'Don't believe every spirit'. 1 John 4:1-6 speaks about evil spirits operating in false teachers, i.e. 'a spirit of error' (verse 6). 1 Timothy 4:1 speaks about 'paying attention to deceitful spirits and doctrines of demons'. In other words, these texts point to an attempted mind control by demons.

16. 1 Corinthians 12:3 'Therefore, I make known to you that no-one speaking by the Spirit of God says, "Jesus is accursed".' Some commentators understand 1 Corinthians 12:3 as implying that Paul's statement is based on the case of a

genuine believer speaking in a foreign tongue induced by his or her occult pagan background.

Conclusions

Demon influence is the action of demonic powers with the intent to corrupt a person (1 Peter 5:8-9). It occurs in various degrees of severity, depending on the resistance the person offers the satanic onslaught (Ephesians 6:10-14; James 4:7). If a believer fails to 'stand against the devil's schemes' (Ephesians 6:11) and yields to this onslaught, the enemy takes all the territory allowed him. Satanic forces operate on the principle: to go as far as they are permitted to go. When they are allowed to operate unchecked (on the mind, the will, the emotions, the fantasy, the bodily appetites), then their influence, imperceptibly at first becomes stronger and stronger (control, enslavement, corruption). There is no biblical warranty to believe that this cannot happen to believers.

In the last 10-15 years quite a number of people have changed their position about this issue. This change has to do with an increase of empirical data and a subsequent review of exegesis.

The New Testament leaves no doubt that Christians do come under demonic attack. The warnings of the New Testament about conflict with Satan and demons are all addressed to believers. Our enemy, who hates God and the believer, is committed to making us ineffective in our personal lives and in our ministry for the Lord. The question is not whether demonic attacks on a Christian are possible, but rather to what extent or to what level they are possible. On this issue people should be allowed to differ. The following quotes may highlight the shift in position about this issue in recent times.

Dr Timothy M. Warner, Professor of Missiology at Trinity Evangelical Divinity School, Deerfield, Chicago: 'My study and experience have convinced me that a Christian may be attacked by demons and may be affected mentally and sometimes physically at significant levels, but that this does not constitute possession or ownership.'

Dr V. Raymond Edman, former Principal of Wheaton College: 'Can Christians be demon possessed? Theory says "no", but experience says "yes". It is theoretical that a demon cannot possess a body in which the Holy Spirit dwells. However, I have known true Christians who were truly demon possessed and who were delivered in answer to prayer given in the name of the Lord Jesus.'

Dr Merrill F. Unger, a leading scholar in the area of demonology and former Professor of Old Testament at Dallas Theological Seminary. He had written in his *Biblical Demonology* (published in 1952) that only unbelievers are exposed to demonization. But in his book *Demons in the World Today* (published in 1971) he confessed that his previous position 'was inferred, since Scripture does not clearly settle the question'.

Dr Fred Dickason, Chairman of the Theology Department of Moody Bible Institute. In his book *Demon Possession and the Christian. A New Perspective* (Westchester: Crossway Books, 1987) pp 185-186 he claims to have seen about 400 cases of demonic influences in Christians.

I myself can cite as examples three lady students who, between 1965 and 1975, in their second, third and fifth year of study at the Indonesian Bible Institute, Batu, East Java, experienced demonic influences.

At times it is argued that since the body of the believer is a temple of the Holy Spirit, an evil spirit cannot also be in his body. This is faulty thinking. Spirits do not occupy space, nor is being Spirit-filled a matter of space. It is rather a matter of the degree to which all my life is lived in obedience to, and under the control of, God's Word and his Spirit. The question is whether Satan or evil spirits can have such a grip on my mind that he can persistently influence my thinking, emotions and/or my actions. The issue is not ownership (demon possession) but whether spirits can have free access to my mind through my failure to use my spiritual defences against it, e.g. persistence in unconfessed sin.

Dr Timothy M. Warner summarised the issue in a helpful way: 'If the relationship between believers and demons is seen in this light, the relationship will fall along a spectrum, running from the level of victory experienced by Jesus Himself at one end, and an entrenched enemy which is camping on ground which has not been brought under the rule of truth and the Lordship of Christ at the other end.'

Tom White, one of the workshop leaders at the Lausanne II Conference in Manila in July 1989, summarised the different levels of demonization in the following way in *The Believer's Guide to Spiritual Warfare* (Eastbourne: Kingsway Publications, 1991), pp 42-43.

Level 1: General warfare against believers
Temptations (Matthew 4:1) are enticement or compulsion (from an external source) to violate God's laws. The solution is resistance (James 4:7; 1 Peter 5:9). Flaming arrows (Ephesians 6:16) could be an external influence of evil spirits intended to attack or inflame weaknesses or hinder ministry. The solution is resistance and using the armour of God (Ephesians 6:10-18).

Level 2: Specific bondage or demonization
Oppression (Acts 10:38) is persistent, ongoing bondage to some bad habit, some distress of body or soul that may be outward disturbance ('vexation') or inward mind-control ('demonization'). How does mind-control function? People listen to deception and lies; they accept them; they become internalised convictions; they become patterns of actions and habits, e.g. habitual sin. The solution is deliverance through renunciation. It is a truth encounter.

Level 3: Deception and bondage of unbelievers
Control (1 John 5:19) includes dominance of the soul by Satan, either generally (covertly) through deception and disobedience (Revelation 12:9; Ephesians 2:2) or specifically (overtly) through the direct control of evil spirits (Matthew 8:28-33). The solution is salvation (Colossians 1:13-14), which involves renunciation and may need to include specific deliverance.

A last quote from Dr Merrill Unger may summarise and conclude this issue. 'It must be stressed that demons cannot indwell a Christian in the same sense that the Holy Spirit indwells. God's Spirit enters a believer at salvation, permanently, never to leave (John 14:16). A demon, by contrast, enters as a squatter and intruder, and is subject to momentary eviction. A demon never rightfully or permanently indwells a saint, as the Holy Spirit does, and no demon can ever have any influence over any part of the Christian's life that is yielded to the Holy Spirit.' (Merrill F. Unger, *What Demons Can Do to Saints,* page 56).

Scripture verses that balance each other
Stewart Dinnen

Verses that tend to indicate that demonization of Christians is impossible:
'No one can snatch them out of my Father's hand' (John 10:29).
'The prince of this world will be driven out' (John 12:31).
'What fellowship can light have with darkness? What harmony is there between Christ and Belial?' (2 Corinthians 6:14-15).
'You cannot have a part in both the Lord's table and the table of demons' (1 Corinthians 10:21).
'He has rescued us from the dominion of darkness' (Colossians 1:13).
'Having disarmed the powers and authorities, . . . triumphing over them by the cross' (Colossians 2:15).
'The Lord is faithful and he will strengthen and protect you from the evil one' (2 Thessalonians 3:3).
'The one who is in you is greater than the one who is in the world' (1 John 4:4).
'The one who was born of God keeps him safe and the evil one cannot harm him' (1 John 5:18).

Verses that seem to indicate that demonization of Christians is possible:
'Satan has asked to sift you as wheat' (Luke 22:31).
'If you received a different spirit . . .' (2 Corinthians 11:4).
'Satan himself masquerades as an angel of light' (2 Corinthians 11:14).
'Do not give the devil a foothold' (Ephesians 4:27).
'Our struggle is not against flesh and blood, but against . . . the spiritual forces of evil' (Ephesians 6:12).
'Satan prevented us' (1 Thessalonians 2:18).
'Hymenaeus and Alexander whom I have handed over to Satan' (1 Timothy 1:20).
'Some will abandon the faith and follow deceiving spirits and things taught by demons' (1 Timothy 4:1).
'False teachers among you . . . denying the sovereign Lord who bought them' (2 Peter 2:1-2).
'Your enemy the devil prowls around . . . looking for someone to devour' (1 Peter 5:8).
'Resist the devil and he will flee from you' (James 4:7).

The Holy Spirit and an unholy spirit in the same body?
Joan Eley

The fact that we have the Holy Spirit does not mean he is automatically in control of every area of our lives. The same goes for a demon which may control or try to control certain areas, obviously areas where the Holy Spirit is not in control. Paul in 2 Corinthians 11:1-4 is expressing his concern that the Christians might have received another spirit. The Greek word for 'another' is *heteros* meaning 'another completely different'. What is more completely different from the Holy Spirit than an unclean one?

Some say that demons can't live together with the Holy Spirit, but the Lord said, 'Do I not fill heaven and earth?'(Jeremiah 23:24). Then where are the demon spirits?

Some say that a Christian is sealed by the Holy Spirit, so a demon cannot break through the seal. But what if demons were already there before conversion, and had never been evicted? Where does the Bible say that the seal is to protect us from demons? The seal of the Spirit is to do with ownership. The armour of God is to protect us, if we put it on. If we don't put it on, what happens?

The Bible does not say a Christian cannot have a demon in his body. Many say, 'Demons were all dealt with at conversion, through the cleansing of the blood.' The Bible does not teach that. Through the blood we are redeemed from the wrath to come, and all our confessed sins are forgiven. There are many different aspects to our Lord's work on the cross but, to be effective in one's life, each aspect must be applied. Salvation and cleansing from sin become effective when we repent and apply the blood of the cross. He bore our sicknesses (Isaiah 53:4, Matthew 8:16-17), yet how many Christians have not been healed until they have applied through faith the healing aspect of Christ's death? He bore the curse for us (Galatians 3:13-14) but how many Christians suffer dreadful failure in their lives materially, physically and spiritually until some curse is revoked and cancelled through applying by faith Christ's victory? On the cross Christ triumphed over Satan and all his host (Colossians 2:15) but how many Christians are defeated by the evil one until they apply that victory?

Will a Christian be shut out of heaven if he dies with demons in his body? No. Neither principalities nor powers will be able to separate us from the love of God in Christ Jesus our Lord (Romans 8:38).

Pigs in the living room: a parable
John Bardsley

Jesus is Lord. Jesus is my Lord. I gave him all of me, years ago, and I was conscious that he had accepted the invitation to live and rule in me. A couple of times he has disciplined me for inviting little tin gods into first place in my life where he belongs.

When I sin, it is as if I go out and fall in the muck. I come home and confess it and Jesus cleans me up.

Now imagine that this sin meets a craving in my life, and that one day I don't confess it immediately, but hang onto it for a while. That's like coming home with a bucket of muck to play in.

Then I miss the presence of Jesus my Lord, and I feel cold and lonely. I realise where I went wrong, and confess it. He cleans me up, throws away the muck bucket, and the sun comes out in my life again. But later, because the muck meets a need in my life, I get some more. It's not difficult to get. It's not far away.

Imagine that the contact I get my muck from says to me, 'Look, you come here so often for muck. For regular customers, we have a home delivery service.' I know Jesus my Lord would not be pleased, so I don't have my contact drive up to the front door with it. But I break a small doorway through the back wall, and he delivers it there.

Then the muck gets too awful, and I feel so bad; so I confess it, and Jesus cleans me up, and throws away the bucket. Bricking over the secret gateway takes time and resources. Jesus my Lord has all those resources, but it makes it slow work for him if I accept another load, and the delivery man breaks it down to get the load in.

Imagine that one day there is such a bumper load of muck, that the delivery man comes in with me to carry it. It comes with free installation and user training, and he shows me several flavours of muck and how to create them; musical variations on muck; muck in games and fun with muck; muck excuses and how to rationalise muck; gift-wrapping muck for giving away; muck on TV and the Internet, and muck, muck more. (Many times a person's first contact with muck is when they receive it gift-wrapped from their parents or grandparents or a trusted friend or relative.)

Just then who should walk in but Jesus my Lord! I am so ashamed and confused . . . and guilty! I get on my knees in a passion of repentance and he cleans me up, and cleans my room. It takes some time. Then the two of us go off together to enjoy each other and refresh our relationship again. It has been a bit stale and static and wooden since I built the muck gate.

I go to the kitchen for a drink, and catch myself thinking, 'What do I feel like? How about one of those spicy new muck flavours?' Then I think, 'Hang about! Two minutes ago I was enjoying Jesus my Lord! Where did this muck thought come from?' I turn around and there is the delivery man, my special muck guide. 'Are you into telepathy then, as well?' 'Of course,' he says. 'But I thought you left when Jesus my Lord came in?' 'Well, I left that room. It got a bit glary for me. I had to find a darker corner. But I have several more fascinating programs to install for you yet.'

I tell him, 'Leave! Get going in Jesus' name, and never return! Take your programs with you! Jesus my Lord, make this muck man leave!' He leaves. Jesus and I enjoy a drink, and the sunny days that follow are wonderful.

Then one day I stumble in an unexpected muck puddle, and the old craving returns. I pick up a couple of bags to take home. It's not so heavy, but the delivery man comes along to carry them, and to help me open the old doorway, unload the muck, and demonstrate the latest. We play for a while, then I tell him, 'You've got to go.' He doesn't seem to take me seriously. I'm not sure if he's gone or not.

I think he's hiding in the basement. The presence of Jesus my Lord never seems quite as clear and bright and joyful as before – as though it was smudged somehow, or as if there was a layer of smoky glass between me and his glorious sunshine.

I'm sick of fighting this war by myself. I ask a friend to be my muck accountability partner. We pray together, and begin. I promise absolute honesty. My friend promises absolute honesty. We're going to get to the bottom of this. Jesus my Lord has promised that we don't have to live like this any more. All he demands is that I set my will towards him. He will give all the strength I need. My friend asks me how it started. Jesus my Lord reminds me. We start right there, and go through systematically, room by room. Everything mucky has to go.

Jesus my Lord comes in with a blaze of sunshine. I really don't know why I ever chose muck.

Can a Christian be demonised? If, instead of going to Jesus my Lord for something I crave, I go to any other lord, then that other lord can have influence in my life. But there is an answer, a complete and total answer! See Strongholds: 'You can be free'.

My flatmate had very strange 'turns'
Norma Hunt

My room mate and I were in Java living with a Christian family while we both studied an Indonesian language in preparation for working in Kalimantan. The place was rife with demonic forces which held sway in the lives of most of the people. However, my experience, which for me was traumatic, took place within the home.

Often during the day and each evening my room mate would have strange 'turns'. A visiting missionary said it was demonic. I was horrified, appalled at such a diagnosis! How could a Christian be so troubled by demons? To me that was not possible.

As time went on she grew worse, although not all the time. Most of the day she was perfectly normal, and was doing much better at learning Indonesian than I was. Because of that, I was loath to say too much to the family we stayed with, in case they thought it was just a case of sour grapes on my part. I prayed constantly for her, and to get her to settle at night I had to claim the covering of the blood of Jesus and the power of his name over her repeatedly. Still I did not understand the problem.

One day, while she was at language class, I was kneeling by my bed praying for her, when something hit me across the back of the neck. It felt like an iron bar crashing down on me. There was nothing there with me! The thought started coming into my mind that it was demonic. Her teacher and mine both thought so too, but how would they know – they were not even Christians! I assumed the devil was putting the thought into my mind, and I fought against it.

Eventually the Lord got through to me and told me to cast the demon out. I didn't know what to do, but I knew I had to obey. I said to her, 'The Lord has told me to cast out a demon.' I thought she would be angry, but she wasn't. She was like a lamb – except that her eyes blazed at me and made me feel that a tiger was going to attack me from within them.

I put my arm around her shoulder, not knowing that I shouldn't do that, and ordered the demon out in the name of Jesus. Immediately I was hit by a terrible force that struck me from the top of my head to my feet. My room mate burst into tears and called out, 'I'm free! I'm free!'

Soon she was in trouble again, and so I shared the problem with the couple with whom we both were staying. They called in the elders from the church, and one told me later that when they came into our room he was almost forced back by the strength of the demonic powers in the room. As we ministered to her together, she gained complete freedom.

A spiritual attack while physically weak
Jim Dawson

Pa Loy was a village pastor's wife and a faithful Christian. She was admitted to the Sukhothai government hospital with high blood pressure and was deteriorating very fast to the point where the doctors said there was nothing they could do to save her.

After a few days she began manifesting an evil spirit and began mocking the church and Christ. The spirit claimed Pa Loy and also declared that the hospital belonged to it. Her husband tried to rebuke the spirit, but it wouldn't leave. Whenever I came to visit her, the spirit wouldn't manifest and she would speak normally. It told the husband that it was hiding when the Christian leaders or missionaries came.

Later, we discharged her and took her in my car to a house to pray for her. Some of the Thai Christians began praying in the town church for her deliverance and missionaries from other provinces also began to intercede. We took a team of six keen Christians and close relatives to pray for Pa Loy in a missionary's house. Some others wanted to come but I had to turn them away as they would have only added to the drama.

We began reading Bible passages that dealt with Christ's victory over the enemy and we sang praises to the Lord. During this time Pa Loy was very weak and hardly coherent. She then began to tremble in her legs and then, lying down in an almost unconscious state, she began to beat the floor with her legs in a violent manner. We sensed that a spiritual struggle was going on and so continued to command the spirit's expulsion from Pa Loy. She then sat up and let out a loud, long scream after which she collapsed again on the floor. I believe this was when the spirit left her.

It was now about midnight and some of the relatives thought that she was going to die and so rushed her to a private hospital nearby. However, we suspected that the spiritual struggle was over. She was admitted to the Intensive Care Unit and they did a CAT scan on her. We prayed for her once more and all went home to snatch a few hours sleep. At seven in the morning some of us gathered at the hospital and found to our amazement that Pa Loy was sitting up in her bed in the ICU with a great big smile on her face and eating rice. The doctors insisted on keeping her in for another day. The next morning her husband discharged her, and she walked to my car as normal as ever and I drove her home.

It seems that the spirit had attacked her while she was in a physically weak state and had tried to kill her. It was a strengthening experience for us all and renewed our confidence in the power of Christ through believing prayer.

A restless, troubled Christian, but we found out why
Bruce and Annette Rattray

Maria, the daughter of an occult practitioner, had found Christ as a teenager. Now a forty year old mother and active in her local church, she was often troubled and restless, and never able to come to a steady walk with Jesus. One day, more agitated than usual, she came to Anne's clinic for medical help. After a thorough check up, Anne called me. 'Her symptoms do not tie in with any sickness. I suspect a demonic problem.'

At first we were reluctant to take her in, stretched to the limit as we were with local commitments and preparation for our Leaders' Course the next month. We knew the hours of prayer and counsel involved in such cases. On the other hand, we also knew that only Christ could deliver her and our refusal of help would mean that her only recourse would be to heathen witch doctors who could only bring her into deeper satanic bondage and ultimate madness.

The first couple of weeks were heavy going. She could not bear to be alone and followed Anne constantly. Often at night she would awaken us as her mind was so tormented by voices and visions of ugly forms. From the beginning we deliberately bound the demon powers in her in the Name of the Lord Jesus. Then we led her in a verbal prayer, sentence by sentence, renouncing all ground she may have given to Satan, consciously and unconsciously.

After a while she was sufficiently improved to receive simple Bible teaching emphasising the blood of Christ as the basis for our forgiveness and approach to God; the defeat of Satan and his demons by the death and resurrection of Christ; the ministry of the Holy Spirit, and what we are to expect him to do. We finished every session by singing a chorus of praise to God together. This seemed to help her as much as anything. Often we sang it several times.

Then the enemy began his counterattack! As we prayed for her, rebuking the demon powers, she told us that they would pinch and hit her. We counselled her to ask the Holy Spirit to reveal to her the ground in her life which allowed the demons to remain. She began to confess her use of powerful witch doctors and asked for forgiveness and cleansing as the Holy Spirit brought them to her remembrance. This really upset the enemy! 'If you keep this up, you will die!' the voices kept telling her. 'Not you, THEM, for they will have to go,' we told her. She found increasing deliverance, often confessing the names of six or seven witch doctors in a single day.

Then she seemed to run into a wall, with no further progress. We knew the enemy can attack a Christian in this way only if he is holding ground legally in their lives. Any use of the occult, for example, puts a person in debt to the devil. We began to ask questions to find the cause. It is imperative that the patient is prepared to cooperate, and being desperate, she was more than ready to do so.

'Have you ever been to the witch doctor when you were ill?' we asked. 'Oh, scores of them,' she said, 'both before and after I became a Christian.' We explained that each visit had opened the way for a demonic attack, and that, as far as possible, every visit must be confessed and renounced. Sin like this is not automatically annulled when a person comes to Christ, but needs specific confession and renunciation before they can enter into a life of victory.

She was amazed. 'My father took me even when I was a small child. It goes back a long way,' she said. 'Ask the Holy Spirit to remind you of every time it happened, then write it down,' we counselled. 'Then each evening we will meet for prayer and ministry.' Amazingly, the Lord did remind her of these times, often in great detail, and she wrote them down.

We taught her from the word of God the basis of deliverance, and led her in a simple prayer of confession, renunciation and cleansing, then putting that area under the Lordship of Christ. Over two weeks she remembered and dealt with over sixty visits to witch doctors!

There was a remarkable change in her, but still not a complete deliverance, with two disturbing manifestations now becoming noticeable. Occasionally she might act like a mad person, talking gibberish, with loud insane laughter. There had been no sign of this before. A mocking look would come into her eyes, giving the impression, 'I've got you beaten. You don't know what to do, do you?' Other times she was quite normal.

As we prayed together, the Lord gave a word: 'A cord of three strands is not quickly broken' (Ecclesiastes 4:12). I suggested we each ask the Lord to speak to us individually, but not share it until we all felt sure that he had spoken.

As I awakened a couple of mornings later, I felt the Lord telling me, 'She has two demons.' I asked Anne, but she said, 'I'm not sure yet,' but after a couple more days she said, 'I believe the Lord is saying she has two demons.' That afternoon we asked Maria. 'I'm not used to hearing from God,' she replied, 'but I have a strong impression there are two demons in me.' Praise the Lord for his word and his Spirit!

I explained to her carefully from the scriptures our authority in Christ over demonic forces, and the procedure for evicting evil spirits. She understood it all very easily.

'I will command the demon to tell you its name,' I said. 'Then you tell me. I will then command it to go where Christ would send it.' After that we will do the same with the second one. Finally, we will ask the Holy Spirit to fill the places left vacant by the two demons, as it says in Luke 11:24-26.' 'Right,' she said 'That's all very clear.'

Standing in front of her, I said, 'In the name of the Lord Jesus Christ, who by his death, resurrection and ascension defeated the powers of darkness, I command the evil spirit in Maria to tell her your name!' Instantly she responded, 'It says its name is Madness.' So I commanded, 'You evil spirit called Madness, come out of

Maria and go where Christ would send you.' The same procedure was followed for the second one.

Then a beautiful thing happened before our eyes. The Holy Spirit did fill those empty places vacated by the demons, and Maria's face lit up with a heavenly joy and peace she had never known.

What a wonderful sense of the Lord's presence filled the room that morning as we triumphantly sang the chorus together, 'Let's just praise the Lord!' It seemed that the angels joined together with us! No need now for someone to be with her. No need for medication to help her sleep. No need for a lamp in her room at night. She read the Bible and sang hymns constantly, occasionally asking us to pray with her as the Holy Spirit brought to her mind unconfessed sins, even as far back as early childhood. Everyone who came in contact with her was blessed and challenged by her radiant testimony of love and gratitude to the Lord. For days and nights, with great joy, she constantly read her Bible, sang hymns and praised the Lord. To this day she has lived a consistent, joyful Christian life. To him who came to set the captives free be all the honour and the glory!

Perhaps the miracle wrought in her life could best be summed up by a letter received by Anne from Maria's sister. This nominal Christian, married to a prominent Moslem official, was at first bitterly opposed to Maria receiving any ministry from us. 'Dear Mrs Rattray,' she wrote, 'I wish to open my heart to you. I have witnessed the power of God's Spirit through the deliverance of my sister, Maria, of whom it could almost be said that she has been raised from the dead. I just want you to know that I give all the glory to the Lord!'

What about Territorial Spirits?
Brian Woodford, John Bardsley, Hans Rothenberger,
Demonic activity linked to a town
Nako in Burkina Faso is the spiritual capital of the animist Lobi. The first missionaries arrived in Burkina in 1936, but until 1989 there was still no church in Nako. The church had tried a number of times to establish a work, but it fell to nought. They realised that it was a battle, and the high priests of the Lobi religion would oppose it. The church conference decided to give time to prayer, to get churches behind a new move, and to send another pastor. The new Christian family arrived in Nako, but their daughter fell ill, then the husband, and they had to leave. So it was a fight over a considerable time, but now a church has been planted.

Demonic activity linked to a wood
In Bouroum Bouroum, Burkina Faso, there is a wood about 400 metres from the mission house. In it are places for sacrifice and links to Lobi initiation rites. Lobi culture is heavily permeated by spiritism. One year the church prayed against that wood and the powers that were present there, that God would destroy the powers and the works of the evil one. After some time, the spiritual leaders of the Lobi tribe went to the local government and accused the church of destroying the spiritual powers in that wood. The reason for the Christians' prayer was that

every seven years in Lobi culture there are initiation rites and every young person is taken for two or three weeks into that wood. These are harsh rites, and usually some children died. There is a lot of occult activity. Church members who had come out of Lobi rites knew about it. They prayed against it every time it occurred. The initiation rite following this special prayer time was a flop! Hardly any of the parents would give their children! The link between prayer and the breaking of localised power is obvious.

In the Jola parts of Senegal there are sacred forests where the initiation rites are held, and there are sacred trees where sacrifices of palm wine are left for the spirits. Oussouye, Senegal is one of the centres of power for the Kasa Jola fetish system. Until recently, Jolas have come to Christ more easily in Dakar than in Oussouye. There are two possible reasons. One is the relative freedom from family surveillance and pressure in Dakar. The other is this phenomenon of localised demons who do not have authority so far away.

Spirits evicted from a grove of trees
Bruce Rattray

My wife Anne and I, with our ten-year old son, and Jonah, a keen young man in our Lay Leadership team, were on our way to take Easter meetings in Taboo River village, which was just opening to the gospel. It was the dry season. The river was too low to go all the way by canoe, so we left our canoe at Fork River village, going on by foot from there. As we walked, I was surprised to see a stand of six or seven very tall trees in the middle of a rice field.

'Jonah, why have those trees not been felled along with everything else? Surely the timber in them would be very valuable.' 'True,' he replied, 'but they are taboo trees. No pagan would dare to fell them. That is where they offer sacrifices to the spirits. They have idols under those trees. Come and I'll show you.' When we arrived at the grove of trees he parted the undergrowth, uncovering several small carved ironwood idols.

Righteous indignation welled up in my heart that Satan had so blinded these people that they offered sacrifices to demons instead of to the living God who had created and redeemed them. 'Let's form a circle around these idols,' I said. 'I want to pray.' I expressed my indignation to the Lord in prayer, then finished by saying, 'In the authority of the Lord Jesus Christ I bind the demons behind these idols from further deceiving these people, and I command you to leave this place, in Jesus' name. Amen.' We sang, 'In the name of Jesus we have the victory.' I felt a lot better as we went on our way. We had a great weekend of ministry, and an uneventful journey home.

Over a year later, I was again forced to leave my canoe at Fork River. To my surprise the headman came down to meet me. 'Leave your motor at my place. Come up and have a drink with me. I want to talk with you.' I had forgotten about praying over those trees, but I sensed this was significant. We sipped our tea.

He looked intently at me. 'You didn't by any chance pray over our idol site when you were here last year, did you?' 'As a matter of fact, I did. Why do you ask?' 'I thought so. The spirits have gone. Last time we went for our offering ceremony we couldn't do it because they were no longer there! We have begun to fell those trees, as there is much valuable timber in them.'

Naturally I took the opportunity to speak of the two masters, the two ways, and the two destinies. So much for idolatry being a mere superstition! They knew the demons had gone!

Demonic powers linked to a city shrine

In the main city square of Kamphaengphet, Thailand, is a beautiful pagoda, a shrine. Locals claimed that the church of Jesus Christ could not be built there because the shrine spirit says what goes in this province. The good news is that the church of Jesus Christ has been planted in Kamphaenghphet. The sobering news is that it took a long time. For years the church struggled to pass what came to be known as 'the 30 barrier'. Every time the congregation grew to 30, there seemed to be a fight, or a serious relapse, or some other disaster resulting in a loss of members. Now, after serious intercession, the church has passed the 30 barrier, and is planting daughter churches.

A language student in India had to walk past a Hindu temple every day on her way to the college where she was studying. Every day she felt hurt inside as she saw the vile customs that went on. She was sad because she could not speak enough Hindi to say anything to anybody about it, but she realised she could pray. She promised the Lord she would not walk past that place without praying for it. Within a week she was visited in a dream by a demonic spirit who said, 'Will you stop praying like that! I can't do my work properly!'

Demonic activity associated with a house

When Dietrich Kuhl lived in a village in Indonesia, he was intrigued by the house next door. Every morning at 6.30 a man's legs would appear over the balcony. Dietrich discovered that he was a medium with occult powers who was standing on his head. After some time he left and the house was left empty. No one would move in, as people knew that house was haunted. WEC considered buying it because it was cheap. After a time, a family from another religion moved in, but they left within weeks. Another family moved in and left quickly. Both families had experienced dark presences. Note the link between location and demonic forces.

In Japan, Christian workers Shuichi and Elaine Kitamura wrote: 'Whenever we move to a new area, the local demons give us a hard time until they realise we know where we stand.'

A Thai teenager had just become a believer. His father, a committed Buddhist, was furious and told him he must give up his faith or leave home. He chose to get out, and went to sleep in the harvest shelter in his father's rice field. There, in the night, he was visited by demons. In the name of Jesus he commanded them to leave him alone and go away. His father had a visit from the village priest to say, 'What have you done with our gods? We cannot contact them any more.'

Verdict about their existence

The concept of territorial spirits can explain the differences in spiritual receptivity among the populations in neighbouring districts or countries. It is evident that certain ethnic groups show themselves more resistant than others. Can we attribute this to a territorial spirit, or are we looking for the cause in cultural, historical or social events? Perhaps both.

There is some scriptural evidence for territorial spirits, but perhaps not enough for us to be too dogmatic. There is abundant evidence from experience, but we prefer not to base our belief on that. We must allow our brothers and sisters to believe differently from us if they draw different conclusions from the evidence.

However, it doesn't matter one bit what we call these spirits. If any spirit opposes the gospel, we have the authority and the right in the name of Jesus to pull down its stronghold, bind it, and set its captives free, on the basis of this verse. 'The weapons we fight with ... have divine power to demolish ... every pretension that sets itself up against the knowledge of God' (2 Corinthians 10:4-5). The Greek term for stronghold describes fortified positions. In other words, pulling down strongholds is an offensive warfare action. God apparently wants us to attack these strongholds.

Sometimes the spirits are easy to dislodge – a Thai teenager or a new language student can do it on their own. Sometimes they are so strong and entrenched it takes years of prayer and fasting by a committed team!

Vicarious repentance – can we repent for someone else?
John Bardsley

Moses repented on behalf of Israel in Exodus 32. Ezra, Nehemiah and Daniel each repented on behalf of the sins of previous generations of their own nation (chapter 9 of each book). In the case of Moses, God did hear his prayer, and forgave Israel. Ezra, Nehemiah and Daniel prayed for the promise of restoration after 70 years to be fulfilled, and it was.

If an individual sins, he repents and confesses, and gets clean. If a whole group sins, who takes responsibility? Sometimes we need public confession, statements of apology, and acts of reconciliation. Hosea 4:1-3 explains that the nation is mourning and the population languishing because of bloodshed and violence! God is holding that group responsible for those actions. An individual in that group can take responsibility.

Can we repent for the sins of our city, assuming that we are partially responsible for not speaking out enough to correct them? Sounds good to me. 'I confess the sins we Israelites, including myself and my father's house, have committed against you' (Nehemiah 1:6).

STOPTHINK&DISCUSS
- Discuss each of the topics, and list the pros and cons.
- Why is it very important to recognise that demons can influence Christians?

CONCLUSION

John Bardsley

And what more shall I say? I do not have time to tell of those who through faith conquered kingdoms, and gained what was promised, whose weakness was turned into strength, and who became powerful in battle and routed armies. Others faced jeers, and were persecuted and ill-treated. The world was not worthy of them. These were all commended for their faith, yet none of them received all of what had been promised. God had planned something better for us so that only together with us would they be made perfect. (Based loosely on keywords taken from Hebrews 11).

When I started praying for Jolas I was young, and our children were still in primary or pre-primary schools. Now I am white haired and pensionable. In this book, among other things, is a record of what God has been teaching me during this time. Now God has just given me the commission I thought he would give me 35 years ago: 'Plant a multiplying church among an unreached people!' How much of this experience will I need in this new venture? All of it, I expect!

What about you? Have you been affirmed in your belief that Satan is defeated, and all we have to do is prove it to him? Have you been encouraged to see biblical ways to overcome the sneaky strategies of the evil one? Have you taken on the forces of darkness in some corner of the world in which we do not yet see Jesus loved, honoured and worshipped? What are you doing, in Jesus' name, for the kingdom? May you always know the strength of the Master.

BIBLIOGRAPHY

Anderson, Neil T. *Victory Over the Darkness*, (Ventura, CA, Regal Books, 1990). Who I am in Christ, and the glorious freedom I enjoy as a result. The book is filled with stories of people who were set free from a range of horrors.

Anderson, Neil T. *The Bondage Breaker*, (Crowborough, Monarch Publications, 1993). The second half of Anderson's teaching. The chapter on forgiveness alone is worth the cost of the book.

Anderson, Neil T. *Steps to Freedom in Christ*, (Ventura, CA, Regal Books, 2004). Prayers, faith statements and renunciations for complete freedom. A little book to give the counselee after deliverance, or to guide anyone towards self-deliverance.

Anderson, Peter. *Talk About the Devil*, (Worthing, H.E. Walter, 1979). Very sound and helpful.

Burnett, David. *Unearthly powers: A Christian perspective on Primal and Folk Religions*, (Eastbourne, MARC, 1988). Scholarly and readable.

Bubeck, Mark I. *The Adversary: The Christian versus demon activity*, (Chicago, Moody Press, 1975).

Bubeck, Mark I. *Overcoming the Adversary*, (Chicago: Moody Press, 1984).

Dawson, John. *Taking Our Cities For God*, (Milton Keynes, Word Publications, 1989).

Dickason, C. Fred. *Demon Possession and the Christian*, (Westchester, IL, Crossway Books, 1987).

Dinnen, Stewart R. *How are you doing?* (Fearn, Christian Focus Publications, 2001). Checklist Ten – '31 tips on recognising and resisting Satan'.

Gibson, Noel and Phyllis. *Evicting demonic squatters and breaking bondages*, (Drummoyne, Australia, Freedom In Christ Ministries Trust, 1987).

Irvine, Doreen. *From Witchcraft to Christ*, (Eastbourne, Kingsway, 2005 [1973]).

Jacobs, Cindy. *Possessing the Gates of the Enemy*, (Tarrytown, NY, Fleming H. Revell, 1991).

Kiev, Ari. *Magic, Faith and Healing: Studies in primitive psychiatry today*, (New York, The Free Press, 1974). A medical and anthropological view.

Kinnaman, Gary. *Angels Dark and Light*, (Ventura, CA, Vine Books 1994).

Lewis, C.S. *The Screwtape letters & Screwtape proposes a toast*, (London, HarperCollins, 2002 [60th Anniversary edition]). Fictional letters from a senior to a junior demon. Wry humour, insightful.

Marshall, Tom. *Explaining Binding and Loosing*, (Tonbridge, Sovereign World 1991).

McAlpine, Thomas H. *Facing the Powers*, Monrovia, CA, MARC Publications, 1991.

Mills, Brian and Mitchell, Roger. *Sins of the Fathers*, (Tonbridge, Sovereign World: 1999).

How national repentance removes obstacles for revival.

Moody Press (compilation). *Demon Experiences in Many Lands: Strange Occurrences in Mission Fields of the World*, (Chicago, Moody Press, 1960). Small but helpful compilation.

Murphy, Ed. *The Handbook for Spiritual Warfare*, (Nashville, TN, Thomas Nelson, 1992).

Neil, Arthur. *Aid Us in Our Strife, vol. 1*, (Cardiff, Heath Christian Trust, 1989). Filled with scripture, densely written and reasoned.

Neil, Arthur. *Aid Us in Our Strife, Vol. 2*, (Newton Abbot, Nova Publishing, 1990).

Penn-Lewis, Jessie. *War on the saints*, (Erith, Diasozo Trust, 1987 [1912]).

Scheunemann, Detmar. *And Led Me Out Into the Expanse*, (Wuppertal, R. Brockhaus, 1980).

Sherman, Dean. *Spiritual Warfare for every Christian*, (YWAM, 1990). A set of audio tapes. Detailed, with lovely touches of humour.

Silvoso, Edgardo. *That None Should Perish*, (Ventura, CA, Regal Books, 1994).

Takaliuang, Pondsius. *Antara kuasa gelap dan kuasa terang*, (Batu, YPPII, 1979).

Takaliuang, Pondsius. *Cara melepaskan orang dari ikatan kuasa kegelapan*, (Batu, YPPII, 1989).

Unger, Merrill F. *What Demons Can Do to Saints*, (Chicago, Moody Press, 1991).

White, Tom. *The Believer's Guide to Spiritual Warfare*, (Eastbourne:,Kingsway Publications, 1990). Tom has taught this worldwide.

White, Tom. *The Believer's Guide to Breaking Strongholds*, (Eastbourne, Kingsway Publications, 1993).

DEFINITIONS

Astrology	Belief that destiny is determined by the position of the sun, moon, planets and stars on the day of your birth, and trying to predict your future the same way.
Clairaudience	Hearing voices, not with the physical ear but in your spirit or your mind.
Clairvoyance	Seeing pictures, not with your physical eyes but in your spirit or your mind. Seeing the future.
Culture	That unique blend of a people's beliefs, value system, language and lifestyle which identifies its members wherever they are.
Curse	A wish, expressed aloud, that something bad will happen to someone. See also 'spell'.
Deliverance	Evicting demons from someone.
Disciple	Someone who spends time with Jesus, learning his ways, then goes out to create other disciples (Mark 3:14-15). The heart of discipleship is worship. The edge of discipleship is multiplication.
Divination	Discovery of what is obscure, distant, or future by occult, supernatural power.
Dualism	A philosophical belief that there are two distinct principles of good and evil, or two divine beings, one good, one evil, equal and opposite.
Fetish	A place where spirits meet humans to accept their gifts and obedience, or an object used to contact spirits. This could include amulets, talismans and lucky charms.
Fey	Having an ability or tendency, developed or undeveloped, to be sensitive to spirits or occult phenomena.
Foothold	Rights a demon has to influence a person's life. A demon can gain a foothold through the sin or curse of an ancestor, or traumatic childhood experience, or wilful sin. A landing pad or entry point for an evil spirit.
Intercession	Prayer in which the one praying accepts responsibility for God's work in some situation, person or group, carrying it until God removes it. Often it comes as a commission from God to act as a responsible 'go-between' for them.
Kairos	A Greek word for 'time' which also means 'opportunity'. It is used here to mean the era when God causes a people to respond to the gospel.
Magic	Activity intended to cause supernatural events. Black Magic assumes an evil intention. White Magic assumes a good intention such as healing, but because it uses occult powers which themselves have evil intentions, the results are also negative.
Medium	A person through whom spirits communicate.

Occult	Beyond the bounds of ordinary knowledge. Secret or hidden demonic activity.
Power encounter	Any occasion when the power of God and the power of evil come into direct competition, for example in healing methods, or in defying a curse. A biblical example is Elijah and the prophets of Baal on Mt Carmel (1 Kings 18).
Powers (1)	One of the levels of authority in the hierarchy of evil spiritual beings. They may have more delegated authority from Satan; they may be more intelligent or more ruthless.
Powers (2)	Political and social structures which may be influenced for good by believers and for evil by those who are under Satan's control, or directly by demons. ('The powers that be' in Romans 13:1.)
Principalities	Spirits attempting to create evil influence in a specific geographical area.
Qi Gong	A system of exercises intended to direct the energy flow (Qi, or Chi) of the body. Related to Tai Chi.
Religiosity	Ritual, symbolism, observance preserved for its own sake.
Shaman	A witch doctor or someone who heals using demonic power.
Sorcery	In the New Testament 'sorcery' is *pharmakeia*, so it means using drugs and potions or a witch's brew to invoke evil supernatural powers or to do evil.
Spell	A form of words used to try to influence supernatural powers to harm someone. Evil spirits like to harm people anyway, so are only too ready to attempt it.
Spiritism	Belief that the dead survive as spirits which can communicate with the living, especially with the help of a medium.
Spiritual mapping	An attempt to locate where ideologies, religious practices, cultural sins, etc. may have invited demons to invade and influence an area.
Spiritual warfare	Pulling down the dominion of darkness in order to build the kingdom of God.
Spiritualism	A religion allowing séances as part of religious ceremonies. Beliefs vary widely.
Stronghold	A foothold that has been allowed to develop. Entrenched forces of evil in a person, organisation, family, community, ethnic group or nation.
Territorial Spirit	A demon with responsibility for influencing everyone in the area allotted to it. This area may be as large as a nation or as small as a room.
Vicarious	On behalf of someone else.
Witchcraft	An attempt to gain power over other people by means of magic, sorcery, spells or charms.
Worldview	A set of presuppositions or assumptions, values and commitments about the basic make-up of the world around us, and the thought system we develop to explain it. Worldview is determined almost entirely by the society in which we grow up. It is something we absorb subconsciously more often than something we adopt after careful study.

Zodiac   An imaginary orbit of fixed stars during the course of a year. It is divided into twelve houses, each ruled by a planet, named after Greek or Roman gods.

SUBJECT INDEX

SCRIPTURE INDEX

CPSIA information can be obtained
at www.ICGtesting.com
Printed in the USA
FFOW03n0347300118
44733430-44765FF

9 780900 828911